Gary Indiana is the author of the hit play *Roy Cohn/Jack Smith*. His novels include *Horse Crazy*, *Gone Tomorrow*, *Rent Boy*, and *Resentment*. He has also published two collections of short stories, *White Trash Boulevard* and *Scar Tissue*. He lives in New York and Los Angeles.

Bleed

essays 1985–1995

Gary Indiana

HIGH
RISK
BOOKS

NEW YORK / LONDON

Library of Congress Catalog Card Number: 95-71068

A catalogue record for this book is available from the British Library on request

The right of Gary Indiana to be identified as the author of this work has been asserted by him in accordance with the Copyright, Designs and Patents Act 1988

Acknowledgements:
The following articles first appeared in *Village Voice*: "Northern Exposure," "Disneyland Burns," "Town of the Living Dead," "Tough Love and Carbon Monoxide in Detroit," "L.A. Plays Itself," "Being and Nothingness American Style," "The P and I," "The Sex Factory," "Otto Hypnosis," "The Dark Side of Gilbert and George," "Death Notices," "Debby with Monument: A Dissenting Opinion," and "The Farewell Party." "The Beauty Treatment" and "Paul Schrader's *Mishima*" first appeared in *Art in America*. The following first appeared in *VLS*: "Writing Dangerously," "Jonathan Ned Katz's *Gay Science*," "Hervé Guibert's *To The Friend Who Did Not Save My Life*," "Emma Tennant's *Higher Powers*," "All I Need is Love," and "Hannah and Her Sister." "Gore Vidal's *Screening History*" first appeared in *Artforum*.

First published in 1996 by
Serpent's Tail, 4 Blackstock Mews, London N4
and 180 Varick Street, 10th floor, New York, NY 10014

Set in Sabon by Avon Dataset, Bidford-on-Avon
Printed in Finland by Werner Söderström Oy

Contents

For Bill Rice and Taylor Mead

Preface

I am writing this little preface about 80km north of Valparaiso, Chile, a port town full of cats, funiculars, and sailors, three things which have given me intense pleasure over the years, though the funiculars have been regretfully few. The seedy obscurity of this city, the "old cathedral town" of the song, with its churches and shanties piled all over each other on an active fault line, has always appealed to my imagination, suggesting as it does what Los Angeles might look like if Hollywood had never been. My second novel, *Gone Tomorrow*, had its point of origin (or one of them, anyway) in a Raul Ruiz movie, *Three Crowns of the Sailor*, set in Valparaiso . . . or so I have come to believe. I've never been able to make heads or tails of that movie, and it's entirely possible that what I remembered of it while writing my book was only dream salad conjured by its vaporizing imprint. This species of uncertainty has a certain charm. The Swiss director Daniel Schmid and I share a vivid, false memory of Anita Ekberg, in *La Dolce Vita*, completely immersed in the Fontana di Trevi, when in "reality" she only goes in up to her ankles. But Daniel and I both saw a poster that showed Ekberg soaking wet, and even Fellini's sublime film was powerless to dispel the illusionism of Cinecita's publicity department.

These essays were written in all kinds of conditions, and were often extracted from deep ambivalence about their subjects, contexts, and in some cases even about why I was writing. Each represents an attempt to map the place where I was at the time—psychically, morally, geographically—and like all maps, they highlight certain aspects of the region while leaving others suggestively blank. They were, sometimes, efforts to say the unspoken about things everyone was talking about. Others, especially the reporting pieces, were staged collisions of my sensibility with phenomena plainly alien to it, tests of my own obduracy. I enjoyed getting hundreds of menacing phone calls from the inhabitants of Branson, Missouri after "Town of the Living Dead" appeared, and I didn't mind the scandal that ensued when the porn movie travelogue showed up as a cover story in the *Village Voice*, but the pieces themselves weren't written to provoke any particular reaction. Rather, I did them to see what I would make out of the material, and also for the experience of travelling outside my own skin. Solipsism is a beguiling infirmity of writers, but for most of my writing life I've devoted some energy to thwarting my own heavy tendency toward it. There is, there must be, some wavering zone of consciousness where more than one of us can, at least for a moment, be in the same place at the same time. I mean besides CNN.

One writes essays to discover what one really thinks. Unfortunately, writing for publication, on deadlines, often results in something a little off what one would like to have said, and I've had to make some small, but to me important, changes in some texts, as a final attempt to get it right.

I want to thank several editors who encouraged me during some pretty dark times, and helped wrestle some of the work into existence: Elizabeth Baker, Nancy Marmer, David Fraenkel, Lisa Kennedy, Jeff Weinstein, M. Mark, Amy Virshup, Karen Durbin, Lee Smith, and Scott Malcolmson. For their assistance in other ways, my gratitude to Guy Trebay, Karen Rinaldi, Vince Aletti, Amy Taubin, David Riminelli, and Hugh Garvey. I especially thank my editors at Serpent's Tail, Ira Silverberg and Amy Scholder, and my agent Emma Sweeney, for their support, advice, and extraordinary patience.

Gary Indiana
La Serena, Chile
December 25, 1995

1.

Northern

Exposure

Funny Mr. Bill

*sixteen and time to pay off: i get this job in a piss factory
inspecting pipe. forty hours thirty-six dollars a week but it's
a paycheck, jack.*—patti smith

Up close, Bill Clinton looks like he's covered in fresh fetal tissue.
His skin is virtually poreless. The high, ample hair (a premium
commodity in this race of semiskinheads), the trim, pneumatic
body, the tasteful but not unduly elegant suit, everything has been
processed into movie star perfection. He could be a retired sports
figure like Bruce Jenner, endorsing a home treadmill. Something in
the grooming suggests one of those miniature species bred to win
show ribbons, a Shetland pony or a toy terrier.

Here amid the authentic wood-grain paneling of the Henry J.
Sweeney American Legion Post #2 on Maple Street, in Manchester,
a large and not unduly elegant crowd of Clinton people has wedged
itself between the floor-level microphone and the cash bar.
Someone, I'm not sure who, introduces Legion Post Commander

Tom Murphy, "who is gonna do the pleasure of introducing Governor Clinton."

The locutions are pure Main Street New Hampshire. Regarding the candidate, Murphy says, "I have read much of what he stands for and espouses to." "It's my distinguished pleasure to honor and introduce to you"—and perhaps he really does say—"the next president of the United States," though the ante here is simply getting the numbers back to where they were before Gennifer Flowers. The will to believe is palpable in the room, if hardly overwhelming. There's a certain mild tension skimming off the synthetic fabrics and plastic cocktail glasses, roughly the voltage of a joy buzzer.

This is a grown-up crowd. There are infants and small kids and grandmothers swaddled in bright ski parkas and knitted beanies, but the main energy emits from men and women of a certain age who buy their clothes out of state and are no strangers to the cash bar of the Henry J. Sweeney American Legion Post #2. I mean that, as Nixon would say, in the best sense of cash bar. Here you have your conservative machine Democrats (what used to be called savings and loan Democrats), mingling with plumbing contractors and Goodyear franchise managers and district assembly-persons, the types that strike all sorts of sweet little deals in places like this on a normal weekday, many 100 per cent behind the candidate but ready to switch horses if the numbers today and tomorrow and next week don't play out as expected.

Clinton doesn't wait on too much fanfare. This is an earnest, flesh-pressing, I'm-not-there-yet-and-I-need-each-and-everyone-of-you speech. The point of the exercise is to find a credible way of projecting "concern" that these people are "hurting," Bush's euphemism for broke. What's Clinton's campaign all about? Three words: "fairness, responsibility, and unity." Where do Republicans make their mistake? Well, for one thing, "most poor people get up in the morning and work" and therefore deserve government help. But let's not slip into socialism. This guy wants "to make more millionaires than Reagan and Bush, but the old-fashioned way." Empower those local governments. Crack down on corporations moving jobs out of the country. And let's have boot camps, military style, for some of our less hardened, first-time-felony criminals. While we're at it, let's enforce child support.

The platitudinous verbal droppings, more like noises one makes to stimulate horses than actual thoughts, also resemble bromides from a soothing commercial for Preparation H: the proctologist, on close examination, has ruled against radical surgery in favor of something smooth and greasy and easy to dissolve in the collective rectum. In case anybody thought he was some woolly-haired tax-and-spend liberal, Funny Mister Bill throws in enough hard talk about welfare recipients and crime to make you forget he's a Democrat. For this particular crowd, he's already demonstrated his Americanism by letting a lobotomized Death Row inmate go to his end by lethal injection—one of three hideously bungled, "painless" executions the same week in America. And if a fair number of conservatives, even New Hampshire conservatives, wince at the stark realities of capital punishment, quite a few think it ought to be as painful as possible.

If Clinton cares jack shit about anything besides getting elected, it doesn't show on that eerily symmetrical face, a visage of pure incipience: soon-to-be-jowly and exophthalmic, a fraction past really sexy, but warmingly cocky, clear-eyed, with an honorary, twinkling pinch of humility. The accent has just enough grain, enough slow roll in it for people to recognize a Good Old Boy with decent values and bootstraps pulled all the way up. His ideas are so lacking in genuine nuance or arresting detail that he might very well pass, if not now then later, as the statistically ideal mediocrity New Hampshire often favors, when it isn't worshipping some pathologically unpleasant, penny-ante fixer like John Sununu. Apart from bland-as-buckwheat officials with no fixed opinions on anything, the Granite State likes pissy, preening, patently empty wastebaskets à la Sununu to push its citizens around from time to time, exploiting them in sadistically unprofitable ways.

There is real social masochism in New Hampshire among the blue-collar immigrant stock of the southland. ("Southland" is my own term for south of Concord, east of Keene, not a New

Hampshire term.) Those for whom "Live Free or Die" has traditionally meant dropping out of 10th grade and heading straight for Klev Bros. and Jody shoe shops, Raytheon, or the mills, feel such depths of cultural inferiority that truly abusive public figures often resonate more winningly with them than reformers and do-gooders. And that's the target constituency, despite today's preponderance of the class three notches above trash. New Hampshirites respect cunning over noble intentions. The Bavarians of New England have never cottoned to obligatory self-improvement or any too reachy sense of community, since these concepts involve sales tax and state tax and the dreaded welfare, which would bring hordes of shiftless coloreds swarming over the border from Massachusetts. New Hampshire makes its money on state liquor stores and highway tolls. Not coincidentally, the state has ranked, for decades, 50th in the nation in support of higher education.

Aside from the daily dose of social Darwinism provided by the Manchester *Union Leader*, New Hampshire's only statewide daily paper, the paradigm of Ignorance in defense of intolerance is no vice has been held in place for decades by the Catholic Church, though the south is full of Catholics who stopped attending mass after Vatican II, when the transubstantial rites of cannibalism switched from Latin to English. (One woman in Derry told me the secularization of the mass was an egregious example of "coddling the young," like the local Rock the Vote registration drive, which unsuccessfully tried to force the Supervisor of the Checklist to register students at the local high school instead of at the town hall. When the Democratic candidates moan about "the first generation of Americans to do worse than their parents," they're waving a blank rhetorical flag. Among working-class parents in this neck of the woods, what was good enough for them is good enough for their brats, and if their brats do a little worse, boo hoo.)

Resentment is running high at the Henry J. Sweeney American Legion Post #2. One woman in a beige parka steps up to the microphone to denounce the State of the Union address, specifically the Marie Antoinette capital gains passage about

Puritans lying awake at night, obsessed with the idea that somebody somewhere might be having a good time. (Our Halcion-sedated chief executive should've recognized Peggy Noonan's winsome hen tracks as relics of the good old days, when people without trust funds didn't realize they were "hurting.")

It takes a member of the press corps, the *Village Voice*'s Alisa Solomon, to mention the A-word: for this bunch, apparently, "health care" doesn't necessarily extend to the politically charged issue of AIDS. Or perhaps it does, but they'd really rather not discuss it. Clinton exudes a pat, uninterested answer about more money for research, et cetera, adding that "President Bush has only mentioned the word AIDS about three times since he's been president." Alisa later notes that this is the first time Clinton has mentioned it at all.

Caliban

> *she's real catholic, see. she fingers her cross and says there's one reason . . . you do it my way or i push your face in. we knee you in the john if you don't get off your mustang, sally—*
> patti smith

The Buchanan crowd is something else again. The Palace Theatre, a porn movie house throughout my teens and later boarded up like most Manchester businesses off Elm Street, has reopened as a legitimate theater. And a grand-looking place it is, with raked seats and ormolu sconces and delicate chandeliers, like a vintage Keith Circuit vaudeville hall.

There is one black man in the cream white audience, wearing a tight black suit, applauding feverishly, a true believer who will gladly salt himself when they throw him into the stew pot, as long as he can be the last one in. Onstage, former Manchester mayor Bob Shaw lectures us about "a little tea party we threw down in Boston a few years ago," flanked by another local hack, the city chairman of Buchanan for President. While the candidate speaks, these two mavens perch on folding chairs nearby, in badly tailored gray suits, one porcine, gangling, and rabid-looking, the other scrunched up like some demented antique dealer with dreams of world domination, Tweedledum and Tweedledee, cackling and stomping their feet. A tableau of jolly idiocy. Potent ecstasy from the audience of functional dipsomaniacs and blue rinse jobs with ropes of synthetic pearls and minks woven circa 1970, LaRouche defectors, Chamber of Commerce ghouls, and assorted bits of space debris. An extremely fat man with inflamed pimples rocks in his seat behind me, muttering "Right on!" every time Pat scores some soaring polemical eureka.

The thrust of The Speech is that America has to be Number One. Not simply Number One in standard of living and capitalization and investments and technology and aircraft construction and car sales, but Number One in unbridled odiousness. The tautological form of The Speech presents a self-evident case that the U.S. is not simply part of the world, but superior to everything in it. Like anyone else from Rockingham and Hillsborough counties, I am able to instantly translate The Speech from its slightly euphemistic idioms into plain English:

We must show these sordid fuckers, the Japs, that we are better than they are because, goddamn it, we're Americans, we're white, we're the greatest nation the world has ever known, and we invented everything. Flat screens and chips and VCRs and semiconductors and the Waring blender. And it's all being taken away from us by a bunch of satanic Nips and totalitarian Chinks and ingrate Koreans and devious wetbacks who've tilted the playing field and by Christ a level playing field isn't the point anyway, we've got to win!

The Europeans—whose gene stock, granted, is the only one worth preserving—are evilly attempting to wrest Boeing and Burger King from America's grasp. Race filth from Taiwan is gobbling up McDonnell Douglas. My god, the bastards will be seizing control of Disneyland unless this belligerent turd at the podium with his socks falling down isn't listened to, and then the residents of Manchester, New Hampshire can kiss the eternal glory of being an American goodbye. Poor little Mickey Mouse is gonna wind up a squalid, syphilitic frog, or a sex-crazed wop, or a stinking guinea, or a bloody wog, or, god help the little rodent, a flaming African jigaboo.

"I've heard about parts of New Hampshire emptying out, the way you used to read about it in the Dust Bowl ... eight years of Reagan, whatever good things he did have been wiped out in these three years ... the World Bank in the last three years has given $3.5 billion dollars to communist China ... at zero interest ... those loans are guaranteed by you ... the Export Import Bank is helping American business locate a new paper mill in Mexico ... has anybody been up to the James River Paper Mill in Berlin? I was up there yesterday ... they're holding on ... they don't know what's going to happen ... they're responsible for 20 per cent of the economy of the North Country ... what are we doing financing paper mills in Mexico when paper mills in New Hampshire are teetering on the brink of going under? [Thunderous applause.] We were the world's leaders in textiles. Number one in steel. These industries are going, going, some of them are gone ... I've been up in the North Country of your home state ... Mr. Bush just had a new guest visiting him, Lee Pong I think is how you pronounce his name ... he's the fellow who ordered the tanks in Tiananmen Square ... that Chinese communist regime is right now selling missile technology ... to our enemies in Tehran ... they dumped all their sweater products in the United States and killed Pandora Mills. ... "

Never mind that most of New Hampshire has always been thinly populated. Never mind that the former Brown Co. Mills have been in decline for 30 years—in steeper decline since their purchase, in 1980, by the Virginia-based James River Corporation, which failed to refurbish the industrial plant when the capital was there. That the population of Berlin has been dropping steadily since 1960, precipitously so since the departure of the Converse Shoe Company in 1979, or that absolutely nobody in New Hampshire refers to Coos County and the wasteland near the Canadian border as "the North Country."

As it happens, Pandora Mills was not ruined by Chinese

sweaters being dumped on the American market. Pandora was ruined by a leveraged buyout of its clothing division following the company's 1983 acquisition by Gulf + Western, as the former president of Pandora Knitwear, May Gruber, informs me after the Palace Theatre loathe-in has dispersed into gelid evening, trailing acrid vapors of Nissan and Honda exhaust. Admit nothing, blame everybody, be bitter—this could easily be Pat Buchanan's campaign slogan, as well the state motto.

Perhaps the sorriest aspect of the Buchanan campaign is the obligation most mainstream journalists feel to declare this boor "interesting," mainly because he customarily feeds at the same trough they do. Yes, he will get 30 per cent of the New Hampshire Republican vote, and so would Adolf Hitler or General Franco. I'm from here, and I've seen this movie before. Buchanan is scary, yes, but so is the more congenial, saner fringe candidate, Chip Woods, an air crash survivor whose reconstructed face at least confronts us with the useful paradox that appearances, which all philosophy since Plato shows us to be false, absolutely dictate the selection of rulers in a televised democracy. By contrast Buchanan is, tediously, exactly what he looks like, a bigoted mick whose pathology runs to fag-bashing and other symptoms of sexual hysteria.

And what of these bullying, cowardly people, stewing in the bilious sweats of their own zeal, bursting into rapturous applause—the heartiest applause of the evening—when Buchanan sneers that AIDS is "still a disease of homosexuals" and "addicts," or vows to rid the NEA of every piece of "scandalous, filthy, or antireligious art"? What about these jumped-up hillbillies, frothing at the dentures to beat up people with AIDS, single mothers on assistance, the homeless, anybody weaker than they? Who regard themselves as the only true victims of history, as "hurting" just because the world is larger than they are, more complex than the country they live in, and not, for the most part, white?

It's standard among the Buchanan set to begrudge any minority the status of victim, to bewail "reverse discrimination" in any attempt at social reparation, so it's no surprise that the *Union*

Leader, Buchanan's principal endorser in the state, has taken up several of Pat's pet peeves. In a January 30 editorial, staffer Leonard Larson attacks "the annual guilt trip over Hiroshima" and complains that "the popular media history . . . will probably define World War II in just two events." And guess what the other one is.

"It's already part of revisionist history that American could have—should have—stopped the Nazi slaughter of 6 million Jews while 20 million other people were also dying in Europe.

". . . So that wasn't a war we were in. There was the Holocaust and everything else was incidental. The revisionists would make it a fact."

I should stress that the *Union Leader* is perfectly capable of going much further than this, of denying that the Holocaust even happened one week, and using the same fictional Holocaust the next week to attack Louis Farrakhan or some other anti-Semite of color, depending on which minority its editrix, Mrs. Nacky Scripps Gallowhur Loeb, widow of the odious William, feels like bashing when she staggers out of bed in the morning.

On other matters, too, the paper has the mercurial temper of a pit viper. It detested Jimmy Hoffa until Jimmy Hoffa became the enemy of Robert Kennedy, and then ran a decade of editorials lauding Hoffa as the savior of organized labor. (The paper threatened to withhold its endorsement of Richard Nixon in '72 unless Tricky Dick sprung Hoffa from the federal penitentiary; Nixon grudgingly obliged.) It devoted eight years of deifying editorials to then governor John Sununu and his albatross reactor in Seabrook, yet currently refers to him as Bush's "pimp," because Sununu refuses to endorse Buchanan. Like the Stalinist-era *Pravda*, the *Union Leader* never simply changes its mind; it "discovers" a pattern of ideological error or flawed character in its former allies, admits to having been "duped," and busily retracts every positive thing it's printed about the latest charlatan. In all of this the paper represents itself as a virgin schoolmarm violated and betrayed by her most trusted pupil, an act so long in the tooth that even its subscribers can't read the *Union Leader* with a straight face.

Back to Buchanan. During Q&A, only two people, May

Gruber—who does not raise the issue of Pandora Mills but instead suggests that Jesse Helm's interference with the NEA amounts to government censorship—and a young woman from Merrimack, who describes Buchanan's position on AIDS as ignorant, challenge the candidate on any of his obvious whoppers. Given the general attitude of Pat's fans, this takes more guts and conviction than the windbag on stage ever possessed in his life. I'd like to think that these two intelligent, humane voices insert just enough dissonance to sully an orgy of ugly feelings, or at least plant a few suspicions that the Wizard of Oz cannot really give the Scarecrow a functioning brain.

On the way out of the theater, an obsessed, elderly, goofily dressed John Bircher strikes up a monologue aimed at the *Voice* photographer, who happens to be African American. The man carries a bundle of literature charting a vast, ongoing conspiracy by the Trilateral Commission and David Rockefeller. "I've had this crap up to here. This country's gonna go right down the goddam tubes. Someday you're gonna have United Nations troops in here. George Wallace got 10 million votes, he said we're fed up with this crap, what happened? Boom. Robert Kennedy knew who killed his brother, all of a sudden, bang, Robert Kennedy, right? Martin Luther King was so exposed he was no longer any use to these people, what happened? Bang!" Like flies to a steaming pile of ordure, the weird creatures of eternal night draw close to the flame that is Pat Buchanan. Meanwhile, some workers roll out the set, a temple-like construction of plastic milk crates, for the Palace Theatre's current production, *The Tempest*.

Fade to Brown

> *i look down at sweet theresa's convent, all those nurses, all those nuns ... to me you know they look pretty damn free down there*—patti smith

In a large auditorium with level seats, pale olive walls, dark neo-Georgian olive trim, festooned with many portraits in gilded frames of men who resemble Alastair Cooke, a number of dewlapped, earnest preppies and environmentally conscious residents of Exeter and nearby towns have gathered at Phillips Exeter Academy to experience Jerry Brown.

Out in the hall, volunteers are stacking Jerry's videotape and piles of Jerry's literature. As I write this, I keep hearing Sandra Bernhard's dialogue from *The King of Comedy* echoing through my head. Jerry.

Jerry Brown has enough sense of humor to joke about the space cadet rap he's getting in the press. Just enough. Perhaps infected by the sober and enlightened atmosphere of this great hall where countless maiden blowjobs began as humid, hungering glances across rows of brilliantined schoolboy hairdos, Jerry strikes a serious yet scrappily boyish note. He reminds us that he is the only candidate with a classical education, schooled in Greek and Latin. For three years he toiled and thought and really examined himself and who he really was in the silence of a Jesuit seminary. He traveled to Japan and spent some quality time in Japan and knows the Japanese, knows the culture and what makes it tick. After that, Jerry spent three months in Calcutta, working with Mother Teresa in her Home for the Dying, eager to see what human caring, human compassion, even in the absence of a mutual language, could do amid so much suffering and dying.

And that isn't all. If I were to write down everything Jerry Brown has done, or even just everything Jerry Brown says he's done, you would still be reading this next Tuesday. Jerry's introduction of renewable energy technologies in California alone would cover many pages, as would his hands-on approach with the state legislature in Sacramento, where he moved into a small apartment right across from the statehouse instead of taking residence in the ugly expensive mansion built for the Reagans. Did I tell you what Jerry did about the dead-end welfare system in California? How Jerry actually lessened crime? The magnificent windmills and other devices that have made PG&E, thanks to Jerry, the most cost-effective and profitable gas and electric utility in the U.S. of A.? No? Sandra, would you please sing "Come Rain or Come Shine" just one more time?

As I listen to Jerry, something keeps irritating me. At first I believe it is the memory of a large crow I once saw bisected by one of Jerry's power-generating windmills outside San Luis Obispo while driving from L.A. to San Francisco. Then I realize it is a small child in a pink padded windbreaker seated beside me who is playing with a Nintendo Game Boy as Jerry speaks.

Just behind me, several young men who had been discussing, avidly, the various clues on Beatles albums pointing to the death of Paul McCartney (for example, on the Sgt. Pepper lyric sheet, John Lennon's finger seems to rest against the line, ". . . at five o'clock as the day begins . . ."—possibly the exact time of Paul's demise) have stopped talking about that and are listening to Jerry with what seems, when I look at them, like respectful skepticism. Good day sunshine.

Jerry wants to take the system back from the politicians and the corporations and put it in the hands of you the people or rather we the people, and that's why he isn't accepting more than $100 from each individual to run his campaign. We can cleanse this system of corruption and provide health care for every American and cure the rot of our inner cities with a few simple techniques. All right, I'm sorry, I don't remember what they are, but Jerry knows them, and if you elect Jerry, he'll tell you himself. Or at least you should take a copy of his videotape. But if you do, be prepared to pass it on to five other people. This is how a grassroots movement gets started.

Jerry is wearing a white turtleneck and a blue denim jacket with brown leather strips on the collar and baggy black corduroy trousers. Jerry has a large bald spot and strangely mottled skin, red in the wrong places, and just between you and me, there is something a little delusional about Jerry, even though I know he really was the governor of California at one time.

Seacoast

In fairness to the candidate, he only sounds this way because America has evolved so far from the notion of direct rule that even people who agree with Jerry understand he has no chance of being elected. One thinks of direct rule in connection with local rather than national politics. Brown does have a constituency in New Hampshire, as would any ecology-minded consumer advocate, because local communities have seen what can be accomplished by write-in drives, petitions, and town meetings. This is, paradoxically, partly thanks to William Loeb and the politicians he supported over the years.

Loeb, by the way, never resided in New Hampshire. For decades he occupied an 80-acre high-security compound in Pride's Crossing, Massachusetts, furtively darting back and forth across the border, it is said, in order to avoid subpoenas. In league with a succession of vacuous New Hampshire governors, Loeb sponsored uncountable schemes to wreck the environment in the interests of various contractors, developers, and high-tech corporations. Sununu's Seabrook nuclear reactor was only the most recent venture to mobilize conservation groups throughout the state.

Before Seabrook, there was Durham Point. In 1973, Governor Meldrim Thomson Jr. (now an occasional columnist for the *Union Leader*) announced his vision that New Hampshire needed an oil refinery. No one had perceived this need before, but because of his campaign pledge of no new taxes, Thomson had to find money somewhere for deteriorating state services. At the same time, employees of Aristotle Onassis's Olympic Oil Co., posing as real estate agents, began buying options on 3000 acres of shorefront in Portsmouth, Rye, and Durham, under various guises: the establishment of bird sanctuaries and hunting preserves, retirement homes, etc. The biggest chunk of optioned land was at Durham Point. Onassis also optioned parts of the Isles of Shoals, a little archipelago 10 miles off the coast.

In November 1973, Thomson announced that Olympic Oil would install a $600 million refinery at Durham Point. Supertankers would offload at the Isles of Shoals, where the oil would be pumped to Portsmouth via underwater pipe, then shunted to Durham Point through another pipeline. Onassis himself would visit the state on December 19. Loeb's front-page editorial announced, "WELCOME To the Two Big O's — Oil and Onassis!"

Appalled property owners in the quiet university town of Durham quickly joined forces with environmentalists to block Durham Point, as the *Union Leader* devoted reams of fawning newsprint to Onassis, whom it characterized as "Santa Claus." According to Loeb biographer Kevin Cash, the Durham Point project would have been "the largest single-unit oil refinery ever built." It also would have transformed the countryside around the University of New Hampshire into a moonscape.

The project met its toxic avenger in the form of Mrs. Thomas Dudley, the town of Durham's representative to the state's General Court. (Mrs. Dudley's given name was also Dudley, therefore Dudley Dudley. She was a descendant of Joseph Dudley, who was governor of Massachusetts and New Hampshire between 1723 and 1728.) A Mrs. Nancy Sandberg, also of Durham, organized Save Our Shores, which opposed Olympic Oil with legal services to optioned property owners, a speakers' bureau, bumper stickers, et cetera.

Mrs. Dudley cast the Durham Point issue in terms of home rule. This had immense popular appeal. Town meetings throughout the Seacoast area rezoned the target properties to exclude the refinery, while House Bill 34, intended to override the local ordinances, went down to defeat 109 to 233. Onassis returned to Skorpios and Maria Callas. Cash speculates that Loeb never fully recovered from the rejection of Durham Point by New Hampshire voters.

Now, it seems, some kind of attitude shift is taking its gradual course in the state—very gradual, if you compare it with the mall and condo boom of the Reagan years, when developers and retail chains, greased by every tax break John Sununu could contrive, swept through southern New Hampshire like shit through a cane brake, transforming a landscape of harsh, bucolic beauty into one of unparalleled hideousness. Steady migrations of "Massachusetts people" into the southland have brought with them, unexpectedly, a burgeoning circulation of the liberal *Boston Globe*. This, combined with a generous cable range, has eroded the Loeb information monopoly. Even if people generally don't like blacks and gays and other menacing elements, now they hear about them all the time.

There is still no alternative statewide paper in which to rebut insane accusations and slanders that appear in the *Union Leader*, but the influx of news from CNN and other sources has miniaturized the paper's impact. Simply to stay marginally competitive with the Maine cable chain and the *Boston Globe*, the *Union Leader* and WMUR-Manchester have to report the unpleasant minority news they used to suppress, even if the paper's editorials—mainly crayoned by geriatric Loeb protégé James L. Finnegan—continue to sound like bulletins from a psychiatric ward. The era when William Loeb's campaigns against local college presidents could hound them out of the state—for allowing gay organizations on campus, or sponsoring "Communist" lectures, as happened with Loeb's untiring persecution of Thomas Bonner at UNH from 1971 to 1974—is over.

Nowhere To Run, Nowhere To Hide

I drive to Keene one bleary morning with Martha and the Vandellas blasting in the car, up Route 3 to Pinardville, down 101 to Milford, Milford to Peterborough. Just before Dublin the Tsongas signs start appearing on trees and fence posts and mailboxes, *I wake up feeling sorry I met you, and hoping soon, that I'll forget you, when I look in the mirror to comb my hair—*

Well, Tsongas has very thinning hair, but this is the least of his problems. In a tiny conference room at *The Keene Sentinel*, surrounded by a restrained crowd of at least 10 people, the candidate is defending his record in Massachusetts, not that anyone is attacking it, and expounding a fairly conservative philosophy of government, conservative but compassionate, and I know he can't help his face but it's full of little moues and funny tics and because I arrived late I am practically sitting in a large potted plant just outside the conference room hoping he will raise his voice above a steady drone. Paul Tsongas looks like somebody who could do a fairly credible Lamont Cranston imitation if he really let his hair down, such as it is, but this morning he's stuck on a tone of infinite reasonableness and gentle self-mockery.

"Look," he says after a half hour, "I'm a Greek from Massachusetts who's had cancer, so I've got to be either really serious about what I'm doing or else I'm crazy."

This is followed by an unfortunate moment of silence. Note to press corps: if you find yourself in Keene next week, Lindy's Diner has terrific oyster stew.

A La Recherche du Debra Winger

> *floor boss slides up to me and says hey, sister . . . you're screwing up the quota, you're doing your piece work too fast, now you get off your mustang, sally, you ain't going nowhere*—patti smith

There was bound to come a nadir, a point below which the tedium of the campaign trail could not dip without degenerating into chaos. I am a student of chaos, absurdity, and life's little ironies. Moved to tears one morning by a CNN report on unemployed factory workers in West Virginia, I then bring my cousin Kathy some lunch my mother's prepared; Kathy has just opened a tax accounting service in town, having left her job at a law firm that lost its major corporate client. Kathy is one of the least neurotic, most industrious people I have ever known. I tell her all about these poor laid-off steelworkers.

"Well," she says, "remember when we were kids in the '60s? And all we wanted was to do something in life where we wouldn't have to work in a factory?"

Of course she's right. It's impossible to listen to these visiting politicians jaw on about restoring New Hampshire's industrial base without remembering the sheer meaningless misery most of our relatives endured, day in, day out, some for twenty or thirty years, gluing on shoe soles or soldering circuit boards, an unending pointlessness for which no amount of quarterly raises and benefits packages could ever compensate. The idea that 40 to 60 hours a week of monotony was good enough for us, for our class of people, was sufficiently appalling to propel us both into college and out of town.

But we came from that factory world, a little more directly than most of the people we know, which is why Kathy and I, in our different styles, have nothing but contempt for New Hampshire yuppies. And why, I suppose, the Conservation Center in Concord, a perfectly benign, tree-rescuing operation in a solar-heated, light and airy facility of dressed knotty pine, activates my class hatred in a way that Phillips Exeter Academy doesn't. I know I'm as smart as any given graduate of Phillips Exeter, but I will never be rich enough to spend all day worrying about acid rain and printing brochures about it on recycled paper.

The gorgeous assistant press officer wants to know if I think they should move the podium for Senator Kerry into the solarium from the observation deck. It is 17 degrees on the observation deck and everyone coming into the solarium shudders when they get a look at it, why on earth do we have to stand outside to hear him? Well, because of the photo op. On the observation deck you've got your panoramic view of a gazillion pine trees and the Route 93 access bridge over the frozen Merrimack River and the dome of the statehouse like a little burnished bubble of junk jewelry, whereas inside you've just got all this knotty pine and several cases of brochures on the culture of Christmas trees and timber management areas and some wall diagrams of the facility and the membership desk. Plus this long knotty pine table where I'm writing this.

"If you get any wind it's going to blow right into the microphone and you won't hear a thing," I tell the gorgeous assistant press officer, who doesn't believe me.

"We've tested it," he says. "You've got good audibility everywhere except in that corner over there."

I am about to say that Senator Kerry is already low enough in the polls without making the press corps stand around in 17 degree weather when the press comes pouring into the solarium, and there's actual excitement in the air, strange considering the candidate, a definite buzz, something's up, something's happened, SOMETHING HAS FINALLY HAPPENED, what can it be?

"The write-in Cuomo campaign has opened an office in

Concord," *Voice* photographer Brian Palmer explains.

On the tail of this news, Kerry's arrival is indeed an anticlimax, his little speech on the observation deck a nonevent of numbing proportions. One of his aides tells me Kerry's numbers have climbed from 6 to 12. Wavering numbers, but the money's coming in, he's planning to hang in until Super Tuesday. Personally, I would ditch the undertaker's overcoat, change the tie, do a nice even rinse on the hair, and try to get him to stop doing that thing with his mouth where he looks like he's sucking a Fisherman's Friend. I now see the wisdom of keeping the podium outside, since most of us would fall asleep if it were anywhere else. At least he doesn't mention The Leg.

"He's gotten more mileage out of that leg," my aunt Beatrice complained when Kerry's commercial came on a few nights earlier. "And he can walk better than I can."

Return To Peyton Place

En route to Berlin, I detour onto Route 140, a hardscrabble two-lane of disintegrating asphalt, for a look at Gilmanton Iron Works. As a child, my role models were Grace Metalious, Emma Peel, and Oscar Levant. Poor tragic Grace ripped the lid off Gilmanton Iron Works in her immortal *Peyton Place*, made a fortune on that and the subsequent *The Tight White Collar* and *Return to Peyton Place*, then drank herself into an early grave. It's a New Hampshire kind of fate.

What I've forgotten is that Gilmanton Iron Works doesn't have much lid to rip off, consisting as it does of a Corner Store and a Post Office. And no one in the Corner Store or the Post Office knows who Grace Metalious was. No one in the Corner Store or the Post Office has decided who to vote for in the primary, either.

"Are there still Iron Works, anyway?" I ask the woman at the Corner Store deli counter.

"There never were any Iron Works," she says. "Not buildings. They used to take iron ore out of Crystal Lake and ship it off."

The Smell

*every afternoon like the last one, every afternoon like a rerun
... yeah we may look the same, both sweating ... but i got
something to hide here called desire ... and I will get out of
here ... and i will never return, no, never return to burn out
in this piss factory*—patti smith

Berlin, late afternoon. Big, bruisy skies with long, gray clouds
rolling through them. Shops on Main Street all offering clearance
sales, 20 per cent off, 50 per cent off going, going, gone. The only
places to get a cup of coffee are the Woolworth's lunch counter and
the local pizza joint. It's 11 degrees.

This is an incredibly bleak town, not really a city anymore.
Snow piled everywhere, ice crunching underfoot, the streets almost
empty. *The Berlin Reporter*, which has just gone from weekly to
daily, reports an increase in head lice at local schools. "AIDS victim
speaks to Berlin high students," reads one headline. "Study finds
shortness of breath among older mill workers."

In LaVerdiere's Super Drug Store, amid a pile of Waylon
Jennings and Lawrence Welk tapes, I find an Ink Spots
compendium I can play on the long drive home.

We always knew of the paper mills in what Pat Buchanan calls
the North Country and we always called "up there": grim clusters
of silos and smokestacks, the Cascade Plant at Cascade Flats, the
Burgess Plant a quarter mile up the Androscoggin River, the chemicals
spreading out through the water, poisoning the Androscoggin,
Tinker Brook, Pea Brook, Dead River, Peabody River, the dead
trout, the cancer-riddled perch, the stillborn smelts, the perpetual
sulfur-and-boiled-cabbage stench wafted on the mountain winds,
covering Gorham, blowing down to Randolph, on a clear day you
could smell it all the way to Shelburne, a smell that stank like
nothing else on earth, a smell like something crawled up inside you
and died, filling everything, like water rising in a sinking ship.

In Harkin headquarters on Pleasant Street, a buxom volunteer
in a harlequin sweater set tells a middle-aged man sitting against

the wall: "You know he's gotten over 50 awards from different disabled groups? Including Veterans with Disabilities? Because he wrote the Americans with Disabilities Act, you know. Which we're all gonna need some day. With arthritis and so on."

The man regards her coolly. He's my age, he resents this. "Well, I hope not."

By and large, an early middle age, late-ish thirtysomething, hyperthyroidal gathering. Working people, lots of beards, lots of mustaches, a number of Alan Alda types, turquoise down jackets, no pretensions in this place, everything ready-to-wear, maybe a certain Cambridge influence, the snack table covered with potato chips, ginger ale, pretzels, Ritz crackers, a jar of Cheez Whiz. Ratty green carpet. Looks like a furniture showroom.

Waiting and waiting and waiting for Harkin. I stand against the wall behind the chairs reserved for seniors and the disabled, with a clear view of the speaking area. It occurs to me, not for the first time, that I could easily have assassinated any of the major candidates. But they seem to be doing a good job of it themselves. A camera crew glides through the place, interviewing people out of work and people who are "just hanging on by a shoestring." Times are tough. The James River Corporation hasn't hired anyone in two years. Harkin's almost here. Some aides are holding open the door. No, not yet, they're still parking the car. Suddenly . . . something in the air . . . quite unpleasant . . . one of these senior citizens has farted . . . I move away from the chairs . . . the smell follows me . . . it's even over here in the middle of the room . . . a thick, rich, bean supper fart . . . wait, though, it's everywhere . . . my god, it's the James River plant!

Yes, folks, just leave a door open on Pleasant Street, and these factories that everybody wants to ram back into high gear have practically stunk out Harkin headquarters. Once the candidate's inside, the door closes and the fart smell gradually dissipates, like a minor motif in a symphony of hot air. A distinguished-looking man, like your favorite high school civics teacher, carefully raked gray hair, a cracker-barrel face that belongs on a dollar bill, light blue shirt, burgundy V-necked sweater, olive gray slacks, a navy blazer—remember Jean Arthur in *A Foreign Affair*, swinging from a ceiling pipe in a Berlin (Germany) speakeasy, singing "Ioway, Ioway"? Harkin has that same wholesome, rolled-up-shirtsleeves quality, and his rap has the plainspoken, blocky style of Harry S. Truman, on whom Harkin's modeled himself. Trailing just about everybody in the polls? Big deal.

"I love history. 'Course you know my favorite president was Truman. One night Truman was speaking to the young Democrats. And he was way down in the polls. Strom Thurmond had walked out with the Dixiecrats, Henry Wallace had walked out with the Progressives, *Life* magazine in that summer had run a picture of Dewey calling him President Dewey. One young Democrat yelled out, 'Who's gonna be the next president?' Truman looked at him, he said, 'Young man, next January, there's gonna be a Democrat in the White House, and you're lookin' at him.' And that's what I say to you. You're lookin' at him. 'Cause we're gonna win.

"I sense a hunger to turn away from the legacy of the Reagan-Bush Administration. Those policies that have made the rich get richer, the poor get poorer, made the middle class pay the freight both ways. Those policies that have cost you your jobs, exporting them out of this country . . . young people can't get a college education, don't know where they're gonna get the money . . .

"If you're a junk bond dealer, a corporate trader, best of times. If you're a corporate CEO with a golden parachute, best of times. But if you're a working person, lost your job, no job training, don't know what to do? Worst of times. If you're a family, unemployed, you don't know how you're gonna pay your health care bills? An elderly person? Worst of times."

There is nothing to argue with in Harkin's broad-brush portrait of America today, though his vignettes about what is wrong are more than a little stale by this time. Free trade is a two-way street. Jobs. Tell Japan to open its doors. Level playing field. Reciprocity. If I ever go to Japan, I won't be taking along the three top auto executives. They can't even figure out to put the steering wheel on the right-hand side. Bring the money home, invest it here. Rebuild our infrastructure.

Tell you the truth, this guy is a little too calculatedly down-home for my taste. Okay, they've all got an answer for everything, but the tone . . . this picture of America as a land of happy workers, raring to go, to pitch in . . . the way everything is us versus them . . . and the way everybody's complaints feed directly into his argument . . . and frankly, he hasn't said one word about minority issues, racial divisions . . . of course, none of the others have, either, except in code. You go to White America, you talk the White America talk.

"WHAT ABOUT THE DRUGS?"

This question punctures the rhapsodic upswing that was supposed to conclude Harkin's speech, and the candidate is clearly irritated, but game:

"We've gotta beef up our coast guard. Anyway, who was it that put Manuel Noriega on the CIA payroll? George-Herbert-Hoover-Bush!" And he goes on. Rather alarmingly. If I understand him correctly, Harkin has no qualms about sending the Marines into South America. With its permission, of course.

"Mr. Harkin," a boozy-sounding woman in the back pipes up, "why should we send billions of dollars to Russia, when they have always been our enemy? And Poland, and Yugoslavia, and all those countries instead of keeping the money in this country?"

Before Harkin can open his mouth—well, it's already open, but before he can say anything—a large, craggy old man with a face like Lionel Stander chimes in:

"Ten billion going to Israel to put these guys to work on the Golden Heights for Russian immigrants! What the hell is this? Everybody afraid of the Jews?"

"Now, sometimes you—" Harkin begins, but the man is implacable.

"I'm not a bigot, I'm not—but on the other hand, they're human beings, but we're human beings, looking for jobs too."

"That's why you need to make sure that they are investing back in this country, that's exactly what I've been telling you."

The woman from earlier is also implacable:

"What I feel, you go into a store, and myself, I buy U.S. made. Made in the U.S.A."

"You bet," Harkin panders.

"If it's made in U.S.A. we keep our own people working, right?"

"That's right," he says.

"But what you see in most of the stores, is Made in China, Made in Taiwan, all that. What's the point of these countries—and if those articles were not on the shelves, people would buy U.S. made. It wouldn't be there. So you pay a dallar more for the product. But our people don't work for nothing, they don't live 12 in one apartment. We have a nice way of living. And we wanna keep it that way. And I don't want to support the Russians, believe me."

Harkin talks about a bill he's introducing, instructing U.S. representatives to the IMF and the World Bank to vote against any loan to any country that spends more on its military than on health and education. This sounds nice, until you consider that the U.S. itself wouldn't qualify for such a loan, though most other countries in the world would.

"They never pay it back. Did they ever pay it back?" the woman screeches.

"There's one country that has paid back every loan."

"Which one"

"Israel."

"Well, the Jews, they have more money than everybody in the world!"

Harkin quickly takes a question from another part of the room. For me, anyway, he has just collapsed into nonexistence. I suppose one can, in these bankrupt times, in a state where the only major paper once ran an editorial entitled "Kissinger the Kike?" expect a little Jew-baiting on the campaign trail. But I cannot imagine Mario Cuomo or Jay Rockefeller letting such remarks just sit there in the room, just to grub a couple of votes. Not in a million years.

On November 7, 1960, John F. Kennedy stood in Victory Park in Manchester, directly across from the Manchester *Union Leader* offices, and said:

"I believe there is probably a more irresponsible newspaper than that one right over there somewhere in the United States, but I've been through 40 states and I haven't found it yet."

The kind of ignorant sentiments sounded at Harkin's Berlin headquarters can be heard throughout the state of New Hampshire, and even if they originated generations before Loeb's acquisition of the *Union Leader*, the paper has fueled them for decades. As a result, bigotry has been institutionalized among the less-educated, who believe their lives have been ruined by the Jews, the blacks, the Japanese, the communists, or invaders from Massachusettes rather than by bad choices, bad leaders, and a refusal to learn from the larger world. The candidates certainly know this coming in, and at the risk of sounding idealistic, I think any presidential candidate stumping through this backward but maybe not entirely hopeless state has some moral duty to offer a corrective example, to show some high-mindedness, instead of just promising jobs and money and material aggrandizement.

During the years of artificial plenty, New Hampshire was happy to sell off the intangible wealth of livably scaled towns, forests, and wide open spaces for a quick buck, three or four extra K-marts within driving distance, and an idiotic abundance of worthless consumer goods. Now that people have to live in the debris, their fields and meadows long vanished under now-vacant malls and abandoned tract developments, they might reflect that this all happened once before, when the great Amoskeag Mills shut down earlier in this century, and that history has repeated itself as farce instead of tragedy. Of course people are "hurting"—you usually do hurt after shooting yourself in the foot. And instead of yacking about wake-up calls and level playing fields and "sending a message" to the rest of the planet that America intends to remain a vicious bully among nations, first in everything but human reason, any candidate worth voting for, however hard the times, ought to offer people an appeal to their better natures, as well as to the part that eats. Nobody did.

1992

2. Disneyland Burns

I flew to Paris with the idea of finding something . . . piquant to write about the Euro Disney resort park in Marne-la-Vallée. It was just a natural for me. For one thing, the various Disney creatures (Mickey Mouse, Donald Duck, Goofy, Minnie Mouse) have always filled me with a high degree of disgust and terror, a creeping fear of idiocy or irreversible insanity that might be brought on by "giving in" to the universe these characters inhabit.

At the same time, I recognize these monstrosities as genuine American archetypes, eerily potent symbols of our culture, about which anybody's personal feelings (even mine!) are utterly irrelevant. "Mickey Mouse will see you dead," as one of Robert Stone's characters says somewhere.

John Berger compares the art of Disney to that of Francis Bacon. He says that the same essential horror lurks in both, and that it springs from the viewer's imagining: There is nothing else. Even as a child, I understood how unbearable it would be to be trapped inside a cartoon frame.

I didn't anticipate a crisis—well, I did and I didn't—that would keep me, for 10 days in Paris, skidding along the rim of an emotional meltdown, my own private volcano. "There is nothing else" was never far from my mind. The harder I tried to push this melancholy consideration away, the more fiercely it asserted itself, the more desperate I became to resolve a slew of painful differences between myself and another person, in spite of her absence.

I would decide the implications of recent bad scenes one way, then the exact opposite way a few minutes later, carrying on both parts of a conversation in my head, often while walking up and down the rue St. Gilles in Montparnasse, where I frequently killed time between lunch at the Hotel Lutetia Brasserie and early evening cocktails at the wine bar around the corner. I sat in a little cement park at the end of the rue St. Gilles, thrashing through *Le Monde* or *The Independent* with the kind of obsessed urgency typical of the mad, the newspaper pages crumpling messily in the faintest breeze, and telling myself: You little imbecile, you really are insane by this time, no wonder she can't stand you anymore. You've fucking lost your fucking mind. I later read the situation in a totally different way, but that was how it was.

The whole prospect of going to Euro Disney became onerous, dreadful, a kind of supreme insult to the operatic emotions I was struggling with. Could I even do my job under such a blitz of heavy feeling, such hopelessness, such ridiculous idolatry of another person? (And sometimes, like a fresh breeze, the thought would come: If anybody's crazy, it's her.)

It didn't help that the Disney press office, no doubt having figured out what *The Village Voice* is, declined to make company executives available for interviews, and restricted our press passes to a maximum of three days. (I was traveling with a photographer.) The Disney people were extremely bureaucratic, cordial, and uncooperative. I had had the idea of bringing various intellectuals and artists out to the park for their impressions, but it now appeared that to do this I would have to lay out the exorbitant entrance fees myself. In other words, I would be heartbroken and penniless in my favorite city in the world and, worse, not even be in my favorite city but inside a huge American plastic bubble at the ass end of my favorite city, in the Brie region of the Paris Basin. No thank you. Brie, as you probably know, is a type of soft cheese. Suitable, I suppose, for Mickey Mouse.

Several years ago I was on the opposite end of a more nebulous romantic impasse, again with a woman, who, as it happens, now lives in Paris, and has lost her mind, or part of her mind (not over me, thank God). She seems to be getting it back, bit by slow bit, but her mind is still like a loose phone wire and when I spent time with her I continually told myself: Keep on like you're going and you'll end up the way she is now, half in, half out of the moment, spilling into another dimension whenever there's a silence or a break in continuity. Unless you've known madness it sounds romantic, like Breton's *Nadja*, to wander the Paris streets with a woman in the throes of subacute schizophrenia, who sees signs and auguries in every chance occurrence. In reality it's exhausting and depressing and made me want to blow my brains out with the kind of pistol one can buy so easily in America, but, fortunately or not, not so easily in France.

It took forever to get motivated, plus one final bracing Remy Martin in the Bar Centrale in the Marais. (I'd read in the prospectus that no alcohol was served in Parc Euro Disney.) Then to the RER train in the giant Métro station at Châtelet-Les Halles, where tickets for Marne-la-Vallée, home of Euro Disney, come in a little folder with a Mickey Mouse silhouette pouch for your return ticket. The train held an unreadable assortment of suburban types, getting off in woebegone places like Bry-sur-Marne and Noisiel, Balzac towns full of hundred-year-old wooden buildings, obdurate necks and ruddy faces, and, on certain RER platforms, huge curved placards featuring the entire family of Disney characters grouped at the bottom, grinning moronically, the legend above them promising, in French: "Where Every Day Is Like Sunday." This automatically recalled the Morrissey song: ". . . a seaside town/that they forgot to bomb. . . . " Very few people were headed for Parc Disney, though 50 or 60 debarked at the end of the line, dispersing by bus or private cars into the countryside.

The RER station is all glass and aluminum or glass and steel, all transparencies and streaks of shiny gray; all of modern Paris outside the city's heart favors this Alphaville or Tonka-toy approach to municipal architecture. It's that cheaply durable mall look that colonized Les Halles with strip joints and hamburger shops when the old markets were torn out 15 years ago. The Marne-la-Vallée metro station sits hublike athwart the various spokes of the Disney wheel, in it but not of it, somehow, like the vaporetto landing at the train station in Venice.

The light was going. I thought it was going to rain. We walked through the gates of the park, into a gaudily landscaped forecourt, the kind of thing you'd find under an atrium at a major Hyatt Regency, with fountains splashing and foaming through a lot of ornamental brickwork. Unhappy children were crying outside the entrance of Euro Disney. For them the dream was over, evidently. A big clock on the front of the main building, with Mickey Mouse hands. A salmon-colored building with little pinpricks of light over every linear surface. The overdone gingerbread effects against the waning, cloud-silted evening sky evoked certain paintings of Paul Delvaux.

Yes, it was late in the day and midgets were casting giant shadows. Really terrible roller-rink music screeched from every imaginable cranny of the simulated rail station, which does in fact have an elevated train passing overhead, but more strategically acts as a barricade to the main park, and functions as a hotel, too, with long ornate arcades at either side of the ticket windows—arcades stuffed with shops selling anything you can think of, mostly bogus 1890s crap, fake memorabilia, fake antiques, globe lamps in frosted glass, old boxing posters, political posters, patriotic posters, anything with a flag on it, everything except that Minnie Mouse Fuck doll we've all been waiting for, creepy little teacups, creepy little desk ornaments, things that working-class people might think genteel or precious, those kinds of pathetic objects one wishes could have an aura or sentimental value, but because they come from a place like this, they can't.

Across the RER station, and partially pillowed in a mist that was rising in the twilight, was a shipwreck-looking huddle of aggressively thematic structures called Festival Disney. From the vantage point of the main park, the angular roofs and facades of Festival Disney resemble the Olympic Village in Munich, which Werner Schroeter used, in *The Death of Maria Malibran*, to evoke the infernal factory landscape of Manchester, England, at the dawn of the Industrial Revolution.

Behind the RER station, the private Disney bus line ferries visitors to the five hotels dotted across a densely landscaped corner pocket of the Disney complex. Though it later turned out you can easily walk to the hotels by passing through Festival Disney and down a corny promenade that looks like a backwater marina in Miami, minus yachts, and along an artificial lake ("Lake Buena Vista," what else), new arrivals, weighed down with luggage, naturally opt for the buses, which crawl along a circuit of trafficless internal roads indistinguishable from the "real" rural autoroutes outside the . . . what do you call it—the compound, the corporate property, the Disney—protracting what ought to be a three-minute zip into 15 or 20 minutes worth of ennui.

Euro Disney can be depicted within a circle, the "Boulevard Circulaire," in fact, which wraps around the amusement park, the resort hotel complex, Festival Disney, the artificial lake, and the property earmarked for Disney MGM Studios-Europe. Outside this enchanted perimeter lie Golf Euro Disney and Camp Davy Crockett, a golf course and camping site respectively, which properly belong to the extended future Disneyville, Disneymonde, or whatever it will ultimately be called.

It seems that the hypothetical planning of Euro Disney knows no final boundaries, that its American proprietors envision a steady, limitless growth, a Manifest Disney surging eastward across northern Europe, like Borges's map that grew until it coincided with the area it charted—eventually folding in private housing, perhaps transforming the countryside into Disney towns and Disney villages.

Note that the perimeter of Euro Disney contains part of the state railway system, a metro station, and a presently inactive TGV trunk line. The wider realm of Future Disney encompasses numerous public roads. There has been, in effect, a complete interpenetration of the Disney corporation and the state: for instance, the privately franchised newspaper kiosk in the RER station is perhaps the only one in France that doesn't sell cigarettes. Cigarettes must be purchased at certain hotel lounges and Festival Disney bars, at a steep markup.

The Disney person I most wanted to speak with was Philippe Bourguignon, senior vice-president in charge of real estate development. But the Disney press office instantly nixed this proposal: I was writing about the park, no? Bourguignon is involved with future projects, of no immediate concern. But of course it's this "future" thing, the vision thing, the prospect of metastasizing all-American amusements transplanted from tropical Hollywood to the damp northern European farm belt that's most arresting and sinister about Euro Disney as a whole. The landmass acquired by Disney in Marne-la-Vallée extends across several towns—Bailly-Romainvilliers, Magny-le-Hongre, Coupvray, Chessy, and Serris, in the corn-, sugar beet-, and wheat-growing flatlands—and is, roughly, one fifth the size of the city of Paris.

Imagine, if you will, a major Japanese corporation purchasing 10 square miles of the Ramapo hills to develop MITSUBISHI LAND USA, a theme park devoted to Japanese comic book and animation characters (and Japanese fast food, Japanese kitsch, Japanese history in broad strokes, and Japanese corporate underwriting), directly across the Hudson from Manhattan. Americans would, I think, burn the place down. (My friend Lynne Tillman thinks just the opposite. "Americans would love it," she assures me. "Besides, have the French—I mean really, when have the French even produced one major rock and roll, one important music group in all this time? They're still going 'ye-ye,' 'ye-ye' . . .")

The French despise Euro Disney—François Mitterrand told a TV interviewer in a withering voice that it was "not his cup of tea"—but, in a jittery economy, look indulgently on anything that promises to bring in revenue. Jeffrey Katzenberg and Michael

Eisner aren't in any immediate danger of being hung, even in effigy, in the Place de la Bastille. On the other hand, despite the massive long-term capital investment (you don't open a dry-cleaning shop unless you're prepared to lose your shirt for two or three years, much less a theme park one-fifth the size of Paris), there's a possibility that the whole project will fall on its face. After all, the Ninja Turtle's Tour crapped out at the French box office, proving that kids are not the same everywhere. So far, Euro Disney isn't getting anything like its projected numbers of visitors or revenue. *The Times* reports that the park will lose $60 million in its first fiscal year.

We're at the Newport Bay Club, a kind of puffed-up New Englandy neocon, pomo sprawl with indoor and outdoor swimming pools, a "yacht club" restaurant, and a plaster bust, I swear to you, of Walt Disney, perched at eye level at the top of the sweeping double staircase leading down to the "Cape Cod" dining room, the "Lake Buena Vista" boathouse, the ferry landing, the enclosed swimming pool, and blah blah blah.

Designed by mediocre architect Robert Stern, the place reeks of bogus gentility and class pretension. It evokes the grand hotels of northern New England, like the Balsams, which have long been converted from upper-class spas to petit bourgeois convention centers, or the grotesquely proletarianized restaurants and hotels of Carlsbad, Czech Republic. The only people in here come from an unbearable strain of French bourgeoisie that actually pays for first-class seats on the Métro, and the kind of American and German swine so bloated from excessive meat consumption they move in an alternative universe of obesity. Of course, you also get your svelte grandmoms and a smattering of debs in Laura Ashley gowns, and the occasional young corporate barnacle nursing a Scotch in the lobby-level piano bar, yearning for a blowjob from his fiancée, or, better, from someone else's fiancée. But mostly you get fat people with fat kids.

The Newport Bay gives off a "subdued" feeling completely at odds with the garish excess people have come here to expose their children to. On balance, however, the room isn't bad. There is, surprise, a minibar, stocked with the standard beers and liquors. The alcohol prohibition, it turns out, applies only to the actual Euro Disney theme park, not to its surrounding franchises. The Newport Bay has 1098 rooms. Nightly tariff in peak season, Fr 1100, e.g., almost $250. In actual Newport (where, if memory serves, there aren't any hotels) or actual New York, this would buy you a luxury suite. This room is slightly smaller than those in the average college dorm.

After our very brief exposure to the blandishments of Euro Disney, the photographer and I are chugging through the contents of the minibar with what can only be called zeal. On the cable TV, an endless montage of advertising for the very resort that surrounds us! Some of the attractions—big-tit girls in Mylar go-go fringe and twanging country crooners—look surprisingly adult, really. It appears that we're just missing Happy Hour at one of the Festival Disney theme bars. The good news is that something called "the Hurricane" is scheduled to happen after 9 p.m. Also, the bars stay open until 3 a.m. This means there is some sort of grown-up life around here, if you stretch the term grown-up a teeny bit. Well, of course, there would have to be: if you had to run Euro Disney according to the ludicrous aporias of "family values," with no chance of at least the head of the family getting trashed and maybe laid by someone not his family-value partner, chances are you would have to locate Euro Disney in Utah rather than France. Naturally, some journalist could easily go to town on Festival Disney, DISNEY'S DIRTY SECRET or what have you.

I am on the phone with the novelist Jean-Jacques Schuhl, with whom I've been drinking and dining in Paris every night. I am under the slightly stoned impression that "the Hurricane" is an actual meteorological event, an artificial storm contrived by those wacky Disney Imagineers, staged in the downtime after all the tubby little snotnosed Mouseketeers have been tucked away in their $250-a-night beds. In my mental world, "the Hurricane" would logically provide the more mature Disney consumer with that reassuring, modern sense of imminent cataclysm.

As it happens, some type of weather *is* blowing up outside, ruffling the gray gelatinous skin of Lake Buena Vista, where a lonely motorized pontoon boat is ferrying schmucks from the Newport Bay to the Hotel New York (Fr 1600 a pop in peak season, or $320 a night). The New York is a vapid exercise in capital P postmodernism by Michael Graves. A plastics convention is in progress over there, across the "lake." I don't mean to sound like a snob, but I can't help contrasting this dinky artificial pond and these pathetic nouveau nothing buildings, the fake grassy knolls and stubby hills bordering the lakeside walkways, with my first glimpse of Lake Como from the Milan-to-Cologne overnight train, or some of the other sublime aquatic views that Europe and nature provide free of charge. I mean, consider Venice in winter. What I'm seeing from this window is a very dim suburban notion of luxury, the kind of spotless, lifeless municipal space provided by a secure tax base in places like the Portland, Oregon riverside. Everything psychotically clean and landscaped for optimum surveillance ease, like Haussmann's makeover of Paris itself, though here every blade of grass has been designed by some eminent wastebasket of contemporary architecture.

"Don't leave the hotel room," Jean-Jacques insists. "Only report what you see on the television."

"I'm tempted by that Hurricane, though, Jean-Jacques. Leave it to Disney." ("Hurricane" turns out to be the name of the Festival Disney disco.)

Jean-Jacques clears his throat. "And is it true, out there, they have prostitutes dressed as Minnie Mouse? Wearing large masks and ears? You must put that in your article . . . even if it isn't true. Because it should be true, don't you think?"

Is It Mickey Or Is It Memorex?

All day Thursday, slogging through the crowds, we came across life-size Tweedledums, Tweedledees, Captain Hooks, Tinker Bells, the gamut, but no Mickey, no Mickey anywhere. On Sunday, however, we spot the little rodent right inside the park entrance.

"Excuse me, is this the only Mickey in the park?"

"Yes, he's the only one."

Rafik, a young Tunisian security man, warily eyes the mob of frenzied children clinging to the only person in the park dressed as Mickey Mouse: each child's hysteria feeds the others', and even some perky young moms and dads are going crazy. The man in the Mickey costume (I assume it's a man) pretends it's all in the day's work, but he's getting mauled pretty seriously. Rafik says it's a constant problem, people mobbing and molesting the main Disney characters, Mickey and Goofy and so on. Many of the swarming children wear Minnie or Mickey Mouse ears.

"How long have you worked here?"

"We can only have them out for 25 minutes. With the heat, they'd collapse."

"No, I mean, you've been working here how long?"

"Twenty-five minutes, then we go in for some time, then at four they will lead the big parade."

"And where's the big parade go?"

"It's here, all along Main Street, U.S.A., like that."

"You're very beautiful."

"Yes, it's beautiful, very busy, very colorful."

"Do you go into Paris? At night?"

As I try recalling Elizabeth Taylor's exact account of the death of Sebastian Venable a young Englishwoman wails ecstatically, "I hugged Minnie Mouse!" People are circling Minnie, Mickey, and the ravening kids with Canonvision, Sony camcorders, etc. We're all in front of the Ribbons & Bows Hat Shoppe and the Franklin Electric Lighting & Appliance Shop in the "Main Street U.S.A." area of the park. A Clydesdale-drawn trolley passes on curving tracks. The noise and the people are too much. Rafik and I spin off into separate orbits.

The most striking feature of Euro Disney is the security force, which comes in all shapes and sizes and all nationalities. Everywhere in the park and its environs roam men and women in suits or shirtsleeves or regulation skirts, carrying large Sony walkie-talkies, conspicuous black earphones plugged into one ear. They seem, at every moment, to be reporting through the handset to some magus, some Walt figure behind the curtain. Lower level personnel, waiters and sweepers and salesgirls and such, are kept under constant surveillance. Anything resembling a potential "incident" is dealt with swiftly, sometimes brusquely, sometimes brutally. The French gendarmes are present as well, empowered to make arrests the security people can't.

We have one report from *Libération* in which a local man was roughed up, then questioned for several hours by Disney Security, for parking his car wrong. He looked suspicious with his shoulder-length hair, had a less than cheery attitude, what have you. The questioning was done in the presence of the French police, who did nothing to protect the victim's civil rights. A mild scandal ensued. As compensation, the Disney people have offered the unfortunate man a free afternoon in the park.

Paris voices, later on:

"I'll tell you, though, the kids love it."

"Kids really go for it. So I guess these stupid stories really do come across for them."

"We might think it's a load of shit, but the kids love it."

"Well, fuck, face it, kids love anything you put in front of them. A Fabergé egg or a piece of cow turd, it's all the same to them."

"I really dread going out there. But I'm sure I'll have to, the kids see it advertised on TV and they want Mickey, they want Donald Duck."

"My son's five, he completely adored it, I have no idea why. You should interview him."

These are the Lands of Euro Disney: Fantasyland, Adventureland, Frontierland, Discoveryland, and Main Street, U.S.A. Like the institutional postmodernism of the resort's six hotels, the superficially varied styles of these lands articulate a heavily overdetermined anachronism, a mode in which any escape from cliché has become impossible.

Adventureland is an Arabophobic and racist pastiche *of The Thousand and One Nights*, complete with "native dancers" from darkest Africa who only lack bones in their noses. Each land has its redeemingly amusing features: Adventureland has "Pirates of the Caribbean," a genuinely fun boat ride through a swampy maze of simulacra (pirate's treasure chests, booming cannons, warring pirates, howling robot dogs, snuffling robot pigs, and dozens of animated skeletons). Really fun, in fact.

Discoveryland resembles the future as envisioned by *Popular Mechanics* back in 1930, "looking ahead" to bejeweled, sausage-shaped spaceships and a world that would represent the ultimate triumph of Art Deco.

Fantasyland is a sort of topiary-and-diorama rendering of classical fairy tales—*Sleeping Beauty*, *Cinderella*, *The Little Mermaid*—that Disney stripped of their complexity, violence, libidinal subtexts, and wonder many decades ago, and which are now so much mannerist piffle. At "Alice's Curious Labyrinth," spermy jets of water leap from pool to pool, the pools set atop six-foot hedges. On the hillside at the rear of the labyrinth, there's a floral arrangement in the face of a Cheshire cat. Inside the face, vermilion flowers. The cat's two eyes are rotating in opposite directions; the cat has a little Marcel Duchamp thing going on there, all based on *Alice in Wonderland*, but without the puberty-terror of *Alice in Wonderland*. There are no shadows, no ambiguities or disappointments in a Disney childhood, no sirree bob. Little children are trapped inside this hedge maze, but not really trapped, there's no real chance of getting lost. If I ran an amusement park, there would be real pirates and gypsies and an authentic criminal element on hand to supply a sense of risk.

This is what I really want to say: Don't throw our love away. The best part of breaking up is when you're making up. Since the day I saw you, I have been waiting for you. Hey, girls, do you believe in love? I got something to say about it, and it goes like this. You know you are in bad trouble when the lyrics of popular songs start making you cry before breakfast.

At the end of the Frontierland area there's something called "Phantom Manor," a virtual replica of Universal Studios Tour's "Psycho House." At least the house is identical—I don't know what happens in there. There are maybe a thousand people—well, I don't know, but hundreds and hundreds—waiting in line to go through this house. The nearby riverboat ride is also mobbed, hundreds packed onto the landing stage waiting to go aboard. The Lucky Nugget restaurant's full of people eating barbecue, under little parasols on the old western wooden porch, on the stoop, on the benches outside. Unbelievable hordes of people.

We have no trouble getting on Les Voyages de Pinocchio the first day, but on Sunday it's inaccessible. The line for the carousel, endless. Well, no, I think you could get on the carousel within a half hour. Aside from Dumbo, a fairly conventional whirling-elephant ride just behind it, the carousel is my favorite. These beautiful horses, tricked out in burnished armor, quite noble-looking, like all horses, and not much different than the ones in the carousel behind the Châtelet Métro station.

There's a very spooked-out looking grandmother sitting all alone in one of the chariots. She's wearing a blue-and-white polka dot dress. She really looks like Margaret Whiting or something, very thin, very old, very dignified, here she comes again, now she looks like Max Ernst, or that actor who played Dr. Mabuse in the Fritz Lang movies. She's got a walking stick. "When You Wish Upon a Star" is blaring so loudly that standing here feels like being trapped in the malefic ending of a Fassbinder movie, where you discover all your paranoid fantasies are true.

Flashback. First night in Paris, dinner at Natacha's: Hanna Schygulla remarks that as a kid during the American Occupation, poking around in the rubble of Munich, she did not acquire much of a taste for the World of Disney, which came along with the Occupation in the form of comics and cartoons and seemed to reflect a fantasy life produced by an experiential vacuum. She turns to our mutual friend V., whose childhood was partly spent in refugee camps after her father was hung with piano wire for his role in the 20th of July plot.

"I can't imagine, V.," Hanna says, "that you had much interest in these Disney things either...."

Adventure Isle. That's where these stalwart adventurers are heading, with their bagels, their $6 franks, their yogurt ice cream cones. So far, I've only seen one shirtless man, who just walked by, middle-aged, a body that hadn't completely run to seed but not terribly attractive, either. Everyone else seems to have clothes on. Adventure Isle, from this side, has a rock formation with the shape of a giant skull embedded in it, and a very large pirate ship. Now we're leaving Adventureland pretty quickly. Here are the toilets. I've had two attacks of pancreatitis since arriving in France. The first was in front of the Hotel Lutetia, the second one here, in *Le Visionarium*, a dumb but effective Circle Vision movie about Jules Verne, H. G. Wells, and time travel: featuring Gérard Depardieu as a baggage handler at Orly airport.

Once again my favorite ride, the one I'd most like to go on, Dumbo the Flying Elephant ride, is completely full, you can't get on it. If it took us an hour on Friday to wait for the not-very-scary, three-minute roller coaster in Frontierland ("Big Thunder Mountain," more like Big Thunder Molehill, thrill-wise), it would take quite a bit longer, today, to get on one of the really nice rides. I don't say Dumbo is so special, except that I really love elephants, especially Dumbo the Elephant. I think Dumbo is an uncharacteristically happy and benign Disney creation, nothing at all like the sinister, brainless yet Manichean Mickey Mouse.

We're now in Adventureland proper, just inside the entrance. People cool their hands in a high tublike fountain under a chandelier. We're right in front of the "bazaar." An African woman assiduously sweeps up cigarette butts as they're discarded by the hundreds of smokers passing through. Here's the artificial *hammam*, the public bath, only it's really a tiled trench full of cold water, and the space is occupied by both sexes, something that would never occur in Morocco. Allah would strike everyone dead.

The cafés are full, the attractions are full, the shops are full. The stir-fry stand, which was entirely deserted the other day, is now mobbed with people. There's a large line for the sandwiches booth, another empty-on-Friday place. There's a pirate ship that cuts across Adventureland, the line for it's endless . . . you have never seen so much leisurewear in your life.

The commodity on sale at Euro Disney is time itself, leisure time, the time of your life: time to wait an hour for a three-minute ride, time to wait for a restaurant seat, time to stand on line next to other people whom you never talk to, never relate to, waiting for an experience that will be entirely private, even though you have it in synchronization with others. The park has been designed so that however small the attendance, the lines will always be impressively long. In practical fact, there isn't much in this place. You could do everything in two hours, go on every ride, sample every restaurant, buy a piece of souvenir junk in every shop, if there weren't stupendous, numbing lines. Since Disney recommends a three-day visit for families, I assume what they're selling is exactly this alienated duration, the time spent waiting in silence, waiting in obedience to some unwritten code of decorum, waiting like cattle at the abattoir. And nobody talks to anybody.

The other thing John Berger says about Francis Bacon's painting, that's also true about the world of Disney: it presumes a universe in which human beings no longer have any minds at all. Where the human beast really is a hunk of chattering brainless meat. Nothing reinforces this view quite as sharply as a half hour in a place like this. When a small child falls on its face, when another one bursts out in tears 'cause he can't find mommy, I think of hapless defective monkeys, wounded baby seals, that sort of thing.

Festival Disney is sort of fun. If you're straight and 18 and really, really fuckable, Festival Disney is your oyster, so to speak. Festival Disney is the lubricious side of this didactically family-oriented theme park. It's basically an arcade, something like the massive arcade in Milan that's practically flush with La Scala. But instead of a glass dome, there are silver and red metal-faced square pylons that rise straight up above the various businesses and are linked by thick wire, which makes the ceiling of the complex resemble a vast circus net.

On either side of the wide main walkway are theme restaurants and theme souvenir shops and theme bars, all done with a maniacal attention to detail. Frank Gehry, the only really interesting architect in evidence out here, has inflated the notion of transplanted Americana into a really disturbing *Twilight Zone* effect. Sitting in the Carnegie Deli simulacrum, you really feel you could be in New York, and not in your favorite place in New York, either.

This impresses me as a very deft stage magician's trick, to reproduce faithfully those quotidian, repulsive details of the American everyday, like the license plates and hubcaps nailed to the rustic wooden beams of Billy Bob's Country Western Saloon, or the bowling trophies and framed pictures of athletes on the walls of Champion's Sport Bar.

At least 200 young cowpokes and their cows are whooping it up in Billy Bob's on this particular evening, jumping, shouting, bumping, and burping to a c&w band so authentic-sounding it has to be fake.

Billy Bob's is a macho scene straight out of El Paso, everybody in cowboy shirts, leather vests, and suede chaps, or those Capezio tops any self-respecting set of bosoms more or less leaps out of, tops tucked into Levis tucked into cowboy boots. Billy Bob's has that crackle of impending violence any real bar for real men offers like a nail scraping a blackboard, and every person in Billy Bob's appears to be clutching at least four mugs of beer and his neighbor's tits, ass, or quiff. Strange to say, for all the noise and booze and confusion in Billy Bob's, it smells like a cedar hope chest in a fresh pinewood closet. Now, a real Western bar smells, as we all know, of piss, vomit, spilled beer, and sawdust. A few drinks down the line, I get a waiter in Billy Bob's to confess that they scrub the entire place down every morning with disinfectant, clean everything including the license plates and wagon wheels, and pipe in that chaste cedar-pine scent. Otherwise it'd be just too raunchy to be a Disney thing.

And what is a Disney thing, after all? It is, first of all, sexless, without sensuality, pitched to the zone of warm, sentimental feelings manufactured by "family" propaganda, something cuddly, something huggable, something with no erotic charge, something that has death included in the sticker price, a code of sentiments wherein everybody means well though everybody makes mistakes, where love conquers all in the form of a chaste enchanted kiss, elephants fly and broomsticks sing, where daddy mommy and baby makes three, four, five, even six little replicas, all squalling and picking their little noses. I guess the ideal Disney thing would be one of those fetuses Randall Terry carries around with him, souped up by Disney's Imagineers to crawl around and deliver a tirade denouncing abortion.

One very peculiar thing you notice walking through Euro Disney: you hear the word Disney uttered hundreds of times by the visitors, like a kind of charm, or a guarantee of authenticity. This must be peculiar to this Disney facility, which has the novelty of being an American amusement park where the elves and androids and talking teapots speak garbled French. What Euro Disney shares with other Disney manifestations is that wondrously mechanistic complacency about its own effect on people, expressed in publicity that tells you exactly what you will feel about its "heartwarming" characters, "thrilling" rides, and "dazzling" 3-D musical films.

At the same time, Euro Disney's publicity contains a heavy element of defensiveness, since the park's very existence is an obvious expression of American cultural imperialism. It's stressed, for example, that Walt Disney was "of Norman ancestry," a descendant of the d'Isigny family (you all know *them*); furthermore, Walt, too young for the army, became an ambulance driver for the Red Cross in France during World War I. The European origin of the Disney characters and stories is emphasized in all the literature.

At around 10 p.m., I find myself loitering between Billy Bob's and the Sport Bar. The Sport Bar, by the way, has a plausibly European expanse of outdoor tables, full at this hour with every sexually active teen from the area—there are, someone informs me, five men for every available woman, the reverse of the usual ratio—drinking lustily and checking out the babes, rubbing their big peasant crotches, posing and preening for the sparse, discreet, but discernible glances of homoerotic interest. Straight men are so damned obvious.

"What, you want a Minnie Mouse or one of these for a hundred francs? Not really?"

Stephanie's accent is Midlands, I think. She's working at one of Festival Disney's sales kiosks, dealing with some fussy British people considering the purchase of a Minnie Mouse ballpoint pen or a Minnie Mouse doll. Since the customers are people from home, she soon feels comfortable echoing their disgust at the outrageous prices. Once they've moved on, I strike up a conversation of the same type.

"Well," she says, "and who wants to pay a hundred francs for a stupid thing like that? It's an outrage. They get a hundred francs for that and you should see what they pay us. I'm not making sod all, standing here all night with a big idiotic smile, and they want to know where I learned French. I tell them, I learned my French at university, certainly not from Disney's.

"You know they did a big recruitment all over the EEC, they got about 12,000 of us over here, I think about 3000 have already quit. They promised me 6000 francs a month, but I'm not getting sod all. There's no place to live out here, they put us in this official housing, it's more than an hour away, and they charge a third of my pay for this miserable little apartment I have to share with two other people.

"Not only do I have to stand here, I've got another kiosk to run over there, and besides that, you've got to attend classes at Disney University, where they indoctrinate you with all this Walt Disney propaganda. It's worse than the Nazis."

I'm not making a word of this up, either. A troupe of acrobats juggling skittles comes bouncing and leaping across the perimeter of the Sport Bar's outdoor tables, then jumps onto an elevated stage beside the entrance to Billy Bob's.

"They're not bad," Stephanie tells me, "when they don't drop the skittles." She tells me she's quitting next month. "I've had it. I went all through university and never borrowed a penny from my mum and dad. Now they've got to send me money every month just to make ends meet. We've all gotten screwed, everybody they recruited. And most of us are quitting, too." Disney declined to comment on employee relations or anything else.

I make a date for an actual interview with Stephanie the following afternoon, but she never shows up; the photographer and I speculate that the security people "got to her." There are so many of them peppered throughout Euro Disney that one feels a heady déjà vu of Prague or Budapest before the end of communism.

"We're not supposed to talk to people," Stephanie told me. "Especially not any press people."

At 6:30 Friday morning, the photographer goes jogging. Out the window, the bleary overcast landscape, the postmodern hotels, the greenish-gray "lake," the boathouse, the emptiness. . . . When I pictured what losing her would be like, I saw my heart being scooped from my chest with a serrated grapefruit spoon, like a custard, a blood pudding. . . . The photographer rematerializes 40 minutes later. He's somehow jogged through the closed park to the main entrance on the autoroute, discovering that hundreds of tractors belonging to local farmers are backed up to the gate. The farmers have made bonfires from pyramids of rubber tires and gasoline.

Sure enough, out the window, a haze of greasy smoke is settling over the middle distance. I shower, dress, grab the tape recorder. We set off for the main gates but where are the main gates? First of all, the rear entrance of Festival Disney is locked, we have to make our way down to the Hotel New York, cross the indoor swimming pool, go out through the garden, and then through a maze of paths, some of which lead to a carport and only one of which ends at the road used by the Disney buses.

Once on that road, we discover that it bifurcates at a sort of sentry box where the usual blue uniforms and walkie-talkies are changing shifts. One branch of the road wraps around the outer park and passes over the rail lines. Looking down from the bridge,

I see that one of the fires is blazing at the distant end of the railway, which looks impossibly far away. To the right of the rail lines, an access road skims several parking lots and a camping ground and extends to a barely visible gate, where it meets the public highway.

"It's there," the photographer says.

"Yeah, but how the fuck did you get there?"

Well, he hadn't expected to run across anything in the first place, so he doesn't quite recall. Beyond the rail overpass, the road abuts an escarpment where several gardeners, all armed with walkie-talkies, are already working on the vegetation. After several false moves and equivocations we decide to split up. I walk back to the overpass and gaze down at the railroad tracks. Out there, at the end of the line, is the public autoroute. It's just a question of getting to it.

I start walking down the access road bordering both the campground and the rail line. The road is unbelievably long. I realize that none of the nonamusement space within Euro Disney is meant to be traveled by foot, or traveled at all: it's like Los Angeles without a car. When the guards at the sentry box see me plodding back to the hotel road from the rear of the park, they demand to see my Euro Disney Pass, and look at me as if I'm obviously demented for wanting to walk around.

Five Black Marias are parked halfway between the sentry point and the gate at the end of the access road. Inside the Black Marias, French soldiers are listening to rap music on the radio. One soldier is taking a leak behind his vehicle. He smiles at me and shakes a little urine off his dick, starts to ask what I'm doing there, then shrugs and gets back in the van. The campground looks empty. The large parking lot around it is dotted with cars, whose cars, who's to say?

The road is at least a mile long. At the very end, a security station, something like a toll booth, and a small white van designed like a police wagon, with an iron grille over the long rear windows. A tall, broad, ugly German in a brown suit stands before the green metal gate, flanked by two Spanish men in unidentifiable, vaguely military uniforms. They all examine me with mild, reflexive contempt.

Well, okay, this big fat German of the authoritarian type I've run across a million times in Germany, the stout-hearted Brown Shirt type, the former Hitler Youth type, the beer-hall type, yes, I stare into his mica blue Aryan-from-Bavaria eyes and he stares into my deep brown one-quarter Jew eyes and what can I tell you, anything but kismet.

"Can you let me through?"

He understands English perfectly but says nothing, just smiles a lipless little smile and shakes his burly head.

"Listen, I'm a reporter, I've got to get onto the main road."

"You have a press card?"

I show him my press card.

"He wants to see the farmers," Adolf Eichmann announces to his Spanish flunkies. "I'm sure, you like the farmers, isn't it?"

"Will you let me through or not?"

"You want to go out? You can go out that way." He points to the auto exit, a fork in the road that goes off a mile and a half in the wrong direction.

"You mean you won't let me out of here? Onto the public road?"

Eichmann replies that if I want to get to the main gates, I'll have to retrace my steps, back up the access road, back to the sentry box, right on the road that goes from the hotels to the park, around the curve where the gardeners are transplanting Serbian spruces and probably planting surveillance bugs in the topsoil, then through the park itself.

There is no percentage in standing here, so I do exactly as he says. It takes a half hour, and once in the forecourt of Euro Disney, I still can't get across it to any of the autoroute entrances. All of which are currently on fire.

The farmers are protesting the current GATT agreements, which mandate huge cutbacks in French agricultural subsidies—supposedly in conformance with uniform EEC policy, but in fact because of egregious pressure from the Bush administration which views the French farm subsidies as "unfair" to American markets. The Reagan-Bush gang, you may recall, crippled small-scale

American agriculture by abolishing our own subsidies, and now wants to "level the playing field" by screwing the farmers of Europe.

A week earlier, the same farmers dumped tons of vegetables onto the autoroute and set them ablaze with gasoline. One of the lead tractors in today's protest is mounted by a farmer effigy with a pitchfork stuck in his stomach. There are three fires going, two at the side gates, one at the main entrance, and another pyre soaked in gasoline that the police stop the farmers from lighting.

I return to the Newport Bay. Festival Disney is still closed, but now the gate's open so I cut through there to Lake Buena Vista etcetera. The air stinks of burning rubber. The wind blows sheets of thick oily smoke through the air. I realize, suddenly, that Euro Disney is modeled like a concentration camp. Each discrete section of the compound can be locked, and by sealing a few strategic routes, security can make it impossible to move from one part of the place to another.

In the "Cape Cod" breakfast room, as I'm writing up notes, an enormous dwarf of some kind, some creature in a big plastic head mask and gaudy costume, whisks the pen from my fingers and apes writing something on its other gloved hand. Giant chipmunks waddle around the restaurant, goosing people, bringing joy and merriment to the hearts of obese brats and their parents, who favor the windbreaker-and-docksider look in the breakfast room. The children all have very spiffy yellow Mickey Mouse rain slickers (Fr 40, a bargain). Meanwhile, out the window, plumes of smoke roll into the atmosphere behind the amusement park, and the stench of burning rubber snakes along Lake Buena Vista, seeping into the somewhat bleary festivity of the "Cape Cod."

The farmers' blockade has left the restaurant, and indeed all the Euro Disney businesses, severely understaffed today: what we have, evidently, is Skeleton Disney, a condition many Disney employees seem amused by, while others are frankly pissed. A guy who works for the Orly-Euro Disney bus line, for instance, tells me that "200 farmers are insignificant compared with the thousands of jobs they've created here," though these jobs, I point out, aren't strictly French jobs, but seem to've been filled by every conceivable nationality. "Well," he retorts, "it's good for the EEC." He also claims that the GATT agreements "have nothing to do with the U.S., it's a European problem."

We are in the Sport Bar in the middle of the day, and I am buying the bus driver large mugs of beer, to "draw him out." He's a small, nervous man with male-pattern baldness and a disconcertingly obvious homo streak in spite of the wife and children; he keeps trying to get me into the bathroom with him.

"See, what the French resent," he informs me, "is that Disney took all these stories, all these fairy tales we had here already, and figured out how to make money with them. We resent the ingeniousness of the Americans."

I keep him soaking up beer, talking, talking, expounding his philosophy of everything, I don't challenge a word, but some kind of internal movement occurs, some shift in his inner wind, maybe his nerves are touchy because of the fires, his buses aren't running, it turns out he hates living out here, he's from Normandy, he'd like to move back there before he dies.

"It's great making money, yes, I admit it," he sighs, completely drunk. "But I have to say, with all due respect, you Americans have got no class whatsoever."

1992

3. Town of the Living Dead

Thirty minutes south of Springfield on I-65, engine sparks spitting under the chassis ignite the innards of an RV, which stops dead on the asphalt, disgorging a family of flustered, obese vacationers moments before the propane tanks explode. It's 90 degrees to begin with, and we're stuck, 12 cars to the rear, waiting for the who knows which fire department and the Missouri highway patrol, as a fat plume of velvet smoke rolls out of the gutted camper. The second explosion sounds like the foot of an angry god stomping on a large sheet of bubble wrap. You can hear a half ton of imitation wood grain furniture and Formica countertops and modular bedding crackle into toxic ash as people waddle from their cars for snapshots. Among the chorus of rednecks gawking at the blaze, there is palpable disappointment, thinly veiled as relief, as the news spreads that everyone got out of the RV okay, including the grandmother.

To put it simply, the fun begins even before you get to Branson, Missouri. Billboards thicken in the fields a few miles before Highway 76. Silver Dollar City. Shepherd of the Hills. Tony Orlando's Yellow Ribbon Music Theater. At the junction of 64 and

76, a cluster of two-story buildings—insurance offices, Baptist and Lutheran churches, clothing shops, and soda fountains—comprise the rural burg that existed before Branson became, in its own words, "America's fastest growing resort." This is downtown Branson—population 4000—all fresh paint and gentrified storefronts and, emphatically, nothing special. It's roughly four square blocks sloping to a narrow arm of Lake Taneycomo, where a waterborne shopping mall in the shape of a riverboat broods near the entrance of a public park.

It would be pointless to look for an authentic, native Branson where the manna of tourist dollars doesn't require at least honorary tolerance of all but the most questionable foreigner. Folks might not cotton to the way you look or dress here, but as long as you're buying something you can count on a smile pasted over the homicidal wish behind the cash register. Now and then an overworked waitress or shopkeeper opines that Branson is "burning itself out," or complains that the "stars" perennially "settling" in Branson, like Bobby Vinton, come in for the quick cash and leave a year later. But Branson isn't Nashville—its indigenous attractions, like the Baldknobbers Hillbilly Jamboree, are the kind of rustic kitsch best exemplified by gift shop miniatures. There is nothing very precious being lost by expansion, except the landscape itself, which no one has much interest in preserving anyway.

Branson is one of those rural sites where temples to local folklore sprang up to attract tourists, who were first drawn to the area by the fishing and boating facilities on Lake Taneycomo. The lake, like the town, is artificial, created in 1913 by the damming of the flood-prone White River. Manmade lakes, with their dynamic impact on aquatic flora and fauna, are a specialty of the region.

There was, in the '30s, a movie house called the Hillbilly Theater, and a Hollywood Hills Hotel owned by a special effects director named Ned Mann. Local histories claim that movie stars stayed there, but fail to mention any by name. In 1949, the manager of the Hillbilly Theater erected a gigantic Adoration

Scene on a bluff overlooking downtown Branson. You know, the Adoration. Infant Jesus, Mary, cattle, the Wise Men, frankincense and myrrh. In 1953, the Chamber of Commerce started, during the Christmas season, an Adoration Parade to light the Adoration Scene.

About the same time, a family named Trimble opened a theme park devoted to the inspirational folklore found in *The Shepherd of the Hills*, a 1907 novel by Harold Bell Wright, which recounts the exploits of The Baldknobbers, an Ozark vigilante gang, and various mystically charged events following a bad drought. *The Shepherd of the Hills* was fashioned into an annual pageant, a sort of white trash Passion Play, performed in an amphitheater at the Shepherd of the Hills farm, which also offers a Homestead Tour, a wagon ride with Clydesdale horses, a blacksmith shop, Championship Frog Races, and a bluntly phallic Inspiration Tower, featuring "a truly awe inspiring panoramic view of the Ozarks," restrooms, and snack bar.

Another theme park, Silver Dollar City, opened around the same time, and another lake, Table Rock, was added to the landscape by another dam. I-65 became clogged with vacationers. A four-lane bypass created an interchange with Highway 76. They opened a Wal-Mart on 76. The rest is history.

From the air—specifically, from a C-500 Hughes helicopter, which you can hire for six minutes for $22.50—Branson becomes a legible metastasis spreading across the woodsy, mountainous Missouri landscape, replicating the same cellular structures over and over: motels, music theaters, "rides," "attractions," souvenir shops, restaurants, specialty stores. This architectural melanoma starts as you hover west from downtown. The lack of any rational planning gives Branson the look of a fever dream, a horror vacuui planted on either side of five miles of graded highway. The theaters, some with seating for 4000, appear as massive swellings beside the weird spires and kooky shapes of amusement arcades, water slides, theme motels, and mammoth parking lots. On branch roads behind Highway 76, huge gouts of forest have been cleared for ever larger hotels and theaters, erected with the speed peculiar to contractors with friends named Gambino and Luchese. At certain hours, traffic is jammed on 76 heading west; at others, the east lane is blocked. Never both at the same time, but always one or the other.

Nearer My God Than You

The woman on stage is singing about Jesus. It is a gruesome tune, emphasis on Crown of Thorns, spear in side, physical torture, sung with a fervor bordering on necrophilia ("Feel his heart beat ... "). She is wearing a mauve dress and clutching a cordless microphone the size of an old-fashioned cocktail shaker. Behind her, liturgical-looking shapes light up the wall above a large assortment of musicians. Deeply moved, the singer belts her way through the Crucifixion and His Blood soaking into the ground and Him being laid away in a tomb, and then, after a histrionic pause, the singer's mouth expands in a smile of blazingly white enamel, because, guess what, when they rolled away the stone, they discovered that He Had Risen, Yes He Had.

It's three in the afternoon, and the Osmond Family Theater is half empty, but also half full, with the staple Branson afternoon audience, bus tours. Down from the fruited plains of Kansas. Up from the parched yet fertile bowels of Arkansas. Over from the purple mountains majesty and prairie towns where cholesterol and deep-fried everything are things to be thankful for rather than feared. People come to Branson in groups. Family groups. Community groups. Retirement groups. Church groups. They come with the love of Jesus and the Right to Life and a hatred of gun control throbbing in their plaque-encrusted arteries in time to "The Wabash Cannonball."

It is safe to say that no one comes alone to see the Osmond Brothers, which is why, sitting in the exact middle of the front row between a woman who has seen the Osmond Brothers 30 times and two very small children attached to a plump, elderly, dropsical-looking woman in pink Bermuda shorts and a thalo-green blouse, I am fully prepared to tell anyone who asks that my wife and children were recently killed in a plane crash.

The Crucifixion number is followed by several couples in shiny red, blue, and yellow, vaguely Swiss, silk costumes, tap dancing. They tap for a long time, faces dilated in robotic grins, with the kind of oblivious energy one associates with amphetamine psychosis. I look behind me. There is a vast bobbing cloud of white hair that slowly separates into individual heads.

Once the Osmonds hit the stage, it's quite impossible to sit still and let the show wash over you. Not because the Osmonds are so special, but because the Osmonds immediately want to know which half of the audience has more enthusiasm. How loud can we clap our hands? How hard can we stamp our feet? Now, let's get to know each other! Shake hands with your neighbor on the right! Shake hands with your neighbor on the left! The woman who's seen the Osmonds 30 times apparently has my number and merely glares at me, though I clap and stomp and smile like an idiot whenever she does, just to see what that feels like. It feels really geeky. I am wearing a dark brown T-shirt and black jeans, a bad choice for a theater livid with pastels and splashy prints. Most clothing worn in Branson resembles daring wallpaper, ethnic restaurant tablecloths, or stuff a motel would use for curtains.

Merrill, Wayne, Jimmy, Jay, and Alan Osmond are all pretty hefty, middle-aged, vocally gifted Mormons. They're wearing white jackets with rhinestone arrows and blue stars and red and white flag stripes, large silver belt ornaments, string ties, and turquoise Indian bracelets. Each Osmond has a little shtick of his own: one fiddles, another one has a guitar thing going on, one yodels Hank Williams covers, another one sings in that froggy Tennessee Ernie Ford baritone, and one brother tells the kind of jokes that used to fly well on *The Lawrence Welk Show*.

There is an inexhaustible supply of Osmonds on stage, in the wings, and on the road with separate acts. Marie and Donny are headliners at other theaters, and often join these Osmonds for a family hoedown, or coven, or whatever you call it, but not today. Instead we have the second-generation Osmonds on various instruments, dancer Heather Osmond, and Amy Osmond, who, somewhere in the middle of the first hour (all shows in Branson run two hours, with a long intermission), provides a spot of Classical

Uplift with a Mozart violin piece. She plays well.

As this unexpected fragment of High Culture sends the crowd into awed mutism, I have time to reflect that the difference between Branson and Nashville is something palpable and programmatic, a satanic bargain between performers and audience based on mutual defensiveness. The audience knows that in the world outside, Branson's headliners—the Osmonds, Glen Campbell, Andy Williams, Cristy Lane—are well past their peaks, which, in many cases, were never exactly soaring. The performers know that the audience—solid white, born-again, lumpen middle- and working-class Americans—is profoundly out of whack with the trajectory of American popular culture, which, for all its inanity, is generally libertarian, multicultural, and secular. The performers cater to the phobia-driven inner life of the audience, devoting lavish stage time to the celebration of family, God, and country. (The Osmonds, like several other Branson acts, wind up their show with "The Battle Hymn of the Republic.") In return, the audience treats them as if they were, currently or ever, major stars.

Precious Moments

At the John Davidson show, the fantastically corpulent ladies on either side of me are getting to know each other and continue talking across me after I sit down.

"Did you ever put up okra with tomatoes?"

"I put up okra with green peppers and onions."

"Well, I like chow-chow. My daughter-in-law went into the hospital last weekend so I'm going to make some for her. I'd like to make raspberry jam, but her doctor told her anyone who munches on seeds and nuts is endangering their colon. She's having half her colon removed. I'm afraid of the seeds!"

"We pay six dollars a gallon for blueberries."

"I'm afraid of seeds!"

Time hasn't been especially unkind to John Davidson, but as with so many Branson headliners he is remarkably thicker and older than one remembers him. It doesn't help that the slide show above the stage opens with a solarized photo of Davidson as he once was, repeated on seven panels. However, he gamely projects a youthful ingenue sort of image to the crowd, which is, by and large, still quite a lot older than he is. When he quizzes married couples in the audience for "the year they fell in love," instantly delivering a song popular that year, the game hits an awkward pause when absolutely no one claims to have fallen in love more recently than 1960.

Davidson works the room like an appliance set to run for two hours even if the roof collapses. He's bent on winning the audience and at the same time seems oblivious to any particular person in it. He's got his material, his fake-opera-with-a-stiff-from-the-audience routine, his sing-along-with-a-Wurlitzer-juke-box shtick, his family-man-who-pretends-to-be-randy thing. This is a low-tech show in a relatively small theater, far from crowded, and Davidson isn't yet really established in Branson. He is not a good singer, yet he sings everything, even his little speeches, creating the illusion that the show has much more music in it than it does. For Branson, he goes rather far. After singing to one dowdy wife in the front row, he imagines her husband telling her back at the motel, "I bet you 20 dollars he's gay."

Later he pretends to arrange motel assignations among strangers in the audience. Having described growing up with a minister father (family photos appear on the slide panels, each with a little story to tell), he does a number in which a ravenously hungry preacher abandons his sermon to devour a chicken that's flown into the church. During a medley of '50s rock covers, he gives a long exegesis of "parking," which was, he says, all about ". . . kissing, since we're in Branson now."

None of Davidson's show would be at all risqué, or for that matter entertaining, outside Branson, but here he fills an obvious void. In a town where fart jokes and speech impediments define the threshold of acceptable humor, Davidson makes fun of religious zeal and alludes to nonmarital sex. The obligatory patriotic finale comes with a slide montage of heroic icons that includes, among several provocative choices, Muhammad Ali and Arthur Ashe. Davidson is, I guess, a safe form of cosmopolitanism.

Shoji Tabuchi is much more identifiably Branson, a cherished local institution. Like Yakov Smirnoff, the Russian comic whose signature line, "What a country!" has congealed into—what else?—the What a Country Theater, Tabuchi functions as an emblem of successful assimilation, of diversity where there is none. A typical story in the promotional literature tells of a veteran who, after hearing Tabuchi's violin, was able "to forget World War II."

Tabuchi is, in other words, the anomaly who refutes the idea that Branson is an intolerant, small-minded, racially exclusive place. It's affectionately noted, everywhere, that Tabuchi is fantastically rich and spent millions on the rest rooms of his theater. In this, and many other things, he epitomizes a stereotype of the "good" Japanese: relentlessly industrious, given to grandiose but shrewd expenditures, and, of course, in his embrace of country and western, endlessly adaptive and unoriginal.

Tabuchi's theater reflects a real-world rather than off-world taste. There are glass bricks in the facade and Deco chairs in one of the lounges, and overall it looks like it was built by an architect rather than a cartoonist. The rest rooms are something from *Citizen Kane*, yes. The lobby is packed full of white people spilling out of their K-mart leisure-wear, snacking and taking snapshots. Shoji Tabuchi artifacts and refreshments are peddled all over the building. During intermission, kiosks offering videos, tapes, and T-shirts appear on either side of the stage.

The show uses a lot of lasers, 3-D effects, and scrims. Tabuchi's little daughter, a tiny spot on a cavernous black stage, sings "Imagine" as a carpet of stars lights up behind her. A flying sofa flutters down from the wings, carrying her into an Arabian fantasia of turbans and dervishes and the kind of choreography the June Taylor Dancers used to execute on *The Jackie Gleason Show*. This goes on for a very long time. A restless brat sitting next to me turns to his mother and says, precociously, "This sucks."

Tabuchi, who dominates a stage of musicians with the restless physical presence of a grinning, wound-up incubus, has at least as much talent on the violin as Victor Borge had on the piano. He can play anything country, and does, though after a few minutes it all sounds like the same thing. The fact that he plays it at all is the source of Tabuchi's popularity; as a Japanese, his status is that of an idiot savant, an alien who shouldn't be able to do advanced calculus in his head but unaccountably does. Tabuchi's shtick is all about being Japanese on other people's turf: pronouncing things wrong, eating raw fish, scrambling the titles of C&W standards, and in general ingratiating himself with hordes of Christians willing to forget World War II, since he's been willing to learn The Tennessee Waltz. Behind the shtick is the scrutable smile of a contented millionaire.

House Of Wax

The mystery of Branson, if there is one, is the quirky way that star worship functions in a repressive microcosm. Maybe because it's compressed into such a small area, Branson is the tightest little cultural sphincter you are likely to find in the United States. There are no shadows in Branson. No whores, no gambling, no drugs, no egregious drinking. There are, ubiquitously, Family Restaurants serving huge portions of the worst food on the continent; "Frito Pie" is a characteristic menu item. Fried chicken, a dish you'd imagine native to the Ozarks, arrives carbonized, like a mutant pork rind.

There are funfairs stuffed with kiddie attractions, bumper cars, water dodgems, convoys of amphibious Duck Boats (something between a cabin cruiser and an armored personnel carrier, "More Duck for Your Buck") that drive passengers into and around the lakes, miniature golf courses, and biblically large families splashing around in heated motel swimming pools flush with the sidewalk along the main drag.

There is Ozarkland, featuring the Koi Garden Oriental Restaurant, T-Shirt Factory, and Basket Man. There is the Calico Cat Country Store, the Hillbilly Inn, Ma Barker's Famous Barbeque, Kenny Rogers' Roasters, Western Sizzlin' Steak House, the D.J. Motel, the Heart of the Ozarks Inn, the Ozark Mountain Inn, Holiday Inn, E-Z Center Motel, the Amber Light Motor Inn, the 76 Mall (Ladies Apparel, Country Fudge, Aunt Minnie's Funnel

Cakes). The Outback Steak and Oyster Bar, Outback Outfitters, and Outback Bungee Jumping Platform. Bonanza Chicken Steak, 36-Hole Indoor Golf and 3-D Cinema, South American Llama, the Cottonpatch Quilt's Gazebo, and the Jungle Boy Outlet.

There is, or are, Precious Moments, a species of ceramic kitsch, the type of droopy-faced little figurine you find in Woolworth's for $3.50, priced from $75 to $400, with legends inscribed "God Bless Our Family," "No Tears Past The Gate," "Mommy, I Love You," "Wishing You A Basket Full Of Blessings," collected by Christians with the gravity of Sotheby's bidders. The salespeople in Branson's many Precious Moments shops do not, as you would imagine, talk about how cute these ghastly little excrescences are, but about their value on the secondary market, how to look for flaws, and which items have been suspended, retired, or discontinued. Motels and show tickets in Branson are cheap. The cost of these objects is the real proof of a parallel universe, where a glazed elf is an investment.

And there is, in some processed, Disneyized, gelded sense, the glittering allure of Stars, Show Biz. A parallel universe, say, in which "top flight entertainment" equals Bobby Vinton and Jim Nabors. It's some kind of allure, supplying that ideal of mildness Lionel Trilling described in "The Fate of Pleasure", an easily digested excitement with nothing profane or suggestive in it.

Elvis, for instance, is hailed from every Branson stage as the King, but every Elvis cover is performed without any incitement to lust, or indeed any reference to sexuality. A star, as any American 12-year-old understands, is someone a great many people would like to fuck. But in Branson a star is a kind of ideal family member, a sibling or parent or child, whose personal life—all details of which are offered from the stage as part of the routine—should closely resemble the lives of ordinary denizens of the Bible Belt.

What the Branson entertainer projects on stage isn't sexiness or eccentricity or extravagance, but ordinariness. Pride in having produced children, in having stayed in the same marriage for many years, in one's own religious fervor, in being as close to some conservative norm as possible, is the acceptable form of overt egotism. "My kid," Wayne Osmond gushes repeatedly after his daughter's violin solo, "my kid." Knowing chuckles from the audience. This is the kind of moist family feeling they relate to. Most performers here mingle with the crowds in the lobby afterward, further proof that they're just like everybody else, only richer.

"The first day I came to work here," a woman selling memorabilia in the lobby of John Davidson's theater told me, "he came right over to me and said, 'Welcome to the family.' That's the kind of person he is." She was selling, among other things, John Davidson brand coffee, a John Davidson line of herbal teas, and John Davidson-initialed varsity sweaters, as well as a "geography game" devised by John Davidson to teach youngsters the often confusing difference between, for example, Canada and Mexico. I heard this again and again from lobby people selling souvenirs for $4.50 an hour: the star had actually spoken to them, welcomed them to the family, was "not at all snobby," but "a regular nice person."

Service industry jobs are about all there is in Branson. A young woman who'd recently moved to another town said, "You've got to work two or three jobs just to live here. A one-bedroom apartment is $500 a month, gas is up to $1.09 a gallon. And tourism is way down no matter what anybody says. For one thing, people think the floods came here, and then other people hear about how crowded it is and stay away."

Unlike Vegas, or Nashville, or any comparable fantasy sprawl, Branson has the provisional feeling of a place that could become an archaeological curiosity in no time at all, like the improvised white flight suburbs of the Northeast that succumbed to mall-and-condo mania in the '70s and '80s. The architecture of Branson's theaters and motels has the Potemkin Village effect of an amusement park, or a studio back lot; a significant percentage of businesses change hands each year, fold, or go bankrupt, and the big country stars who "locate" in Branson, like Loretta Lynn, generally abandon the place after one or two seasons. ("She's had so much tragedy this last year," a coffee shop waitress confides to a couple from Iowa, "that she's decided to give up her theater.")

It may be uncharitable to say so, but artists tend to flee places like Branson rather than settle in them, and for anyone with a viable career elsewhere, Branson has to be a purgatorial stop on the road instead of a destination. Of course there is money, quite a lot of it, to be skimmed off the 4 million tourists passing through every year, and beautiful homes or compounds to be carved from the vegetation around Table Rock Lake, but it's hard to imagine being young and vigorous and talented and not going stark raving mad in Branson sooner or later. The town smells of embalming fluid.

Appropriately, one of its major sidebar items is Long's Wax Museum, in a ranch-shaped building near the Osmonds' theater. A maze of moisture-buckled plywood paneling and display cubicles behind Plexiglas, the wax museum offers an assortment of stuffed, moulting avian and mammal specimens, many of them extinct; myriad vintage firearms, in less than mint condition; and an array of rusted or rotted farm tools and primitive household conveniences (icecream dipper, ice shaver, bung hole auger, cabbage cutter, etc.). The wax displays are a weird mixture of celebrity fetishism and campy religious piety, musty sermons in wax epitomizing the Branson ethos.

Along one corridor, we find the plywood pasted over with assassination headlines: RFK, JFK, Martin Luther King. Inside a cubicle is "the '61 Cadillac in which Jacqueline Kennedy drove to President Kennedy's funeral," with an oil-on-velvet portrait of JFK; in the neighboring alcove, wax figures of Mrs. Kennedy, John-John, and Caroline at the funeral; in an adjacent display, his connection to the Kennedy funeral unelucidated, Michael Jackson, with glove and red leather jacket, waves into space, a dozen gold records dangling near his head.

Next, a procession of tableaux from old movies, the figures in decaying period costumes, the skin tones more than slightly off, and, close up, bearing almost no resemblance to the actors they're based on: Mary Pickford on a swing, Gary Cooper surrounded by hostile Indians, Marlene Dietrich in a tuxedo, Jean Harlow and Clark Gable in a red boudoir. John Travolta, looking like Milton Berle; Clint Eastwood, Barbra Streisand, Dolly Parton, and Burt

Reynolds. Marlin (sic) Brando in *The Wild One*. Mae West in *She Done Him Wrong*. Karloff as Frankenstein. Hedy Lamarr.

The show business figures are mixed in with other ones: John Wilkes Booth crouching behind Mary Todd and Abraham Lincoln at the theater, Judge Roy Bean observing a hanging, Ronald Reagan standing behind a seated Oliver North, Mahatma Gandi (sic) in the lotus position, the Assassination of President McKinley. In an overlit passageway, glass coffins contain dummies of Hitler ("who committed suicide in his private bunker at Berlin . . . so it is reported by captured Nazi officials. THERE IS DOUBT TO ITS TRUTH"), Eva Braun, and Mussolini "as he actually was just before burial in a secret grave." Mussolini is green, leering, and full of bloody perforations; he resembles the Incredible Hulk, who's also replicated a bit further on. On the opposite wall, there is an odd square object with hairs embedded in it. It takes a moment to notice the nipples. It has sarcophagus-shaped, Egyptian decorations painted on it. Beside it is a wooden spear identified as an "ancient heart stake."

In the depths of this macabre inventory, the Life of Christ appears like a moth-eaten road show, a little melted from travel, in narrative sequence—Journey to Bethlehem Nativity, 12 Year Old Jesus in Temple, Baptism of Jesus, First Miracle, Christ at Mary and Martha's, Last Supper (with place cards), Peter Denies Jesus, Pilate Washes Hands, Scourging Jesus, Bearing His Cross, Casting Lots, Carry to Tomb, Ascension.

Salon De Musique

I could not face Jennifer in the Morning, or the Jim Owen Morning Show, or Moe Bandy's Americana, or the Pump Boys and Dinettes Theater, all of which, in any case, were plunking and twanging and picking and clog dancing all over the Vacation Channel, along with off-world comedy bumpkins with missing teeth. It was a bad town to wake up in, strangely desolate despite the traffic, and the honorary friendliness of shopkeepers and waitresses seemed to mask a sinister back-narrative, as if they had stepped out of *A Boy and His Dog*.

In one place that resembled a normal, adult-oriented steak house, McGillies, a few sullen young people could always be found drinking heavily on the patio. You could tell they were local and they dressed like kids who wanted to be somewhere else they had seen on television. The patio had pleasant landscaping and a waterfall but for some reason was bathed in green fluorescent lights. One waitress in McGillies claimed that a newly built star theater was sinking in its landfill, and seemed to detest quite a lot of what Branson had to offer. But malcontents were scarce. Malcontents in places like Branson always tell you some new building is sinking into landfill.

I saw exactly three black people in Branson. Two were in a white panel truck behind McGillies, maybe maintenance men, and one, a boy of about 13, was walking down Highway 76 with two white kids. He had a bangee boy haircut and his shirt off, which made him three things you just don't see on the street in Branson. I wondered who this boy was and what he was doing there and wondered if he felt as oppressed and eager to leave as I did.

Inevitably, I went to the Anita Bryant Morning Show at the Ozark Theater.

I hadn't given Anita Bryant a thought in over a decade, except once, over a year ago, when a play I was writing, set in the late '70s, cried out for a line about her. In some glitch of memory concerning the year or two just before AIDS, I had a blurry mental image of Anita Bryant being reconciled with the gay community of Dade County, dancing in a gay disco, something like that, the kind of little "ironic" item you find in the front of *Newsweek*—but of course it never happened.

What happened to Anita Bryant was, she lost her job with the Florida Citrus Commission, her TV thing, after organizing against a gay rights bill in Miami. Then something else happened to Anita Bryant when she got a divorce: she lost her religious-right constituency, her rabid claque.

Anita Bryant went into the wilderness.

Now she is back, if having your name on a theater in Eureka Springs, Arkansas (the next Branson), and doing a morning show at the Ozark Theater in Branson can be called back. She appears, first, in a long white jacket over a beaded gown, a jacket that looks like vinyl and has red and blue Constructivist stripes that also look like vinyl. The entire outfit is covered in sequins that look like vinyl. The auburn hair is whisked up in a surprisingly butch do, the face perfectly sculpted, with good bones behind it. She marches right down into the audience, singing what, I don't remember, but the voice, to give her her due, isn't bad.

Anita Bryant's thing is to take us down memory lane while working the audience like a slot machine. This isn't unusual for Branson, and neither are her rapid jumps from bluegrass to Patti Page covers to the obligatory Hank Williams numbers, "Jambalaya," "Your Cheatin' Heart," etc., which everyone does. Anita also does an impression of Elvis and shakes her moneymaker more than I would have anticipated. She sits down at a dresser on stage, fixes a ponytail into her hair, changes into a skirt and sweater, and relives someone else's '50s girlhood while singing "At the Hop." She gets two musicians into semidrag to accompany her on some Andrews Sisters songs. She selects a tall, bald, befuddled man from the audience to sing a duet with her and cracks surprisingly cruel jokes at his expense. In fact, there's a slightly nasty edge to Anita's act, some evidence that as far as she's concerned she's still the Queen of Show Biz and it's no fault of hers that she has to perform for busloads of geriatric bohunks at ten in the morning.

This may simply be the attrition from the other side of Anita Bryant's act, which contains a lot of spiel, much of it a melodramatic rehash of her glory days and even more of it a deft reinvention of, and apologia for, her Fall.

The word homosexual never passes her lips, but Anita refers, often, to her Troubles, her loss of the orange juice contract and the evil boycott that effectively ended her career, though she knows she had only done what was right. Everyone knows what she's talking about, that unspeakable Godmocking "lifestyle" corroding the very springs and shock absorbers of This Great Country. And then—her voice drops, oozing snappily phrased sincerity—even more devastating was that painful divorce, the last thing on earth she ever wanted, and Being Judged by Strangers. Mud was splashed all over her by the media. She felt humiliated and worthless. It's all there in *A New Day*, her autobiography, on sale in the lobby, "the book I said I'd never write." The blacklist. The persecution. The lifestyle that a few people on their AIDS-deathbeds renounced in her presence as she Gave Them Succor. The years of songless exile in Atlanta, where, in the depths of the fait accompli, her Depression Became So Great That She Seriously Thought About Taking Her Own Life.

But then a good friend made her pray. Made her pray for the Lord's "tough love" and shoulder her cross and accept and love herself for who she really was. After a long healing process, during which she also realized that she had to become a corporation and put her fag-boycott-and-divorce-devastated finances in order, she experienced "the blessing of total self-forgiveness."

Anita recounts nearly every Precious Moment of her career, with almost defiant panache, as if she had been, before the fags ruined everything, as big as Madonna. She warbles not only her early Coca-Cola commercial but also her Florida Orange Juice theme. ("Orange juice with natural vitamin C! From the Florida Sunshine Tree!") She is, after all, the youngest person and only woman ever inducted into the Florida Citrus Hall of Fame. She regales us with the 11 Bob Hope USO tours, more tours than any other guest performer, the long rewarding years of bringing the gift of song to lonely servicemen on desolate foreign soil. She tells the story of the army jacket she's changed into, a jacket festooned with cloth decorations—more military decorations, in fact, than any other performer has ever received—that has her last name on the ID patch: once upon a time, she was performing free at an army base, and asked the general there for a fatigue jacket to put all her decorations on. She had four stars from General Westmoreland, and all these patches from all those USO tours, and they brought her this jacket, which already had the name tag, and it turned out that a Private Bryant had donated his.

She didn't meet Private Bryant at the time, but she talked to him on the phone. She sent him some goodies in exchange for the jacket, and they started a correspondence. He was sent to Vietnam. They wrote to each other for a year. He became her special friend. And then, one day, she got a call from the man's wife. Private Bryant had been killed in action.

Anita Bryant then performs the theme song of every armed service of America, instructing everyone to stand when she gets to the song of the branch they served in, or their spouse served in, and behind her, a giant American flag beams across the back wall of the stage. At the end of this medley the whole audience is standing, ready to trample out the vintage where the grapes of wrath are stored. By the end of her show Anita Bryant has pushed every Branson button so hard that this audience would forgive her if she confessed to murdering the Lindbergh baby.

Monkey Do

Later that night I caught the magic show at the Five Star Theatre. There were lots of young, dancing magicians materializing tigers and sawing women in clear plastic boxes in half, and a long episode of flamenco dancing that featured male and female ingenues with beautiful bodies, some of them distinctly ethnic. The Five Star had drawn out a noticeably younger crowd than I had seen anywhere else, and the dancers led me to imagine some secret disco in the hills where stir-crazy performers under 50 went to party.

There was Bobby Berosini and his world-famous performing orangutans, an act that called upon the orangutans to kiss and clamber around a kind of jungle gym and make farting noises with their mouths. This became more and more horrible as it went on. Later Bobby Berosini appeared in the lobby with "Tiga," the orangutang who costarred with Clint Eastwood in *Every Which Way But Loose*. An endless line of parents and children formed, to have their pictures taken with Tiga. Tiga looked very much like the stuffed Tiga dolls being sold in the lobby, except around the eyes. Around the eyes, Tiga looked extremely despondent, starved for affection, and, if this is possible for an orangutan, bored. Bobby

Berosini looked like an enterprising oil slick.

In the parking lot I struck up a conversation with a young couple from St. Louis who seemed to have strayed into Branson by accident. With little prompting they expressed dismay at the use of rare animals for entertainment. They had only caught this one show and were driving home in the morning. We talked about animals and ecology for a long time. At last, I thought, after all this time, real people. The young man had been to New York. He had a friend who lived in Woodmere.

"Now, I've got nothing against the Jewish people per se," he said, launching into a long story I was afraid to follow because his presence in Branson was about to make sense. It was the last night in Branson. I went to McGillies and got drunk.

1993

4.

Tough Love and

Carbon Monoxide

in Detroit

The assisted suicide trial of Dr. Jack Kevorkian opened with a "bombshell" from defense attorney Geoffrey Fieger, who announced that the deceased, a young man named Thomas Hyde, had died outside the jurisdiction of the Detroit court. The bombshell left a residue of herring rather than gunpowder. Fieger, a flamboyant attorney given to cosmic pronouncements, threw the venue issue in as acquittal insurance. Although the Michigan Attorney General ruled, at the request of Prosecutor Timothy Kenny, that the trial could proceed in Wayne County, Judge Thomas Jackson decided to let the jury determine if the place of death was correctly stated in the indictment.

The only witness to Hyde's suicide was Kevorkian himself, who administered carbon monoxide gas to the "patient" in the rear of a VW van. (Before his license to prescribe was revoked, Kevorkian used a lethal injection device he called the "Thanatron"; he now uses a barrel of CO attached to a rubber hose and a face mask.) Whether the van was parked behind Kevorkian's apartment in Oakland County at the time, or on Belle Isle, the Wayne County park where he delivered the body to police, only Kevorkian really knew.

Having raised the issue in the first place Fieger later declared it trivial, and flogged the press for "inflaming" it. His ego was at stake. He saw himself as an avatar of a great social movement, the Clarence Darrow of humane euthanasia. "The trial of the century, the most important case that's been tried in American jurisprudence in 70 years . . . and to ask me such banal questions about the goddamn venue," Fieger shrilled at one noon press conference. He went on to cite Article 8 of the Nuremberg convention: "When a duly constituted law is immoral, you have a duty not to follow it." The Nuremberg law cites a duty to disobey unconscionable orders, for instance to shoot a prisoner of war or to perform involuntary euthanasia; its application to Kevorkian's volunteer work as an itinerant suicide helper was, in Fieger's view, too obvious for discussion.

So the banal question hovered, dampening the atmosphere, for if the law was immoral and Kevorkian's defiance of it a heroic deed, why was his lawyer trying to get him off on a technicality? Unlike Gandhi, to whom Fieger likes to compare him, or Galileo, to whom he compares himself (along with Einstein, Thoreau, Nelson Mandela, and Margaret Sanger), Kevorkian seemed unwilling to take the rap for what he clearly, and in his own eyes nobly, had done.

While Fieger enjoyed lecturing the court and the press that "all of us," especially those of us with terminal illnesses, were on trial, one couldn't avoid the impression that Jack Kevorkian and his intent constitute a pesky aesthetic problem that had come to overshadow any larger issue. In the absence of clear medical and legal guidelines for assisted death, a cadaverous-looking retired pathologist and his adoring followers had pioneered a do-it-yourself, try-this-at-home approach to "self-deliverance."

The aesthetic problem is not small. It encompasses Kevorkian's theories, his feverish proposals for statewide suicide parlors ("obitariums"), his vision of a "mature" social future in which the terminally ill would be joined by the mentally ill, the severely handicapped, and condemned criminals as worthy candidates for medical experimentation and organ harvesting as well as "medicide" (Kevorkian's term). There is his abysmal career, thwarted, in his account, by the primitive, superstitious squeamishness of colleagues toward his discoveries: that you can, for example, transfuse whole blood directly from cadavers to live patients, or fix the exact moment when resuscitation becomes useless by gazing into the eyeballs of dying patients.

A Taylor Mead poem comes to mind: "I had the right idea in the wrong brain." Those who don't oppose Kevorkian on principle may still find something unseemly about buying the farm in a "battered VW van" and having a dead body delivered to the wrong police station like a Domino's order gone awry. Under Fieger's questioning, Kevorkian accounted for a lifetime of quirky, morbid, marginal preoccupations as "the boy in me." As someone who had previously given him little thought, I found this wholly accurate. Kevorkian exudes the excited pedantry of an adolescent autodidact. On the plus side, his sincerity is obvious and uncontrollable.

Seated at the defense table every day in the same white windbreaker and blue sweater, Kevorkian immersed himself during hostile testimony in a textbook, *Reading Japanese*. He traced Japanese characters on the page with a spindly forefinger. Outside the courtroom, he sported a crumpled white fishing hat and regaled his wellwishers with fortifying wisdom: "Ever study the Inquisition in school? That isn't a trial, it's an Inquisition."

His claque (Hyde's family and friends, people connected to previous Kevorkian cases, and right-to-die advocates, joined by the occasional class of high school civics students) sat behind him and off to one side near the jury. They were emphatically suburban, ordinary Middle Americans, dressed, like the jurors, in colorful ready-to-wear, as suitable for a barbecue or a cocktail party as a courtroom. Lynn Mills, the local head of Operation Rescue, sat at one end of the front bench, right beside Thomas Hyde's family, sometimes fingering rosary beads atop her Bible, at other times peering into a book called *Fit or Fat*. (Mills is not fat, and bears an eerie resemblance to the young Lee Remick.) She was, aside from the prosecutors, the only Kevorkian enemy present.

One can easily include Geoffrey Fieger in the category of aesthetic problems. A tall, fleshy, beaver-faced man who looks like a tennis scholarship gone to seed, Fieger routinely dismisses even his mildest detractors as "assholes" and "sacks of shit," thinks his long-term client is the Messiah, and spends recesses and lunch breaks extolling his own brilliance to anyone who will listen. Fieger is the type of B actor who summons awe among the semieducated, a sound-bite lawyer who stirs the illusion of passion in anemic settings. The Detroit Recorder's Court, a fairly small basement chamber with octagonal seating and wan-looking travel posters framed on the slatted walls, had a blasé, laid-back feeling, punctured only by Fieger's histrionics and, at trial's end, by the angry, tearful testimony of Heidi Fernandez, Thomas Hyde's common-law widow.

Fernandez described in grueling detail Hyde's disintegration from amyotrophic lateral sclerosis, or Lou Gehrig's disease. Fieger had, shrewdly, shown the jury an appalling videotaped interview of Hyde by Kevorkian, getting it in during the prosecution case, when its contents were immune to cross-examination. He showed it again during closing argument. Fernandez broke into sobs three times on the stand, making the trial feel like a senseless persecution. Off the stand, Fernandez was a rebarbative presence, warming up for her big moment in a succession of dramatic outfits and hairdos, yacking to friends during testimony, and chewing a big wad of gum, delighted to be, along with Dr. Jack, the cynosure of all eyes. As Laurie Anderson recently said of Barbra Streisand, Heidi's thing was about "Love me or I'll kill you." As lubricant for Fieger's closing argument, which involved a ponderous quantity of sudden hushes, whispered rhetorical wheezings ("Are we not human?"), and grandiloquent allusions to the civil rights movement, Fernandez's testimony was untouchable. Prosecutor Kenny, a gangling, woeful figure with the flair of a rural undertaker, had the bad sense to cross-examine her.

As it happened, *Michigan* v. *Kevorkian* was not a case in which aesthetics carried much weight with the jury. Suicide has traditionally been informed by a sense of style, but medicide is a

K-mart kind of suicide for a democratic era, when aged and bedfast dependents of even the average joe often find themselves attached, at life's end, to wildly expensive feeding tubes and respirators that keep them technically alive for weeks and months in a state of vegetable oblivion.

All states have given this problem some imperfect consideration, recognizing, for example, living wills, which allow the patient to forgo "heroic measures" to prolong life. These are often ignored by hospitals unless the patient has vigilant relatives or attorneys. The Michigan statute, hastily contrived solely to restrain Kevorkian, does allow physicians to administer potentially lethal doses of painkiller to the terminally ill. Assisting those too debilitated to end their lives without help is either the logical next step or the crest of a slippery slope.

In many ways the Kevorkian trial was a moot issue. No fewer than three Michigan judges had declared the statute unconstitutional; it was before an appellate court. A state commission on death and dying was studying the statute for revision, and the current law was set to expire six months after the commission's recommendations. Now, following the trial, the appellate court has invalidated the law but also reinstated two murder charges against Kevorkian, emanating from two assisted suicides in 1991—a case of the state stupidly ratifying Kevorkian's persecution complex.

In any event, the jurors—mostly youngish, mostly black, mostly female—could, along with everyone else in the courtroom, imagine themselves in Thomas Hyde's hapless, unbearable predicament. In the videotape he can barely talk, has almost no use of his limbs, and says he wants to die. As Fieger accurately predicted, empathy (compounded by a few side issues) swept away any slavish attention to the jury instructions.

The second theme of Fieger's presentation, intent, opened an absurd yet viable loophole. Once the prosecution rested, the circus of bad faith began. Kevorkian's expert witnesses are familiar figures in Michigan, true believers who step up to the mike whenever Jack ushers a fresh patient into the Great Beyond:

Dr. Barry Bialek, an emergency room physician in Ontario, testified that the Hippocratic oath was actually devised by the Pythagoreans, that he doesn't believe in the Greek gods mentioned in the Hippocratic Oath, and that the final treatment measures he could take with ALS patients would do nothing to relieve their pain and suffering.

Kenny: "Would you use carbon monoxide as a pain reliever in the emergency room?"

Bialek: "Yes, if it were made available to me."

Dr. Stanley Levy, internist, told Fieger "it was a heroic effort by Dr. Kevorkian, heroic in the sense that it was not standard, something others would not have thought of," and that Hyde's death in the back of Kevorkian's van was a form of "New Age hospice care."

Kenny: "Do you consider carbon monoxide a poison?"

Levy: "I consider all therapeutic modalities potentially poisonous."

Kenny: "Why is it that you haven't prescribed carbon monoxide?"

Levy: "I haven't thought of it."

Kenny: "Would doses of carbon monoxide provide ALS patients with temporary relief?"

Levy: (without irony) "I think relief would be permanent."

Interspersed with the experts, Thomas Hyde's brother, his hospice care worker, and Kevorkian's associates demonstrated an identical inability to link carbon monoxide inhalation with death. The gas, they said, was administered "to relieve his pain and suffering," pure and simple, a phrase that gradually took on the empty familiarity of a jingle. The rote evasion exasperated Kenny, particularly when it came from Kevorkian himself.

Kenny: "You had an expectation that he would die?"

Kevorkian: "That his suffering would end. I surmised he would die. A surmise is a guess."

Kenny: "It was just a guess, after 18 occasions? Were you startled, sir, to find out after 20 minutes that he was dead? . . . Did you provide enough carbon monoxide to cause his death?"

Kevorkian: "No. Enough to end his suffering."

Kenny: "And death ends all suffering."

Kevorkian: "Not if you're religious it doesn't. Some people believe you go to hell when you die."

We hear from Neal Nicol, who described himself, Kevorkian, and Kevorkian's sister Margo Janus, as a "think tank" that evaluates medicide candidates and follows through on their treatment. Nicol looks like the actor Pat Hingle in *The Grifters*, stolid and steady-eyed. He is a medical technician; Margo Janus is a retired secretary. Far from encouraging people to end it all, Nicol said, the think tank urges them to keep going, especially "if we know about a procedure and medication the patient doesn't know about. We make sure the families are involved. We always suggest they get religious counseling."

"If a patient changes their mind," Fieger inquired, "can they come back to you?"

Nicol: "No, if they're uncertain, it means they have emotional problems."

Nicol's testimony was avidly seconded by Margo Janus, whose role in the think tank includes videotaping her brother's consultations and consoling the soon-to-be-bereaved. Janus was florid and irrepressibly upbeat about her brother's practice; every statement was a testimonial. Kevorkian "tries to contact the doctors whose names are on the [patient's medical] records," carefully documents all meetings "to assess for himself that this is a case of true physical distress and mental competence," and "discusses all facets of a life—the social, the economic, the political if you will." Kevorkian "has to satisfy his own high medical standards." Janus was like an adorable parrot, embellishing her answers with buzz phrases about the "blatant unprofessionalism" of the police, the "serenity" achieved by medicide patients, the "last soft and tearful goodbyes" between Thomas Hyde and Heidi Fernandez. Why, Kenny asked, if Hyde's death took place in Oakland County, did Kevorkian drive the corpse to Belle Isle?

"Because it's a very beautiful isle."

While Margo Janus made Thomas Hyde's final hours sound like

an especially heartwarming bake sale, expert witness Dr. David Schwartz, a psychiatrist, preening imperiously on the stand, painted a grim picture of what Hyde's end would have been like had Hyde experienced the choking death typical of ALS patients:

"Picture a moment of choking or strangling to death ... the person would have to become tremendously angry and psychotic—hateful!—there would have been no positive feelings ... all the remembrances of living, in a broad sense, would have been taken away ... his hate for what was happening would wipe out anything good that had happened in his life."

Like earlier expert testimony, Schwartz's was over the top, and an adroit prosecutor would have ripped it to pieces. People do, after all, die naturally from ALS and other ghastly diseases without becoming "psychotic." Kenny, lackluster at best, instead returned to the topic of carbon monoxide, which Schwartz predictably declared of "therapeutic value" vis-à-vis "relieving pain and suffering."

A large part of the defense strategy was to show how assiduously ("that means carefully," Fieger instructed one reporter) Kevorkian limits his practice to the hopelessly ill and how scrupulously each case reflects, at every step, the wishes of the patient involved. A key element of the process, stressed many times, is an absence of doubt or ambivalence. If anyone changes his or her mind, even at the last moment, Dr. K. simply folds his tent and moves on.

None of Kevorkian's "fail-safe" measures has any accepted medical or legal value except as exculpatory evidence. Still, they do represent an effort to organize assisted suicide into a semblance of medical propriety. It's worth noting, then, that the pledge to withdraw assistance from ambivalent patients has been inconsistently applied in certain of Kevorkian's cases.

The most controversial case was that of Hugh Gale, an emphysema victim who used the carbon monoxide technique in February 1993. Mr. Gale died at the home of Neal Nicol. Right-to-life activist Lynn Mills, who believes that God led her directly to Nicol's sidewalk garbage, abducted a large bag of it after Gale's death and discovered inside a form labeled "Michigan Obitiatry Zone-1," "Final Action," and "Confidential." On it, Kevorkian had typed an account of the procedure used on Gale:

> *A plastic tent was put over his head and shoulders. . . . The patient then pulled a string tied to his left index finger, other end attached to a clip, which was pulled off a crimped plastic tube, opening it from the outlet valve of a canister of CO gas to the mask. In about 45 seconds the patient became flushed, agitated, breathing deeply, saying "Take it off!" The tent was removed immediately, the mask removed, and nasal oxygen started. . . . The patient wanted to continue. After about 20 minutes, with nasal oxygen continuing, the mask was replaced. . . . In about 30-35 seconds he again flushed, became agitated, with moderate hyperpnea; and immediately after saying "Take it off!" once again, he fell into unconsciousness. The mask was then left in place. . . . Heartbeat was undetectable about 3 minutes after last breath.*

However, a police search of Kevorkian's apartment turned up an altered version of this document. The lines pertaining to the second request to remove the tent and mask had been whited-out and typed over with the exact number of characters:

"*. . . moderately increased rate and depth of respiration, and muscular tension without overt action (an exaggerated response seen in cases of marked loss of pulmonary reserve). Agitation abated in 10-15 sec., with unconsciousness, calmer gasping breaths for . . .*"

Gale's death was investigated as a homicide. But authorities eventually accepted a benign explanation of the discrepancy: Kevorkian had simply typed up the procedure in a state of distraction, mistakenly recording the first "take it off" twice. Still, according to his own stringent protocol, he ought to have desisted after one request.

Kevorkian also says that assisted suicide should only be performed after consultation with the patient's regular physician.

Yet he never contacted Hyde's doctor. Questioned on this by Kenny, Kevorkian said that Hyde's doctor "might have alerted the authorities" to Hyde's impending suicide or even tried to intervene himself.

This fear of interference furthers the argument for decriminalizing medicide, perhaps, but also suggests, like much else in the trial, that Kevorkian's need for secrecy preempts the best interests of his patients. He has, for example, told several patients that his access to carbon monoxide was threatened by state officials, which may have alarmed people into dying before the gas ran out, rather than when they wanted to.

In Kevorkian's mind, opposition to his practice is monolithic and conspiratorial, requiring secrecy and guile. The AMA and the Catholic church are in league against him, though "half the doctors" secretly support what he's doing. At the same time, he insists that medicide is a medical procedure that needs to be regulated by the medical profession, in other words by the same people persecuting him. But since society is "still in the Dark Ages," Kevorkian must go it alone, devising through lonely trial and error the ideal way to give human beings "the same compassion we give dogs and cats." In short, Kevorkian intends to do things his way until a law is passed that allows him to continue doing things his way.

Popular sentiment in Michigan favors legalization of physician-assisted suicide. As the trial proceeded, a Hemlock Society petition drive to put the issue on a state ballot reached the 100,000 signature mark. A somewhat uneasy truce exists between Kevorkian's followers, who view euthanasia as a privacy matter outside the law, and the Hemlock Society, which seeks constitutional protection for the right to die. Janet Good, the head of Michigan Hemlock, scoured the courthouse for signatures during lunch breaks. A pleasant, articulate feminist whose involvement in the issue has nothing of Kevorkian's egocentricity about it, Good saw the trial as drawing energy away from the petition drive, but backed Kevorkian firmly. They have common enemies.

Hemlock distributes Derek Humphry's bestseller, *Final Exit*, a book that provides advice on at-home suicide by plastic bag, prescription drugs, and other methods.

"It lists everything," Good told me, "but the fact remains that no matter how much you know, and I've become almost a pharmacologist, you still have to know people's weight, and so forth . . . if you don't have a compassionate physician, you're still up a creek. People with money and education are more likely to know someone who can dispense drugs. It's a class thing. Like everything else."

It did seem to boil down to class, and style: if *Michigan* v. *Kevorkian* proved anything, it was probably that "death with dignity" has become an extremely elastic term, especially among lower-middle-class people who rightly fear the lengthy suffering and expense produced by mortal illnesses and technomedicine. Dignity, for Kevorkian's clientele, equals "taking control" of death, rendering it economical and relatively painless.

Kevorkian's services are free, therefore a smart consumer option—a working-class alternative to pricey high-tech hospitals and a drearily protracted end. Those with insurance and/or money can afford hospice care (arguably the best option for most of the terminally ill, though hospices, even for the well-off, are few), and as Janet Good said, the upper classes know how to secure a stockpile of Seconal, or at least how to contact the Hemlock Society. For less adroit, less affluent, or less imaginative people, Kevorkian is a brand name, recognized nationally, proven effective in 20 known cases. For the happy few approved by the think tank, death becomes a shrewdly chosen commodity, suicide a group activity the whole family can, at least to some extent, participate in.

"We needed the jury to look at more abstract notions," Prosecutor Kenny mused when the not guilty verdict came in. But death and suffering are the least abstract of human problems, and the last thing the jury saw before deliberating was the video of Thomas Hyde, a former outdoorsman, reduced to a groaning envelope of degenerating tissue. His fate could be anyone's. In the face of such distress, the hyperbolic, crude stratagems of Fieger's defense looked less ignoble than the state's prosecution of an essentially pointless case.

Yes, where it actually happened was a factor in the verdict. Yes, they acquitted on the specious separation of cause from effect, i.e., carbon monoxide from death. At least one juror offered the thought that people have a right to do this but that Kevorkian is going about it the wrong way. Fieger won, but his whole case seemed ineluctably tainted by a steady whiff of cynicism and contempt: the aesthetic problem remained.

As the huge sales of *Final Exit* a few years ago proved, the way people die in America is unacceptable to millions. Most people want the right to decide when life is no longer worth living, and access to the means to terminate "mere existence." The dangers of abuse inherent in legal assisted suicide may be grossly exaggerated by its opponents; after all, thousands go out that way every year, illegally and quietly, with the discreet help of loved ones, and sympathetic doctors. It seems self-evident that we own our bodies, that no law can tell us what to do with them when we ourselves find staying in them intolerable.

On the other hand, since suicide is a private matter, the depersonalization implied in "regulating" it, offering it as a standardized service, and having specialists in it like Kevorkian roaming the landscape, or presiding over McSuicide Clinics, offers Americans nothing more than another dismal method of jamming life into death, surrendering the last remaining mystery to faceless consumerism. This is hardly a legal argument but simply a question of taste or, to be more exact, tastelessness. Had Kevorkian ever treated Thomas Hyde, or anyone, for anything besides "that long disease," his life, the service he provides might well look like the mercy of a friend instead of the dubious kindness of a stranger.

1994

5.

LA Plays Itself

The Edward R. Roybal Federal Building in downtown Los Angeles is a salmon-and-gray miniscraper two parking lots away from the Museum of Contemporary Art, a Molotov cocktail's toss from Little Tokyo to the south and Olvera Street and Union Station to the north. The structure closest to the Roybal Building has a family resemblance to other postmodern monoliths in the landscape, its pointlessly angled, blocky ostentation garnished by diagonal glass-enclosed ramps with exposed support beams that twinkle at night under evenly spaced flood spots. Razor-slit windows perforate the facade like holes in a computer punch card.

This edifice, connected to the Roybal by a raised plaza with Grecian pretensions, is the Metropolitan Detention Center. It graces the cover of Mike Davis's *City of Quartz*, and is, Davis notes, "the largest prison built in a major U.S. urban center in generations." Its proximity to the Roybal suggests a smooth two-way flow of major felon traffic from one building to the other, a kind of glitchless, architecturally ideal passage from indictment to incarceration. The defendants in the case at hand, *U.S. v. Stacey C. Koon, Laurence M. Powell, Timothy E. Wind, and Theodore J.*

Briseno, however, arrive from the suburbs every morning in private cars, playing peekaboo behind the morning's *Los Angeles Times* with a variable number of television cameras.

The defense team and their clients are from Central Casting: the perpetually scowling, high-domed Sergeant Stacey Koon carries himself with the tranquil arrogance of a bulky, dangerous mammal accustomed to pushing weaker mammals around, chomping into them when irritated. His attorney, Ira Salzman, is a tall, long-faced, dark-complected man with no lips, whose cornily handsome features are marred by deeply pitted skin, bad teeth, and an air of insufferable sanctimony. Officer Laurence M. Powell has the jowly potato face and put-upon, porcine expression of a slow-witted high school bully. Michael Stone, his lawyer, is squat, rosy-cheeked, humorless, and wears a bad haircut settled above the cringing mug of a malefic toad. Probationary Officer Timothy E. Wind, the Greta Garbo of the case, is a tall, darkhaired, fairly pleasant-looking Midwesterner whose counsel, the long-winded, basso profundo Paul DePasquale, suggests what the mating of Don Rickles and Mussolini might look like.

Finally there is Officer Theodore J. Briseno, cast against type: Briseno is almost handsome in a sallow sort of way, with nicely cropped black hair and mustache. He is short, willowy, with quick, delicate gestures and eager, hangdog smiles, searching eyes, and a manner so earnest and anxious to do the right thing that the only word that comes to mind is "twitch." Briseno is represented by Harland Braun, a lanky, pallid, bland-looking WASP with a goofy mouth and an oblivious attitude.

We each come into these things with our little preconceived notions, of course, but even if these people were the Greenpeace board of directors I think I would still consider them an unfortunate-looking bunch. On the other hand, maybe not.

At the Temple Street side of the Roybal Building one finds a two-story Jonathan Borofsky sculpture: four identical, flat, white silhouettes converge on each other nose-to-nose in the attitude of a fistfight, like one big angry dude who's been squeezed through an egg slicer and tastefully arranged for serving. The figures are pocked all over with holes, as if they've been sprayed in a drive-by. On the plaza side, where wooly bits of vegetation and sprigs of magnolia poke from decorative tubs and containers, a half-circle of marble columns arcs around a fountain whose centerpiece is a reclining marble infant holding aloft a little marble globe; the columns are festooned, Hindu temple-style, with stubbylimbed, vaguely Sumerian figures, naked, wearing expressions of hapless imbecility and bewilderment. These architectural doodles are the work of Tom Otterness, a sculptor who once shot a dog for a little film he was making.

The six o'clock television feeds tend to lead into the day's events in front of the Borofsky, with cutaways to the lunch break briefings of the defense team, which are held on the plaza. The networks file on Eastern Standard deadlines, which shaves off the last hour or two of testimony every day. Amid the first slew of motions in *U.S. v. Stacey C. Koon, et al.*, petitions for better media access raised some artificial suspense in the press room, where, throughout jury selection, all but three pool reporters—invariably, two networks and a major newspaper—were parked around speakers wired to the courtroom two floors above.

Since this is a federal trial, it is not being televised. Recording devices of any kind have been banned from the building. The pool system favors corporate media, which have the time and resources to keep abreast of the shifting whims of the U.S. Marshal's Office, which decides who gets access to the courtroom and on what basis. The starstruck federal marshals will do almost anything to accommodate *The New York Times*, *The Los Angeles Times*, the networks, or CNN. Those of us attending on an irregular basis, on the other hand, have been repeatedly threatened with the revocation of our courtroom passes, thanks to the idle lobbying of the major media jocks (with the notable exception of the CBS reporter) who don't show up every day, either, but want extra seats for Rodney King's testimony and, of course, delivery of the verdict.

During voir dire, at least 70 members of the jury pool are packed into the courtroom every day, so there are, in fact, only a few seats open for reporters. Keeping the bulk of the press in audio contact two stories down produces an odd sort of redundancy or dyslexia, with everybody straining to follow the badly miked proceedings and devising charts to track individual jurors. To further complicate matters, the jurors are identified by number to protect their anonymity, with another number designating their potential place in the jury box. At lunch recess the day's three pool reporters breeze into the press room to offer their impressions: "White male, late 30s-early 40s, blue Oxford shirt, faded jeans, beard and mustache"; "Bleach-blond white woman"; "White male former marine, 50s or 60s." (These potted descriptions, emphasis on race and placement in the food chain of Southern California, are disseminated more or less verbatim throughout the country.)

The briefing is followed by a scramble for the elevators and the midday soundbites of the defense attorneys out on the plaza, another pass through the metal detectors, and lunch in the cafeteria, where one can view the defendants feeding at one end and the current crop of potential jurors at the other. Most reporters generously pass along what they believe has happened in the courtroom on any given day, or tell you which person in the cafeteria is Juror Number 531 or 689, but they are quite often mistaken, and the voir dire comes to resemble a protracted game of Gossip, in which rumors spread like brushfires, and are doused at the end of the day by some simple piece of information that's been garbled by the loudspeakers.

The sensation of groping needlessly in the dark for data that should be brightly lit and readily available also suffuses the actual voir dire, which pits each jury candidate against his or her previous responses to a 52-page Juror Questionnaire. (The questionnaire has been a long-tossed bone of contention between the media and Judge John Davies, who has refused several times to provide copies of completed questionnaires to the press; blank ones are available from the marshals.) Several jurors are disqualified when, under questioning, they amend their written answers, or betray a greater knowledge of the case than they've indicated on the questionnaire, or are shown to have more opinions, or claim to have fewer opinions, than they've expressed in writing.

Like so much of the defense's version of the case, and some of the prosecution's as well, this jury selection almost uniquely demands a collective suspension of disbelief, to wit:

It will fall upon the prosecution to prove, beyond reasonable doubt and according to the two counts of the queerly worded new indictment, that the four officers in question, acting on the authority of Sergeant Stacey C. Koon, willfully kicked, beat, and stomped the person often identified in the press as "motorist Rodney King" with the intent of depriving Rodney King of "his right not to be deprived of his civil rights," though even well-informed partisans of the government's side cannot say with exact certainty which aspects of the beating received by Rodney King on March 3, 1991, in strict legal terms, directly violated his civil rights.

It will be the defense's task to demonstrate, as it successfully did to the jury of the previous trial in Simi Valley, that a large drunken man surrounded by more than 20 law enforcement personnel from three separate jurisdictions (the Los Angeles Police Department, the Los Angeles Unified School District, and the California Highway Patrol) was not beaten with excessive force by the four LAPD officers on trial, that on the contrary the suspect exhibited superhuman strength and actually "controlled everything that happened on or about March 3, 1991" by refusing to assume a "felony prone" position and continually threatening to spring up from a "weak push-up-position," forcing the officers to continue striking him, when there is ample videotape evidence to the contrary, evidence that has been viewed at least once by all but one juror (a young Latino man, the last juror seated), and indeed by most citizens of the United States with access to a television set.

With respect to the jury, it is tacitly understood by all the players that few residents of Los Angeles County in their right minds want to serve on it, and therefore the 300-something potential jurors who have not deliberately disqualified themselves prior to voir dire comprise a small, determined core of Angelenos who desire, for one reason or another, to qualify for this specific trial. Since a strong desire to be on the jury, in this case, indicates an equally strong reason for a juror to be rejected, the voir dire, which in most federal cases is mainly handled by the judge, has been turned over to the attorneys.

Listening for days to the muzzy, halting responses of jury candidates, one can't avoid the impression that each has discerned from his or her predecessors what kinds of answers will fly with both sides, or will at least forestall a peremptory challenge. There are, of course, a number of potential jurors who answer spontaneously, candidly, without calculation, and these people are, sooner or later, bumped from consideration, as is anyone who seems able to form two consecutive thoughts without assistance from the judge or the attorneys.

Expressing any too-developed opinion or feeling about the massive insurrection that followed the acquittal of Koon, Powell, Wind, and Briseno in the Simi Valley trial, leads to closer scrutiny, eventually to dismissal, as does any evidence of an analytical or "political" bent—for instance, an Asian woman, Juror 497, who watched the entire Simi Valley trial on television while recovering from neck surgery, makes the fatal gaffe of confessing emotion about the verdicts "because of how I feel about inequalities among poor and minority people." Juror 497 is replaced as Juror 2 by Juror 448, a white male, former Marine Corps machinist, who "had no reaction to the state verdicts last year."

Juror 383, "white woman, 40s, manager of commercial marketing education for insurance firm," sounds as if she's been put in the jury pool for comic relief: she can't stop talking about herself, especially about her job, where "I teach agents to sell, and naturally I always drive the point home . . ." She has no time, she says, for anything besides work and education. The volume of information she volunteers points to a mild personality disorder, particularly since none of it is interesting. "I'm extremely disciplined. I went to a Catholic boarding school." There follows a long digression about her eyesight, which once had an 800+ correction but is now 20/20, thanks to "historic eye surgery." Exhausted, the attorney questioning her (Paul De Pasquale, Timothy Wind's lawyer) queries: "You won't feel slighted if I don't ask you any more personal questions?" After several other jurors have been questioned about whether they intend, if seated, to publish books or articles about their experience ("I'm a capitalist," asseverates one, "being an American, so naturally we all think of that."), 383 asks to be heard and states that she has no intention of writing a book.

Neither side wants to waste a peremptory on 383, and neither side wants her on the jury, either. Just from her voice, one can conjure an unbearable scenario of 11 decided jurors, for or against the defendants, and one egomaniacal insurance bureaucrat staging an epic filibuster until she gets her own way. The prosecution waits for the defense, defense waits for the prosecution, neither makes a move, and 383 gets seated.

"The mood of the city is uneasy anticipation," writes Al Martinez, a columnist in the *L.A. Times*, "like that of a child huddled down in darkness, searching for monsters in the shadows . . . The emotions are not dissimilar. Will morning come before the things in the night leap out and devour us?"

It's a widespread assumption that unfavorable verdicts in what is usually called "the Rodney King trial," or in the immediately subsequent trial of the L.A. 4+, *The People of the State of California* v. *Damian Williams, et al.*, popularly known as "the Reginald Denny trial," will trigger another uprising. Although not everyone is clear about what would constitute favorable verdicts in either case, the worst scenario, insurrection-wise, would obviously be a second acquittal of all four white police officers, followed by unanimous felony convictions of the young black men accused of attacking truck driver Reginald Denny at the intersection of Florence and Normandie last April 29.

The semantics of both trials, and of the events of last April, suggest the agitated mixture of accommodation and polarization existing in L.A.: "Reginald Denny" figures less in certain conversations than "the trial of the L.A. 4," or "L.A. 4+." People who have more than a cursory interest in the subject tend to use "insurrection," "uprising," or "rebellion," while "civil disturbance" and "urban unrest" are the politically neutral phrases used by social service agencies, city bureaucrats, and politicians. The average white citizen of Los Angeles uses "riot" automatically; none of the African Americans and Latinos I've spoken with have failed to make the choice of something other than "riot" an emphatic one.

The child-huddled-down-in-darkness theme is, as you might assume, most disingenuously struck in the gated communities of North Hollywood and the Valley, the Armed Response zones on the west side, white flight netherlands like Palmdale and areas north of Wilshire and west of Vermont patrolled by Neighborhood Watch groups. It is not a theme that plays too well Downtown in the region charted by Mike Davis as the "Homeless Containment Core," the "Narcotics Enforcement Zones" of Central Avenue and MacArthur Park, Koreatown, or in Compton, Watts, Inglewood, Crenshaw, and Florence, where the logic of last year's events is less elusive and shadowy, where people have been huddled down in darkness long enough to know that the biggest monsters don't live in darkness but merely collect the rent on it, and where the terms of the equation are visibly intact. Barely a dime of useful relief money has ever reached South Central Los Angeles.

Peter Ueberroth's "Rebuild L.A.," however well-intended, has bogged down in a morass of red tape. As for Federal Emergency Management Agency and its multimillion dollar allocation for L.A. disaster relief, Cynthia Robbins, the directing attorney of Urban Recovery Legal Assistance, characterizes FEMA as "the second disaster that follows any federally declared disaster."

"We've seen a pretty big share of people who are trying to get emergency benefits," Robbins says. "I think it's appalling that at this date we are still helping people to access emergency benefits as a first shot through the system. It's appalling that many of our clients who did ultimately get help got it in August, September, and October, which means that somehow, through the good graces of friends and relatives and people in the community, they were able to hang on by a thread from early May."

"We also have people who haven't gotten any benefits at all," says Becky Rosenthal, a paralegal at URLA. "We have a lot of recent immigrants, people who aren't sophisticated, who don't have accountants, swap meet people, they don't have safety deposit boxes for their papers, and often what records they did have were destroyed. The place they worked was burned down or their shop was looted or something like that. They're just not able to provide the federal tax forms, a lot of it's usually cash transactions, so there are no sales receipts whatsoever. For FEMA, if you can't produce the kind of documents they want, you don't qualify for the benefits."

"These are exactly the people," Robbins adds, "who were intended to be beneficiaries when this legislation was passed by Congress."

Juror 202, a Hispanic male, has two children and is involved in coaching. He has had a "generally good" experience with law enforcement. He was arrested on a DWI charge at the age of 23. Does he believe police generally catch the right people and do their jobs right? No, he doesn't think so. He is involved with Neighborhood Watch. Though he sounds like a good enough juror, the defense eliminates him on a peremptory.

Juror 488 is dismissed after stating unequivocally that "what they did was wrong": he says this with a winning mixture of reasonableness and disgust, as if he couldn't be bothered to play out the charade of objectivity.

Juror 598, a black female, works for the U.S. Postal Service. Was she surprised by the outcome of the first Rodney King trial? Yes, she thought there were a lot of facts leading to a conviction. However, she feels that justice was done in that case. She understands that these are two separate cases. In the absence of a defense challenge, she's seated.

A startling number of people in the jury pool have contacts in law enforcement: Juror 574 has a close relative on the Whittier Police Department; Juror 639 has friends on the California Highway Patrol and the Oxnard Police Department; Juror 649 knows a detective and a parole officer. Juror 519's father was a cop in Detroit. Yet another juror's two children had "considered careers in law enforcement." Many, but not all, are rejected. Judge Davies wants to pick up the pace—even for a "sensitive" case, this thing is moving like molasses.

During the lunch recess, Attorney Stone complains about "a volunteer jury." Ira Salzman, the attorney for Stacey Koon, remarks with some asperity that "speed for the sake of speed is bad."

Salzman describes Juror 598, the black postal worker, as "a perfect juror," a remark that backfires a few days later. Having seated one black juror, the defense proceeds to exclude on peremptory the subsequent four black candidates. The strategy seems to be to get the "racial balance" issue out of the way with one token person of color. Prior to the trial the conviction that the threat of black violence would force a guilty verdict—"It's like telling a juror, 'We put dynamite in your home and if you vote not guilty we're going to blow up your house' "—was publicly trumpeted by Harland Braun, who is known in L.A. as a "flamboyant" figure, meaning he's an uncontrollable blabbermouth. For this, he had a gag order slapped on him; it was later lifted by an appeals court, so the defense lawyers can work the press while the prosecutors remain incommunicado.

When the defense moves to exclude Juror 473, an elderly black man whose voir dire answers are inconsistent with those on his questionnaire, the prosecutors, Barry Kowalski and Steven Clymer, finally invoke *Bateson* v. *Kentucky*, a federal finding that prevents lawyers from using peremptory challenges to exclude jurors on the basis of race. They proceed to argue that Salzman, Stone, DePasquale, and Braun have consistently questioned black jurors differently than white jurors.

The next morning, Judge Davies rules for the prosecution. The defense immediately wants to invoke *Bateson* v. *Kentucky* itself, claiming that the prosecution has demonstrated a "consistent pattern of excluding on the basis of race and age, only choosing to exclude whites over the age of 50." Since the jury pool is overwhelmingly white and middle-aged, Davies dismisses this objection out of hand; soon after, the defense claims to have been contacted by an excluded juror with the news that Juror 598, the black female postal worker, had made remarks impugning the fairness of the Simi Valley trial. Once again, Davies rules against the defense.

The defense has, in fact, shown a pattern of excluding black jurors. But Juror 473 probably shouldn't be on the jury anyway. For one thing, he never entered his neighborhood on the questionnaire, and has lived in Watts for 25 years. If I heard correctly, he also claimed not to have been personally affected by the riots, had no curiosity about the Rodney King incident when he saw the videotape on TV, and in general seemed willing to say anything that would get him on the jury. Moreover, the defense's objection to Juror 473 is being allowed to stand throughout the proceedings, and will surely be cited as one basis for appeal.

On the other hand, the government is playing this case very carefully—because of the videotape, the prosecution in the state trial was disastrously self-assured, a condition the defense seems to be suffering in the present case—and no doubt has a handle on what the standing objection will be worth later on. As far as that goes, Juror 473, who becomes seated Juror 3, has at least as much business on the jury as seated Juror 10, a white male in his 30s who, while working as a security guard, apparently beat up two people, or seated Juror 2, the sixty-something former Marine Corps machinist. Despite the ruling, after 473 no more black jurors are drawn from the pool and 535, the last person called, is also the last non-Anglo person picked.

"The whole question of juries is going to have to be revisited in this country," Congresswoman Maxine Waters tells me one afternoon in her South Central office. "Somehow we're sliding backwards, in terms of jury selection. We must take a look at how lawyers are able to use this process to exclude potential jurors.

"We're going to have to go back and take a look at what it means to have a jury of your peers, and a change of venue, and all that. I'm not only talking about this case, but the Harold Ford case down in Memphis, where the prosecution convinced the judge that Harold Ford was too popular in Memphis to hold his trial there. So they went 100 miles away to Jackson, Tennessee, bused in potential jurors to choose who would sit in judgment of this man over in Memphis. We got the Justice Department to intervene, to petition the court not to swear them in. The court disagreed with the Justice Department; as of Monday they swore in 11 white jurors, and one black, from 100 miles away, from a judicial district that's maybe 17 per cent black, rather than choosing from Memphis, where the population is 40 or 50 per cent black, I think."

When the state of emergency was declared on April 29, 1992, the LAPD began assisting the Immigration and Naturalization Service in sweeps of Los Angeles, in direct violation of laws prohibiting the LAPD from detaining persons based on their immigration status or handing them over to the INS unless they have been charged with multiple or serious misdemeanors or felonies. Six hundred and eighty-one of 747 Mexicans detained were summarily deported—81 Salvadorans, 44 Guatemalans, 27 Hondurans, 4 Nicaraguans, 4 Cubans, 3 people from Belize, 1 Italian, and 1 person from Costa Rica. The following are two of many stories collected by the Central American Refugee Center:

"Lucia A., a 24-year-old woman who is four months pregnant, was walking with her husband on Olympic near Alvarado on Monday, May 4, shortly after midnight, when an LAPD car pulled up and two officers demanded to know the pair's country of origin. When they were unable to produce papers, one of the officers said to her in Spanish, 'You're going to be visiting your country very soon and for free.'

"The officer grabbed her by the hair and pushed her up against a wall, referring to her as a prostitute, and then cuffed her tightly with plastic bands. The day after her arrest, INS presented her with a voluntary departure form and told her she could avoid detention and a high fine if she signed the paper. She signed.

"On May 4, about ten LAPD officers forcibly entered an apartment in Pico Union without a search warrant and began seizing items. The police accused three men in the apartment of looting and demanded Social Security numbers and green cards. All of the residents are legally present in the United States. The men were ordered to produce receipts for all of their belongings, including a television, a stereo, and a radio or face criminal charges for looting."

Somewhere during opening statements, Paul DePasquale enters a motion to dismiss the case against Officer Wind. A number of matters bunged up, some to do with internal affairs transcripts obtained by the prosecution, "avoiding taint from impermissibly compelled statements," violation of Wind's due process, and other opaque issues. These segue into a request from Wind to have his trial separated, on the grounds that DePasquale had once been a law partner of one of the other defense attorneys. This is settled in a nebulous fashion: DePasquale will give his opening remarks after the prosecution rests its case, which means, apparently, that Wind's case will be separated from *US.* v. *Stacey Koon et al.*, but Wind himself won't.

During a recess, when asked if he is worried about a military doctor on the prosecution's witness list who would testify regarding the blows to Rodney King's head, Stone snaps that there were only five blows to the head, "which was less than 5 per cent of the blows," and furthermore there was "no tissue injury consistent with baton blows." He goes on to claim that the police manual's statement that officers cannot force compliance with baton blows is "nonsense": "We know what they mean but they didn't say it right."

The courtroom is packed, and it is quickly evident that the arched ceiling makes the cramped space look very big. Exhibits— equipment checkout sheets from Foothill police station, a map of the Foothill area, etc.—are blown up so large that if they're shown to the jury neither the lawyers nor the judge can see them. So the defense, the prosecution, and the judge all have video monitors planted in front of them, and the clutter at the front of the room resembles the jungle of wires, cameras, and lights that confront the studio audience of a television talk show: you're there, but you can hardly see anything.

Prosecutor Clymer's opening remarks are accompanied in places by the world-famous Rodney King videotape, which is, by the way, in color, though it's usually shown in an enhanced black-and-white version.

Rodney King was speeding on the 210 Freeway in a 1988 Hyundai XL at approximately 12:30 a.m., with a patrol car in pursuit. His blood alcohol level was high. He was on parole for a robbery. He left the freeway at the Paxton Street off-ramp, and pulled off the road near the intersection of Foothill and Osborne.

Powell and Wind pulled up in their car. The passengers in Rodney King's car got out and laid down on the ground. King forgot to take his seat belt off, and his first attempt to leave the car was hampered by the seat belt.

Other officers had arrived. King was given different commands from different locations. He knelt on the ground. He resisted Powell's attempt to handcuff him, knocking Powell off his back.

Koon fired his Taser, a battery-powered device with a toggle switch that, when pressed, launches two darts. The darts won't operate if they land in clothing—they have to connect with flesh. Then, when the toggle switch is held down, the darts send 50,000 volts of electricity into the suspect. (The LAPD trains its officers not to rely on Tasers.)

We see King's muscles convulsing. After 5-to-10 seconds the Tasers wore off.

George Holliday was filming the event from his balcony. On this copy of the tape, the FBI has installed a date- and time-counter in the upper right frame.

Rodney King's car is in the middle of the screen. We see Powell knock King to the ground with his PR-24 side-handle baton. (The LAPD prohibits officers from hitting suspects with batons or kicking them to make them obey orders.) Powell continues to strike him in the face. (Unless lives are threatened, L.A. police cannot hit suspects in the face or head.) King tries to get up, but Powell knocks him down. Briseno reaches over and touches Powell's baton to restrain him. King falls to the ground and stays there. (If a person poses a threat, officers may use more and more force, but must de-escalate force when the suspect ceases to threaten.) The officers yell for King to put his hands behind his back. King attempts to. Briseno stomps on his neck. King sits up on one of his legs. Wind kicks King as Powell continues beating him with the baton. Powell gives Briseno a set of handcuffs. Briseno throws King from his seated position to a prone position on the ground and handcuffs him.

A blizzard of radio and computer messages between the patrol cars and Foothill station:

Powell describes King as the "victim of a . . ."

Koon: ". . . victim of a beating . . ."

Powell laughs.

Koon sends a message over a Mobile Digital Terminal: "Bigtime use of force."

Powell: "Ooops! . . . I haven't beaten anyone this bad in a long time."

Rodney King was taken to Pacifica Hospital, but only partially treated there: a doctor going off his shift stitched up the inside of his mouth. At the suggestion of Powell, apparently, the doctor wrote on the medical report that King was on PCP.

Powell and Wind were to transfer King from Pacifica to County-USC Medical Center. They left Pacifica with King at 3:30 a.m. They arrived at County at 5:30. During the two hour lag, they drove King to Foothill station. Powell left King in the car with Wind, went into the station, and got other officers to go out and look at King.

When Powell and Wind finally got King to County Medical, they told the emergency room nurse the PCP story. Blood and urine samples taken at the time showed that King had no PCP in his system.

Rodney King's right cheekbone was broken in three places. His right and left maxillary sinuses were smashed. His zygomatic arch was broken. He had facial nerve damage. His leg was broken. He had multiple contusions.

The prosecution says that Powell and Wind changed the log at Foothill station to read 4:45 instead of 3:30 as the time they left Pacifica Hospital. That contrary to regulations, Koon never entered a report of the beating on his Sergeant's log.

The defense strategy is clear as creek water: Rodney King is a bad person, a convicted felon, who, driving while intoxicated, led the police on a terrifying, eight-mile high-speed chase, and then resisted arrest. Despite the heroic restraint exercised by the defendants, King literally forced them to beat him senseless. Salzman tells the jury that Koon did nothing illegal, indeed he upheld the standards of the LAPD and even exceeded them. True, King's blood test showed no PCP, but police are taught to rely upon reasonable observations, and the LAPD has standard procedures it follows when "objective symptoms of PCP" are observed.

What are the objective symptoms of PCP? Profuse sweating. Rodney King waving at a police helicopter overhead, like King Kong swatting at the airplanes. Los Angeles police officers are tested on how to conduct themselves around PCP users. They must not, for example, go in for a "tie-up," i.e., physical contact. In a tie-up, an officer's weapon is too close to the subject, who may grab hold and shoot him. Salzman cites the "idea of the officer's weapon retention." This is, he stresses, for the safety of the suspect. The beating with batons and the stunning with Tasers—surefire methods of avoiding a tie-up—were done to prevent escalation to deadly force.

Salzman's presentation, and the one following it by Stone, seems designed to conflate the alleged perception of PCP use with the real thing, to convey the idea that Rodney King, though he wasn't on PCP, manifested the supposed superhuman strength of someone on PCP, so he might as well have been on it. The image of the brute black superman being evoked has heavy overtones of Willie Horton; I'm not sure about the jury, but I remember from the years I lived in Los Angeles how often the PCP defense used to cover all sorts of egregious acts by the LAPD. Back in the mid '70s, the police shot a naked man on Silver Lake Boulevard, something like 13 times, claiming that he seemed to be on PCP, struck a karate pose (rendering his body itself a deadly weapon), and would not obey their commands. The man was deaf, as it turned out.

The defense has prepared its own version of the videotape: on one go-round, pan of the screen is masked to "eliminate camera movement." Second time around, even more of the frame is blocked from view to isolate the action. Another time the image has been enhanced for better contrast. In slow motion—we are fated, today, to see the Holliday videotape in every conceivable permutation—the beating looks like an underwater ballet, and the cause-and-effect relationship between the baton blows and Rodney King's reactions unravels visually. At normal speed, though, it looks like a bunch of cops beating up a helpless drunk. Clymer and Kowalski, unlike the Simi Valley team, have figured this out; they also realize that the tape has much more impact if the lights are lowered in the courtroom.

Even better than the doctored video, the defense has worked up a sort of countervideotape, a montage of colorized black-and-white photos, with cars matted in, illustrating the high-speed chase that led up to King's beating; these show the intersections, freeway off-ramps, and other landmarks the chase involved, shot from several angles. The emphasis is on red lights the suspect ran, endangered vehicles along the path of the chase, and the efforts of CHP, the Unified School District, and the LAPD to apprehend King. By dramatizing the duration of the chase and its potential dangers to pedestrians and motorists, and depicting the chaotic and uncoordinated movements of the three law enforcement units as a concerted effort worthy of Interpol or the FBI Bomb Squad, Salzman apparently hopes to transform a traffic violation into a major felony.

Rodney King "had a blank stare and just looked through" the officers. He "swayed back and forth like a drunk on New Year's Eve." King was "patting the ground." While Koon "verbalized," King "grabbed his ass"—his own ass—and shook it at a female officer of the CHP, Melanie Singer. King "continued to resist" after being hit with the Taser. In fact, he "stood up and started dancing."

So far we have a black convicted felon, DWI, possessed of superhuman strength beause of the PCP he wasn't on, waving at helicopters as if to pull them down from the sky, who makes an obscene gesture at a lady cop and has the effrontery, or just the natural rhythm, to get up and dance after being electrified. And we have the slowed-down, cropped, masked, and wobble-corrected video that shows, not Rodney King being beaten, but Rodney King refusing to lie entirely flat enough to satisfy Koon, Powell, Wind and Braun—and 20 other cops standing around watching—that he was truly defenceless. It's rather like seeing the Zapruder film while someone explains how John F. Kennedy assassinated Lee Harvey Oswald.

But the best moment of the day comes when Braun explains that Ted Briseno is "right-footed," and is therefore bracing on his strong foot while resting his weaker foot on Rodney King's neck. Braun then holds up a boot. The boot looks a little like a high-top Nike Air. This is not, Braun tells the jury, the exact boot worn by his client on March 3, 1991, but it is similar, as they can see, it's very lightweight. Briseno's actual boot, however, was even lighter than this boot. It was, Braun says, "almost like a ballet slipper."

Since day one, it's been apparent that the defense feels it did all its work in the Simi Valley trial. Having won once by slowing down the video and adding its exegesis, it has approached the federal case with nothing new. The prosecution on the other hand, has made several preemptory strikes against the kind of thing that went over with the Simi Valley jury, admitting at the outset that Rodney King was drunk, that in the first few minutes of the incident he did indeed give the officers trouble, that he was on parole for a felony—his fear of going back to jail for parole violation being his reason for not pulling over in the first place— but stressing repeatedly that whatever kind of person Rodney King might be, he is not on trial, and the thing that must be decided is whether excessive force used by the LAPD violated his civil rights. The fact that he was not on PCP, verified by the blood and urine tests taken at County Medical, gets underlined so often in the prosecution's opening remarks that the jury may well view the defense's interminable observations about PCP as irrelevant.

And the prosecution has new witnesses, including Rodney King himself, who does not lose his composure on the stand, sticks to well-rehearsed answers under intense baiting by the defense lawyers, and has lost a considerable amount of weight—he so little resembles the angry giant of legend the defense feels it has to show the jury photographs of King with a few more pounds on him. His uncertainty about whether the officers called him "killer" or "nigger" doesn't damage his veracity nearly as much as the sound of the word "nigger" in the courtroom damages the defense case. And his admission, when asked to read back testimony, that he cannot read, simply makes him seem more a pathetically helpless victim.

The prosecution's claim that Powell brought King to Foothill station instead of County Medical in order to display him to other officers gets shot out of the water by an Officer Gonzales, who turns out to be the only cop who viewed King at Foothill, on his own initiative. On the other hand, the defense's claim that King was taken to Foothill for "remote booking," and that doing so even saved time in getting King checked into County Medical sounds extremely suspicious—why not simply have County alerted via police radio? Prosecution witness Dr. Harry Smith, an expert in biomedical engineering with degrees in medicine and a background in physics and mechanics, testifies that at least three of King's head injuries were caused by baton blows rather than impact on the pavement as the defense has been claiming. If King had simply fallen as per the defense, his nose would have been broken, but it wasn't.

There is, additionally, eyewitness testimony from neighbors, and from members of a band who passed the scene of the incident in a bus; the Simi Valley trial had no eyewitness testimony. The use-of-force expert produced by the prosecutors, Mark John Conta, is exactly the son of gung-ho, streetwise cop—he worked in South Central for a year—likely to impress the conservative, mostly white jurors.

But as the Simi Valley verdict proved, you never can tell.

Research assistance: Ed Leibowitz

*

Closing Time

LOS ANGELES—"Okay, I live in the Hollywood Hills. So I can be away from all the crap." The woman driving me to the radio station in Pasadena was, like so many people I encountered that week, considering a little vacation. The short-term goal was a little time off just before the verdicts. The long-term goal, maybe depending on how the verdicts played in "the community"—that mythic place where everybody else lives—was departure on a permanent basis. A poll published that week claimed that a majority of Angelenos would move elsewhere if the possibility presented itself.

"A week ago I start hearing gunshots, like, every night, coming from behind the house. And I think 'I do not live here to experience this.' You know? It's either a crime spree in the neighborhood, or somebody doing target practice.

"I visit these friends, and there's a loaded gun on the coffee table in their living room. Their teenage daughter's alone in the house. I said, 'Nicole, what is a loaded gun doing out here?' She said, 'When the shit comes down again we have to defend ourselves.' I said, 'Are you people crazy?' "

In the closing days of the trial of the four police officers accused of violating Rodney King's civil rights, it was impossible to get through a conversation without mentioning the current status of *U.S.* v. *Stacey C. Koon. et al.* In a surprise move, the defense rested Thursday morning, April 1, without calling officers Timothy Wind, Laurence Powell, or Ted Briseno to the witness stand, leaving the prosecution very little to rebut. The trial suddenly churned into overdrive; gun sales in Los Angeles County hit a peak.

That afternoon the prosecution moved to show the jury a video of Ted Briseno's testimony in the earlier Simi Valley trial. In that case Briseno had characterized Powell and Wind as "out of control," and said Koon had failed to report the use of force as required by the LAPD. The prosecutors had stated their intention to do this early in the trial, but it had been supposed they would show the tape, or attempt to show it, while presenting their case, rather than during rebuttal. Judge John Davies ruled to allow the tape, providing the government confer with him and the defense over the weekend to decide which bits of Briseno's testimony were admissible. As Davies delivered this decision, Briseno's attorney, Harland Braun, popped up from his seat at least four times to object; Judge Davies finally told him that the 9th Circuit Court of Appeals was right across the street, and that he should go find a judge to overrule him and issue a writ, to "take it off my shoulders."

I was traveling to promote a book. People who interviewed me started with questions about my novel and inevitably swerved to the King trial, and the almost desperate question, "You've been in that courtroom, what's going to happen?" It was useless to say that the atmosphere of the courtroom was one of vertiginous queasiness and crushing boredom, that the jury was utterly opaque and looked like what you'd see if you sliced a crosstown bus in half and peered in, that the prosecutors were extremely competent but had to operate with less than a full deck of admissible evidence.

It was also useless to say that in this case, as in so many others, reality and the law have collided in a way that exposes the contradictions of the system we live in—of any system, really, where masses of people are kept in check by fear of the police and the threat of incarceration or execution, rather than by a shared sense of possibility.

Los Angeles is a city whose gross physical expansion in the past 20 years has been predicated on the segregation of the underclass from the cash nexus. In L.A., the white population has become a minority, and the wealthiest part of that minority sees itself embattled in much the same way that the white minority of South Africa does. It feels threatened not only by the jobless young black men who have left hopelessly underfunded schools in South Central to join gangs, but also by the economic alliances between African Americans, Asians, and Hispanics likely to form in the next decade, if the city itself doesn't further disintegrate into Balkanized war zones.

L.A. feels as if it's wobbling between halting efforts at multicultural accommodation and Bosnia-Herzegovina. Most of the old power structure seems to prefer the latter. In the mayoral race you have Richard Riordan, a millionaire industrialist, who wants to lease LAX and contract out most of the city's functions to private companies, the way Detroit was sold to private interests in *Robocop*. You have Joel Wachs, duenna of Tribeca and the Valley, calling for the National Guard and military occupation during jury deliberations in the police officers' trial, enhanced security for white homeowners' associations, and the breakup of the Unified School District. Across most of the mayoral spectrum the themes are "putting more cops on the street," diversifying the capital base, and an implicit endorsement of trickle-down economics. In other words, protect our investments with more cops and we'll take care of South Central when L.A. is out of bankruptcy. Only Michael Woo seems to offer a coalition-building, Clintonian program. He will probably win, but we are already seeing the weaknesses of the Clinton approach. Tom Bradley was good at coalition-building, too, and, like Sam Yorty before him, sold out most of his constituencies to real estate developers.

As for *U.S. v. Stacey Koon*, apart from the defense lawyers and the defendants themselves, I never encountered a single person in L.A. who thought the police should be uniformly acquitted. Most favored a split verdict: conviction for Koon and Powell, a lesser conviction for Tim Wind, acquittal or some mild penalty for Briseno. I did not see how the jury could possibly acquit all four officers. But absolutely nobody thought they would be acquitted in the Simi Valley trial, either, so the general expectation is now running the other way. I wanted not to agree with the American Civil Liberties Union that *U.S. v. Koon* constituted a case of double jeopardy (in this instance, who cares?) and at the same time thought that if acquittals came in again, Los Angeles would've been put through a judicial charade, a cruel joke that simply underscored the realities of Southern California: that no white cop ever goes to jail for violence against a person of color, that the LAPD mainly exists to beat up erratic drivers and to keep the 17 per cent African American population out of affluent neighborhoods, and that the "wake-up call" of last year's insurrection (which, perhaps more than any other single factor, handed Clinton the backing of the nation's power elite) merely inspired a heavier application of cosmetics to a festering wound. Wake-up to makeup.

Nor did I understand the willingness of people everywhere to assume that widescale rioting would break out as soon as the verdicts were read: surely the riots would come later, probably in August, if the Reginald Denny matter goes from jury selection to verdict by then. The constant flaunting of combat readiness by the LAPD, the National Guard, the CHP, and the Sheriff's Department pointed in the opposite direction, i.e., an unspoken expectation by the Mayor's Office and law enforcement that the likelihood of massive disturbances was small. As many radical members of the African American community pointed out to me, the entire National Guard would be unable to quell another full-blown rebellion. And, given that L.A. covers over 700 square miles, even the 8190-officer LAPD seems inadequate to such an event. But in the event of little happening, it could be claimed that the transformation of Los Angeles into a virtual police state had saved the day.

Assignments, however, had already been made by the wire services, networks, magazines, and newspapers: if you wanted to know which reporters would be at Florence and Normandie or down in Pico Union when the verdicts were read, it was easy enough to find out. There would, no doubt, be a few third-stringers assigned, for comic relief, to Frederick's of Hollywood, and some sidebar people reporting from poolside at the Beverly Hills Hotel.

If rioting does follow the verdicts, whatever they turn out to be, one would have to credit the timing of the judicial process itself, and the mass media, though the causes of last year's disturbances— lately blamed, in a revisionist coup among most of the mayoral candidates, on "bad people" rather than hopeless conditions among the poor whites, blacks, Latinos, and others who participated—haven't changed an iota.

"The model really appears to be the old patronizing thing, corporations coming down, helping out, chipping in a little bit, rather than long-term stimulus," says Ruben Martinez, author of *The Other Side* and a frequent commentator on the mysteries of L.A. "It's not like you can see tangible results. I don't think anybody's at work at a single job that wasn't around before the riots because of Rebuild L.A. Given that the economic outlook is still piss-poor, and that that's what set people so much on edge, how can you think there's not going to be another riot eventually, whether it's after the trial or some other occasion?"

Attending any trial for protracted periods of time makes one blearily aware that "justice" is a consensual fiction, a haphazard interpretation of Byzantine legal language by lawyers, judges, and juries, all of whom are, consciously or otherwise, deeply biased, in the sense that bias is simply another word for human personality.

For example, it was Judge Davies's particular, biased reading of the law that kept out of evidence an incident of 1986, "in which defendant Koon lied about and failed to report a use of force incident." On that occasion, LAPD officers pursued a stolen car. The car crashed. The driver and a 17-year-old passenger fled. Koon captured one of the suspects at gunpoint.

According to court document 143, "After Koon apprehended the juvenile, Officers Jang and Sharpe arrived on the scene. Officer Sharpe pushed the juvenile against a wall and punched him in the head. While Officer Sharpe was holding the juvenile, defendant Koon kicked the juvenile twice in the chest. The officers then knocked the juvenile to the ground, handcuffed him, and took him back to the location where the car had crashed.

"The LAPD requires that a 'Use of Force' incident report be completed whenever force is used by a police officer. Koon falsely replied that no force was used."

In a related order, Judge Davies excluded from evidence a 1990 incident cited in court document 145, in which defendant Laurence Powell and his partner "detained a juvenile and his companion for jaywalking. When the juvenile's companion ran away, Powell and his partner handcuffed the juvenile, placed him in the rear seat of the patrol car, and drove away in search of the companion . . .

"Powell's partner hit the juvenile in the chest with his elbow.

Defendant Powell stopped the car, opened the rear passenger door, and began to punch the still-handcuffed juvenile with his fist, cursing him as he did so. Defendant Powell struck the juvenile repeatedly, bloodying his face. . . . At the station, defendant Powell falsely reported that the juvenile's injuries resulted from his own resistance while being handcuffed."

Even Ted Briseno, arguably the least culpable of the four defendants, has a prior history of stomping, also kept out of evidence by Judge Davies. In 1987, a child-abuse suspect named Daniel Foster was restrained in his apartment doorway by two police officers. This incident is outlined in court document 144: Briseno arrived at the arrest scene, "grabbed Foster, forcing the rookie officer to lose his grip. Foster began to resist again in response to Briseno's intervention. . . . Briseno took Foster to the ground, where Foster was handcuffed behind his back as he lay prone on his stomach.

"While Foster laid on the ground, Briseno struck him twice with the baton. At least one of the blows connected with the back of Foster's head. Briseno stopped striking Foster only after the veteran officer told him to. . . . Shortly thereafter . . . with what the rookie officer described as a 'stomp,' or a 'sharp, rapid' downward movement of his foot, defendant Briseno caused Foster's head to 'thump on the ground.' The stomp occurred while Foster lay prone, handcuffed, and unresisting."

The rookie cop was later able to recognize Briseno in the Rodney King video simply because he'd "know that kick anywhere."

For every item of evidence introduced in the trial, there is at least one and sometimes many that've been left out: deleted draft passages from Koon's memoir of the King incidents, *Presumed Guilty*, in which Koon referred to King's apparent buttshaking motion as a potential "Mandingo sexual encounter" between King and Officer Melanie Singer, for instance. Sifting through the documents of the case, one can construct many alternative cases. But the jury doesn't know that, and as far as it is concerned, Koon, Powell, and Briseno are first-time offenders.

On Tuesday, April 6, Ted Briseno's Simi Valley testimony is duly shown, a day after the 9th Circuit denies the writ requested by the defense lawyers. It's hard to make out the video from any part of the spectator section, since much of it consists of Ted Briseno's hand and arm, in extreme right frame, pointing to sections of the Holliday videotape of the beating: we are watching a monitor within a monitor, the beating tape even smaller and less distinct than it usually appears, with voiceovers.

Dramatic as Briseno's earlier version of events is—Powell's baton strike "was not accidental," King made "no combative movement," Briseno moved to stop Powell because he believed Powell "would keep beating and beating"—and despite its contradiction of most of the defense's case, it's hard to imagine that anyone in this courtroom hasn't long ago reached his or her saturation level. I catch myself looking away from Wind's attorney Paul DePasquale's monitor, to Laurence Powell's father, a stocky, nice-looking man who usually sports one of three differently colored Mickey Mouse ties, but today is wearing one with a sort of Vorticist design. The only jury member I'm ever able to focus on is a big-bellied blond man with long hair on his face and head, who always wears T-shirts and looks like a retired Hell's Angel.

After the lunch break, Briseno's attorney, Harland Braun, attempts a bit of his usual inane humor, circulating an anonymous note that reads, "Judge Davies asked me to give you this so you can be an even bigger prick." Below Braun's scrawl is an ad for a "Male Enlargement" device.

Testimony drones along. Yes, Briseno saw misconduct by Koon. He thought Koon had reported the use of force and only discovered later that he hadn't. Briseno was afraid of Rodney King, who was "twice his size." (True. Briseno is tiny.) He did think Rodney King might be on PCP. He told Powell to "get the hell off" King, several times.

The defense gets a "sur-rebuttal" the next day, which Judge Davies crops from three to two witnesses in hopes of getting the case to the jury by the weekend. First we have Daniel Sullivan, a deputy chief of police in the Valley between 1961 and 1986; he testifies that in 1982 the upper body control hold was "taken away as a police resource." At the time, Sullivan said it was "preposterous to do away with the one tool that prevented having to beat people into submission."

As Sullivan testifies, I notice that a sketch artist sitting in front of me has made a feature-perfect sketch of the entire jury, contrary to the orders of the judge. I'm not sure, but I guess this means he's committing a federal crime. We'll probably get the sketch on TV after the trial closes.

Prosecutor Steven Clymer, a certified dreamboat whose composure throughout the trial has perhaps swayed the jury more effectively than the histrionics and jokecracking on the other side, deflates Sullivan's testimony with a few questions about why the upper-body hold was removed from the LAPD repertoire: too many suspects were choked to death. (And, parens mine, the city had to pay out too many millions in wrongful-death suits.)

The last witness is Sergeant Stacey Koon, who states under questioning by Michael Stone that he placed himself "on the outer perimeter" of the King incident. There, he "could be more objective in my analysis of what was going on." He was about 12 feet away from the first baton blow. His "best recollection" is that this blow connected with King's right clavicle. Koon supposedly yelled, "Don't hit him in the head!" No baton blows hit King in the head.

Clymer, on cross, brings up Koon's memoir, in which he writes that Briseno "gave a false motivation for his own behavior." Koon, however, is now conciliatory, since Briseno has recanted his Simi Valley testimony, claiming that after viewing the "registered videotape"—the one worked up by the defense from the Holliday video—he believes that excessive force was not used. Different officers, Koon magnanimously states, have different perceptions.

And that's a wrap. The next day will be taken up with instructions to the jury, followed by closing arguments. As we leave the courtroom the reporter from a great metropolitan newspaper of record asks L.A. Weekly's Ed Leibowitz if those will be important to cover. Leibowitz, whose reports on the trial have been scalpel-sharp and vastly more insightful than those of the mainstream press, drolly replies that since the jury instructions determined the outcome in Simi Valley, they might indeed be worth dropping in on. (Several of the mainstream trial reporters could be seen on any given day congenially lunching with the defense attorneys in the courthouse cafeteria, which gives you an idea what kinds of stories provided continuing access to Messrs. Salzman, Stone, DePasquale, and Braun.) In closing, the defense is up first. Michael Stone delivers a four-hour rhapsody to the unsung ardors of police work. That his client laughed and bragged about the King beating for hours afterwards is no more damning, according to Stone, than the giggling fits some people experience at funerals. Koon's attorney, Ira Salzman, who delivers a rambling, incomprehensible soliloquy running for three and a half hours, at one point weirdly compares the prosecution's use of Briseno's videotaped testimony to the "my sister, my daughter" scene in *Chinatown*. DePasquale, more or less abandoning any solidarity with the other defendants, paints his client, Timothy Wind, as the hapless rookie who fell into bad company. Just following orders while his supervisors went bonkers.

Finally, Harland Braun, dependably grandiose and sophomoric, compares Ted Briseno to Jesus Christ: 2000 years ago, he notes, another prisoner was brought before a judge amidst widespread rioting, and to calm the rioters . . . well, as it's Easter Weekend, the analogy couldn't be timelier, or more grotesque. A lucky thing, Braun says, that Prosecutor Clymer wasn't around then—he would've indicted the Apostles!

Prosecutor Clymer is characteristically terse, using the videotape to show that King was not, in fact, charging at Apostle Powell when Powell struck him in the head with a lead baton, something the defense has claimed throughout the trial.

As I write this the case is with the jury, which has picked Juror 5, a real estate salesman thought to be sympathetic to the defense, as its foreman. On its first full day out, the jury requested a transcript of Officer Melanie Singer's testimony—Singer had burst into tears while recounting the King incident. Judge Davies turned down the request, perhaps in the interest of speeding deliberations, instructing the jurors to rely on their memories. (This sounds, off the top of my head, like a fresh basis for appeal in the event of convictions.)

Several jurors have been attending church services. Their priests and ministers have been asked by the U.S. Marshal to refrain from mentioning the trial, the impending verdicts, or the possibility of riots following same. Apparently, the ministers and priests have accommodated this request, no doubt to the complete bewilderment of their congregations. Few pulpits in L.A. have been addressing anything else for weeks.

By the time you read this, the jury should have reached its verdicts. Whenever they come in, Judge Davies intends to delay reading them, possibly waiting until 3 in the morning when most people—bad or otherwise—are asleep.

Is L.A. burning?

1993

6. Being and Nothingness American Style

These are the generations of America.

> ... *And Lee Harvey Oswald shot John F. Kennedy. And Jacqueline Kennedy shot Mark S. Goodman and Mark S. Goodman shot Beverley Davis. And Beverley Davis shot James Willwerth. And James Willwerth shot John J. Austin. And John J. Austin shot Nancy Jalet. And Nancy Jalet shot Leah Shanks. And Leah Shanks shot Christopher Porterfield* ... —J. G. Ballard, The Atrocity Exhibition*

On November 7 of this year, the usually infallible Bernard Weinraub ("Special to *The New York Times*," and to each and every one of us) assured his readers that Oliver Stone's forthcoming *JFK* "will be the most widely discussed movie of the Christmas season." Not The Addams Family! "The fact that the movie, budgeted at $35 million to $40 million, feaures Mr. Costner, one of the top stars in Hollywood, and is supported by one of the more prestigious studios, Warner Brothers, adds considerable weight to the impact of the film's thesis, which presents the killing as a conspiracy but does not pinpoint the conspirators."

Notwithstanding Oliver Stone's recent description of prestigious Warner Bros. as an organization of "cocksucker vampires," it does seem that the lavish bankrolling of a studio film supporting the four-shots-from-the-grassy-knoll theory has started a lot of talk. The *Times*, for example, titled Weinraub's article "Substance and Style Criticized in 'J.F.K.' ", when neither the style nor the substance of Stone's film had yet been viewed by anybody. *The Washington Post* and *Time*, twin pillars of credibility, have been poo-pooing Stone's assassination theory with uncharacteristic fervor for months, apparently on the basis of a stolen first-draft script of the film.

Stone's partisans in the a priori controversy swirling around his movie include Carl Oglesby, founder of the Assassination Information Bureau, Herbert L. Schiller, professor emeritus of communications at UC San Diego, and Zachary Sklar, coauthor of Stone's screenplay. These people sense dark forces at work to discredit Stone, and to keep the searing truth about the Kennedy Assassination from reaching the American public. The same dark forces, perhaps, which converged that fatal day in Dealey Plaza. In the scenario favored by this particular mindset, a public awakened to the possible collusion of the Mafia, the CIA, and even J. Edgar Hoover in the murder of an American President is a public that will march on down to the government and put a stop to this sort of thing. "One purpose of our movie," Stone asseverates in a letter to *The Washington Post*, "is to see that in at least one instance history does not repeat itself."

Given the resumé of the current White House occupant, there would seem to be little danger of history repeating itself in quite the same configuration any time soon, but Stone's faith in the public's thirst for truth is nevertheless admirable. Granted, the conclusion reached by the House Select Committee on Assassinations in 1979 that there had, in fact, been a conspiracy to kill Kennedy caused barely a flutter in the pop heart and mind. The House Committee, however, is no Oliver Stone. A Gallup poll commissioned by Stone revealed that 70 per cent of people questioned had "a positive interest in seeing an Oliver Stone film on the assassination," a clear leap in numbers over those who had a positive interest in seeing one about Jim Morrison.

Troubling to *Time* and *Washington Post* reporter George Lardner Jr., Stone's script closely follows the 1988 book *On the Trail of the Assassins* by Jim Garrison. In 1967, then New Orleans district attorney Garrison indicted Clay Shaw, "director of the International Trade Mart and fixture of New Orleans high society" (Garrison's description) for conspiracy to murder Kennedy. Lardner flatly states that "Garrison's investigation was a fraud." Clay Shaw was found not guilty after less than an hour of jury deliberation. (Lardner was very much on the scene in those murky days and months that followed the assassination. He was, piquantly enough, the last to see one of the key conspiracy suspects, David Ferrie, alive.)

To digress for a bit: by this time, close to 30 years after the fact, at least half the American people believe the Kennedy assassination was a conspiracy. Many believe that Oswald was a patsy set up by the conspirators, that the conspiracy was covered up or ignored by the Warren Commission, and that the assassination was a virtual coup d'état. Plenty of evidence supports these notions. Oswald's supposed weapon was a mail-order Mannlicher-Carcano rifle with a defective scope. To kill Kennedy he would've had to fire it three times in six seconds with preternatural accuracy. Oswald was a poor shot. The spent cartridges were found in a neat arrangement near the sixth-floor shooter's window, whereas, vide Garrison, "when a rifle is fired the cartridge is flung violently away." Bystanders on and near the famed grassy knoll saw puffs of smoke and heard rifle fire coming from behind them. A fresh bullet nick on the freeway escarpment indicated a direct trajectory between the area of the picket fence at the top of the grassy knoll and the death car.

Somewhere between impact and autopsy, Kennedy's brain disappeared. Or the brain wasn't sectioned for trajectory data at autopsy and could not be subsequently located. The coffin bearing the corpse out of Parkland Hospital was a different coffin than the one it arrived in in Washington. Doctors at Parkland Hospital saw a man whose entire rear skull had been blown off; autopsy photos from Washington show a single, tiny bullet hole in the top rear of a virtually intact head. If Kennedy had been shot from the rear, i.e., from the sixth-floor window of the Texas School Book Depository, he would have slumped forward with his face obliterated. Instead he was knocked backward and sideways. Certain incongruities, such as Governor Connally's back and wrist wounds, were accounted for by the so-called magic bullet theory: a single bullet exiting Kennedy's body struck Connally and passed through his body and was found, later, undeformed, despite impact with numerous bones and organs. This is ballistically impossible. The Warren commissioner responsible for the magic bullet theory was Arlen Specter, the rat-faced Republican inquisitor of the Hill-Thomas hearings. I rest my case.

At this juncture, the underwater narrative of conspiracy becomes one of suppositions and shadows. One scenario has Jack Ruby traveling to New Orleans in mid 1963, ostensibly to hire strippers for his Dallas clubs, secretly meeting with mob bosses Carlos Marcello and Santos Trafficante. Through Chicago mob boss Sam Giancana three hit men from the Sicilian Mafia in Marseilles are hired to whack Kennedy in Dallas. Meanwhile, dupe Oswald is set up by anti-Castro nut and former highranking FBI official Guy Banister whose Anti-Communist League headquarters were located at 531 Lafayette Street in New Orleans. The same building, with a different entrance at 544 Camp Street housed Oswald's Fair Play for Cuba headquarters!

Enter David Ferrie, described by Lardner as "a vain, nervous flight school instructor," and by others as a virtually hairless chicken queen whose eyebrows and toupee were held in place with Elmer's Glue-All. After the assassination, "authorities" were tipped that Ferrie "knew Lee Harvey Oswald and might have hypnotized him, that he might have gone to Dallas as a 'getaway pilot' for a presidential assassin," etc. Lardner claims that Ferrie, one of many collateral actors to die mysteriously, was "employed as a private investigator for attorneys of reputed Mafia kingpin Carlos

Marcello ... [and] had been sitting outside a federal courtroom in New Orleans waiting for the verdict in a case against Marcello (not guilty) until several hours after Kennedy was killed." Moreover, "he went to Texas for a weekend trip . . . but went to Houston and Galveston, not Dallas." That (not guilty) speaks volumes. Marcello, Trafficante, Ruby, Ferrie, Shaw, and Banister float through many scenarios besides Garrison's, sometimes in connection with "maverick elements" of the CIA, veterans of the Bay of Pigs, the army, and an array of malcontents.

To wade through a fraction of the existing conspiracy literature is to feel oneself inexorably sinking into quicksand. We may never know what really happened, any more than we will ever know the true identity of Jack the Ripper. Vital parts of the jigsaw puzzle, like Kennedy's brain, have vanished forever; you can keep shifting the other parts around as long as you please, but there will always be gaping holes in the big picture.

For this very reason, the Kennedy assassination lends itself to fictional treatment, see William Richert's classic movie *Winter Kills*, based on the Richard Condon novel, and Don DeLillo's brilliant novel *Libra*. The submerged, partly unknowable quality of the assassination narrative has always struck a welcome chord in lovers of suspense. In actual fact, most people don't really care who shot Kennedy; as the one element everyone agrees on, Kennedy is the least interesting figure in the story. The atmospherics give the thing its malignant tone: the feeling that something sinister was taking its course under the American veneer of prosperity and two car garages, something that ultimately brought disillusionment and cynicism into a world that had seemed shadowless and full of possibilities. After all, look what happened afterward: expansion of the Vietnam War, race riots, more assassinations, hippies, LSD, Kent State, Woodstock, Altamont, the Black Panthers, and then all that unpleasant stuff in the '70s followed by 10 years of Reagan-Bush Incorporated.

The coup d'état angle, the suggestion of powerful, implacable enemies of democracy masquerading as businessmen, flight-school instructors, pedestrian gangsters, and nightclub proprietors, has plenty of allure. Throw in the embittered Cuban exile community and the lunatic fringe of the VFW and it's hard to imagine who wouldn't like the story. As with Jack the Ripper, there isn't enough hard evidence to make any particular version of the story stick; one's free to believe whichever variant provides the satisfying twists and turns of good fiction.

In the immediate wake of the assassination, of course, the deranged-loser-acting-alone scenario also held great charm. Oswald: a tiny, insignificant figure who failed despite the myriad opportunities offered by a flourishing America. Kennedy: the pinnacle of other-directed success and the most important person in the world. There seemed at first to be a tragic and very legible lesson in this disparity, an illustration of absolute good and absolute evil, and Oswald's murder, following 23 hours of mysteriously unrecorded interrogation by the Dallas police, drew down the silence of Iago on the meaning of the bloody deed.

Since that faraway era of violated innocence, the conspiracy industry has furnished sufficient motive to make Kennedy's murder seem practically belated. Judging only by Stone's pronouncements about JFK, and his demonstrated compulsion to recast the entire 1960s in the image of his own dippy, Iron John notions of truth, justice, and the American way, Stone intends to show exactly why JFK was bumped off. This information is so explosive, so menacing to the established order, that the minions of darkness have already mobilized against him. In case Oliver Stone gets assassinated and all the prints of *JFK* are destroyed before the truth can reach the American people, I feel obligated to reveal a secret that has flummoxed historians and all concerned Americans ever since the tragic afternoon in 1963 when those three, four, five or six shots rang out in Dealey Plaza: Kennedy wanted to pull troops out of Vietnam, end the Cold War, and normalize relations with Cuba. Pass it on.

Those of you who have not already taken to the streets upon hearing this news may wish to ponder the evolution of motive in relation to the JFK hit. In the deranged-loser-acting-alone schema, Communist Oswald, who had once defected to the Soviet Union, was trained in Moscow to kill the President, in which case he wasn't really acting alone; but if he was acting alone, it probably had something to do with his love of Castro and Cuba, our communist foes, because he did have that Fair Play for Cuba thing going in New Orleans and even got into a scuffle while handing out leaflets. (In the conspiracy scenario, this scuffle becomes a piece of theater intended to make Oswald's presence in New Orleans stick in certain memories.) He'd also tried to assassinate General Edwin A. Walker, a John Bircher, plainly demonstrating his left-wing sympathies.

The idea of a commie-inspired hit by a lone nut, though ideologically soothing at the time, was also rather frightening. Visions of nuclear war were never far from the public mind in those days, especially after the Cuban Missile Crisis, and what if the government found Castro or Moscow at the bottom of the assassination, what then? Soon enough, however, our government was able to brush away those suspicions and paint Oswald as a disgruntled crackpot. Given the obvious ineptitude of the Warren Commission, it seems fair to say that the commission's purpose was not to discover anything really scary, but to "prove" Oswald acted alone.

As the Kennedy killing receded in time, and America generally proceeded to fall apart, the conspiracy models gained plausibility. There was the Mob angle: as attorney general, Bobby Kennedy had been out to break up organized crime, and JFK had done nothing to stop him. Furthermore, the Mafia pined for its lost casino empire in Havana, which it had hoped to win back when assorted bits of Miami-based flotsam of the Scarface variety washed up in the Bay of Pigs, but Kennedy failed to provide air support and the coup failed. Jimmy Hoffa wanted Kennedy dead. Carlos Marcello wanted Kennedy dead. The Five Families who control all the tiles of that gorgeous mosaic, New York City, wanted Kennedy dead in a big way. To read some of the literature on this subject (i.e., *Contract on America: The Mafia Murder of President John F. Kennedy*) is to become convinced that a hefty percentage of the populations of New Orleans, Miami, and Dallas, as well as a daunting number of federal employees, wanted Kennedy so dead that a list of possible assassins could easily fill all 26 volumes of the Warren Commission Report.

For a long while, these sounded like sufficient reasons for JFK's murder by the Mob and/or the Cuban exile community. More recently, the apparent wish of the Kennedy brothers to force J. Edgar Hoover's retirement has added another motive, one that ropes in the FBI, Lyndon Johnson, and Hoover spouse-equivalent Clyde Tolson. Even more recently, the theme of Kennedy-withdrawing-from-Vietnam, a notion rather flimsily supported by a peace-oriented speech Kennedy gave in June 1963, has been cranked up by assassination theorists who claim that the end of the Vietnam involvement would have jeopardized the CIA-Mafia heroin network in Southeast Asia.

What emerges in these latest revisions, strangely enough, is a fantasy rewrite of the Kennedy administration's agenda. Oliver Stone's public statements about JFK reflect a strong wish to reenchant Camelot and its clanking Cold Warrior ghosts with their long-faded myths of nobility and good intentions. In the Stone paradigm, historical cause-and-effect is direct and obvious; if the policies of the Kennedy administration, coldly examined, seem continuous with what happened before and after, i.e., imperialistic, conservative, given to military adventurism, then Kennedy's death must be accounted for by an impending reversal of those policies. Thus, neatly, a single cause, Kennedy's assassination, accounts for all the icky things that followed.

Stone may be very mistaken about this: read Taylor Branch's *Parting the Waters* for a dispiriting picture of a Kennedy whose relationship to the civil rights movement was both cynical and expedient. Read Stanley Karnow's *Vietnam* for scholarly evidence that the Vietnam buildup was proceeding at the time of Kennedy's death, unimpeded by anything except an eye for public opinion. Skim the many volumes of case abstracts issued by the Subversive Activities Control Board covering the era of Bobby Kennedy's attorney generalship, replete with federal suits against the Civil Rights Congress, the Labor Youth League, the Communist Party, et al.

It's hard to conclude that Kennedy was philosophically much different from Nixon. But he was different in a way that Hollywood is uniquely able to convey: he had the charisma of a movie star. Though the right wing still doesn't get it, the fact that JFK was boning hundreds of women in the White House merely adds to his protean legend as chief executive. We have been ruled by gray, dropsical, humorless men with mob ties and the so-called intelligence community ever since, excepting always our strange interlude with the humble peanut farmer from Georgia. (Carter is the only living ex-president who devotes his time to public service rather than the collection of payoffs.) Stone is quite correct when he claims that America changed after JFK's killing. The style of government has become ever more imperial, secretive, and punitive; the Presidency is now a vortex of negative glamor. The substance of government has always been kept out of public view, in secret memoranda and drunken jigs around the campfire at Bohemian Grove.

Stone may also be right when he says that some elements of the media have been working overtime to discredit his movie. Lardner, intelligence and CIA reporter for *The Washington Post*, has perpetrated several jeremiads against Stone, Garrison, and the conspiracy model, taking the droll position that all questions were impressively settled by the Warren Commission. Lardner threatened a libel suit over Stone's description of him as a "CIA agent journalist." "The only subject I have covered for years is sin and corruption," writes Lardner. Though no spook, Lardner does seem imprudent when he brags about being the last person to see David Ferrie alive, at four in the morning, as if that automatically refuted the idea that Ferrie was bumped off. Ferrie "died of natural causes," Lardner writes. And left two suicide notes. Which seems to rule out homicide. Sort of.

It may also be true that Stone's treatment of the Vietnam War, Wall Street, and the Doors has made many people wary of his broad-brush technique, and his melodramatic penchant for personifying Good and Evil in absolute terms. And in a more general sense, some just naturally resent having a history they can remember tailored into a two- or three-hour entertainment that may, things being what they are, come to represent "historical memory" for still others whose memories begin after the events being pictured. This resentment takes on a certain edge when the entertainment in question costs $20 to $40 million to produce, and anywhere between $5 million to $20 million to advertise: its claims and representations can't be meaningfully contested by a review or a letter to the editor. Young people do not read books, and so whichever interpretation of the long-ago recent past reaches the screen first tends to be definitive. Stone himself is sensitive to this rule of market research; allegedly he muscled a competing JFK-kill flick, based on DeLillo's *Libra*, into turnaround through his clout at CAA.

The representation of "living history" can never satisfy the people who lived through it, either at the center or on the periphery. Every human memory is an incessant editor uniquely adapted to the primordial wishes of its owner. Visual evidence and visual fiction can both play havoc with what we think we have stored in our neocortex. Many years after the Kennedy assassination, a poll revealed that an overwhelming number of Americans—at least as many as believe the Dallas events were part of a conspiracy—believed they had seen the assassination live on television, though the Zapruder film was in a vault at Time-Life until five years later.

Like so much of modern life unanticipated by the Constitution, the saturation booking of 2000 theaters for a single director's version of Gandhi or Jesus Christ or the shooting of JFK is something we just have to live with, along with the easy purchase of Uzis and AK-47s. It's part of the touching megalomania of film directors to imagine that people should only quibble with this state of things after the finished product is on display for $7.50 a pop. At least some of the negative feelings aimed at films and filmmakers taking on large, still-resonating chunks of recent history have to do with the industrial scale of the product itself, which renders ex post facto analysis and criticisms practically moot. On the other hand, the people most upset about Stone's *JFK* have an unseemly investment in the lone-gun explanation of every American assassination—as someone once wrote of the fall of the Austro-Hungarian Empire, "it just sort of happened."

If it does nothing else, Stone's film will at least teach a fresh generation of video renters that nothing bad just sort of happens in America.

1991

7.

Gore Vidal´s

Screening History

Screening History
by Gore Vidal

The three lectures collected in *Screening History*, and delivered at Harvard in 1991, give us Gore Vidal at his most relaxed and digressively avuncular. His first sentence refers to that ever approaching Final Exit we must all take sooner or later—Vidal speaks of his Now as the springtime of his senescence—yet I detect no slackening of the nimble, wacky mind that summoned Myra Breckinridge in 1968. It must be said that Vidal, half politician that he is, tends to hone certain themes into aphorisms and to repeat these for years on end. Fortunately, they are usually heretical enough to bear repeating.

In the work at hand, the story of Vidal's childhood and youth in the '30s is shown through the prism of surrounding history, the perception of which was then and is now strongly determined by the fiction films and newsreels of the period. Movies, Vidal says, are the *lingua franca* of the 20th century; the printed word, especially the novel, is superannuated, and "to speak today of a famous novelist is like speaking of a famous cabinetmaker or speedboat designer." Once upon a time, books were famous, among both those who did and those who did not read them. Today, the literary artist "is not only not famous, he is irrelevant to his time."

Vidal compares the switch from print to image culture with the fifth-century shift "from the oral tradition to the written text." This notion has been around since Marshall McLuhan, and it seems, unfortunately or otherwise, true. But Vidal, a genuine media celebrity, has escaped the obscurity of his less telegenic colleagues. To a degree, *Screening History* is about his own fame or inscription in history, and that of his family.

Vidal's grandfather was a much-elected blind senator from Oklahoma (a state, Vidal claims, that his family invented). His father was FDR's Director of Air Commerce, and the founder of several commercial airlines; his thrice-married socialite mother, less famously, managed "to drink, in the course of a lifetime, the equivalent of the Chesapeake Bay in vodka." It was Vidal Sr.'s dream that every family should own, not just a car, but a plane as well. Thus the author, at age ten, was captured by newsreel cameras piloting a Hammond Y-1.

Vidal's maiden appearance on the big screen left less of an impression on him than the spectacle of Mickey Rooney in Max Reinhardt's 1935 film *A Midsummer Night's Dream*. Vidal wanted to be Rooney and to play Puck. (At the time of his Harvard lectures, Vidal notices, Rooney is doing a book signing at the Harvard Coop.) Other key films of the period were *Love Song of the Nile* with Ramon Navarro, *A Tale of Two Cities*, *The Scarlet Pimpernel*, and *The Mummy* with Boris Karloff. The latter inspired Vidal's fleeting wish to become an archaeologist, while another Karloff film, *Isle of the Dead*, mysteriously impelled him, years later, to complete his stalled first novel, *Williwaw*.

Regarding *The Mummy*: "Fifty-eight years later, I watched the movie for the first time since its release and I became, suddenly, seven years old again, mouth ajar, as I inhabited, simultaneously, both ancient Egypt and pre-imperial Washington DC." Our relation to memory is paradoxical in a culture of images, where history is easily altered, edited and suppressed. The movies and television allow us an easy form of time travel, which Vidal, in numerous fictions, has given three-dimensional palpability. In *Myron*, 1973, the hero/ine plunges into the television set and lands inside the 1948 filming of *Siren of Babylon*, starring Maria Montez. The characters inhabiting Duluth in *Duluth*, 1983, are sometimes real, sometimes the fictional creatures of a romance novelist with three names, and slither back and forth, according to the whims of the Creator's word processor, between the world of Today and that of Hyatt Regency England. Vidal's latest novel, *Live from Golgotha*, has late-20th-century TV executives ferrying via laser beam to the period of the Crucifixion.

Vidal's sense of time as a porous and flexible medium is fascinating when applied to his own many years on the public stage. He's so good at playing himself that his undoubtedly authentic memories sound almost too neatly trimmed, as though contrived for the occasion. His descriptions of Old Washington movie emporiums is marvelous—the Belasco, the Capitol, Keith's; he remembers the Dentyne stuck to the seat bottoms at the Metropolitan, the smell of honey in the Translux. Vidal works such seminal movies as *The Prince and the Pauper*, with Errol Flynn and identical twins Bobby and Billy Mauch, into his memories of the Depression, demonstrating by his own intense identification with these screen figments the complex way in which modern reality is invariably mediated through the symbolic.

The book has even more than Vidal's usual tossed-off hilarity. The bemused, sardonic ring of his speaking voice is clearly audible throughout: "Generally," runs one sparkling line, "a narcissist is anyone better-looking than you are." Epiphanic observations flash through the text with striking casualness. Of the U.S. in World War I, for example: "The world was not even made safe for democracy, a form of government quite alien to the residents of our alabaster cities, much less to those occupants of our fruited plains."

Vidal moves us through the Depression into the immediate prewar period (*The Three Musketeers*, *Fire Over England*, starring

Laurence Olivier and Vivien Leigh, *The Prisoner of Zenda*, and of course, *Gone With the Wind*.) We see him at age 13 on a school trip to Europe; he, inevitably, spots Daladier in a military parade, and sits very close to Mussolini at an outdoor opera in the baths of Caracalla. Early on, Vidal can't resist yet another swipe at Truman Capote's mythomania; even Capote might've thought twice, though, about throwing Daladier and Mussolini in the path of the same 13-year-old. But Vidal said it, I believe it, and that settles it.

The final lecture, "Lincoln," winds things up with more Washington memories, war and postwar recollections, and some apt, canny remarks on George Bush's world view, the Persian Gulf bomborama as a television fiction, the Japanese acquisition of Hollywood, and the odiousness of the *New York Times*. All in all, a stirring performance, not least because Vidal has covered much of this territory many times before yet manages rather pithily to make it new. He remains the most useful, entertaining and, why not say it, wise speedboat designer in America.

1992

8. The Beauty Treatment

On Sept. 12, 1984, the Museum of Modern Art in New York opened what must be one of the most extensive and carefully orchestrated retrospectives ever awarded a living photographer. The photographer, Irving Penn, is surely the best-known commercial photographer in America, rivaled only by Richard Avedon. Employed steadily since 1943 by major fashion magazines (*Vogue*, primarily), Penn has probably done more to make the iconography and technical nuances of fashion presentation seem like art than anybody besides Diana Vreeland. In the words of John Szarkowski, at the end of his essay for the catalogue of this seminal event in photography, "Penn's private, stubborn, artistic intuitions have revised our sense of the world's content. His essential work is Spartan in its rigor, in its devotion to the sober elegance of clarity, in the high demands that it makes of us regarding poise, grace, costume, style, and the definition of our selves."

Szarkowski concludes, with a drop of valedictory wistfulness: "We have failed to meet those demands—naturally—but we will not forget them."

One would do well to consider the relativity of "our," "us" and "we" in connection with the work Szarkowski is describing, since so much of it was commissioned by, and appeared in, magazines whose primary audience is the upper middle class of suburban America. Since it is phrased in the Churchillian rhetoric of universal values being mobilized against an implacable barbarism—i.e., an unregenerated world view—one could easily assume that Penn had, stupendously, revised everyone's sense of the world's content by making its consumer products look more desirable than they actually are, and by making demands of grace, poise, costume and style which every person is anxious to define himself in terms of. Yet even the slightest familiarity with everyday life, as lived by most people, demonstrates not only "our" failure to meet the exacting standards of poise, grace and et cetera set by Penn's Jell-O Pudding and nail polish ads, but the indifference of "most people" to the entire world in which Penn's professional life has been, as it were, lived. Stubborn and private and artistic as Penn's vision reputedly is, it has ever offered the perspective of a particularly snappish, lavishly favored lapdog, gumming the hands that feed it without ever piercing the skin. The demands of this vision could easily be forgotten rather soon after Penn stops making them, but this is an optimistic view. Penn is already a role model for a new generation of incessantly clicking acolytes, busily devouring the world in the interests of enlightened consumerism.

The phases of Penn's career are easily capsulized, to wit:

Early work. 1939-45. Arty. Found objects, poor people, war residue, buildings and landscapes in conditions of advanced decay, showing how really pathetic and sad, yet beautiful, the homely life of disadvantaged and displaced people really is when photographed.

Sensitive portraits of famous people. 1947-ca. 1960. Witty and funny, a privileged view of special persons and the odd mannerisms they take on to make their personalities show in their faces. Brooding especially evocative in writers; knowing stares tell you everything about painters. Actors acquire character through their clothing.

Fashion pictures. 1947 to the present. The model expresses a compositional idea somewhere between the human and its parody. The viewer must wish, simultaneously, to kick that smirk off the model's face and steal her clothes.

Ethnographic portraiture. 1948, '67-'69, '70-'71. Shows how everyone, even in remote villages, dresses up in "primitive" outfits that are really fashion-perfect in their natural state, and belong in *Vogue*.

Art photos (still lifes, nudes). 1947-50, 1972, 1980. The photographer can give a striking appearance to almost anything. If something is beautiful, it can be made strangely beautiful. If something is ugly, it can be given the appearance of transcendent candor and unflinching realism. If something is ordinary, it can be rendered emblematic.

Workers. 1950-51. Against the right seamless backdrop, they make us realize how human they are, and how arbitrary our prejudices against them.

Garbage and dirt. 1975. For those whose lives are never touched by them, garbage and dirt, studied closely, have a beauty few would suspect. But then everything is beautiful if you look closely. A single splash of milk, captured in a microsecond, looks like an imperial crown.

Flowers. 1967-70. Who has really looked at a flower? Penn has.

Celebrities in mid-, late career. 1962-80. Age and finally death claim us all, and our faces change accordingly. Pores become large, but the dignity we have acquired because of our accomplishments makes these pores . . . expressive of the real human being under all that publicity.

High art. 1980 to the present. Take a bone, a lipstick broken off. A square of steel, a skull. Those homely little bits of nothing lying fallow in the studio. Look closely. See? Everything that is, is somehow . . . you know, beautiful. Under the right light, anything can, sort of, say everything.

Few photographers have prospered in recent years without following some version of the itinerary which Irving Penn pioneered. Genre pictures emanating from these categories include Rock Stars, Politicians, Punks, Suburbanites, Landscape

Curiosities, Prison Inmates, Body Builders, Gay Pride Marchers, Heiresses, and unaccountable others. To appropriate the world for easy consumption is a routine chore for any photographer. To make the world in its troublesome complexity chic is a Promethean effort of technical rigor combined with a bottomless cynicism about life and reality.

In the world of fashion gush, it is customary for such efforts to be greeted as towering artistic achievements; *Vogue*, quite naturally, supposes that the MoMA show "place[s] Penn unquestionably in the first rank of living American artists," since "he has seen things his way and, in the manner of great artists ... has relentlessly urged us to see them that way, too." But while a few ardent debutantes and jewelry designers may have had their sense of the world's content irrevocably zapped by Irving Penn's photographs, most people, including most *Vogue* subscribers, recognize some basic differences between an artist like Penn and one like Velasquez (to whom *Vogue* compares him, along with Balanchine, Jasper Johns, and Francis Bacon).

I am not referring to the difference between painting and photography, nor even the difference between "high" and "low," these artificial distinctions are, in any case, firmly reinforced by the art market, according to its own loose and seasonally revised interpretations. I am referring to the difference between the real world, as eccentrically perceived and conveyed by artists, and the advertising world, which operates within the margins of quotidian, consensual perception, disinfecting and retouching the obvious and packaging it for sale.

The label "advertising" may sound unduly punitive when applied to the prodigiously varied thematic material encompassed by Penn's retrospective, and would indeed be misleading if its scope were confined to product advertising. (Penn's commercial photographs are amply represented, but are candidly identified by such tags as "Frozen Foods" and "Low-calorie Drink.") However, in an era of mass manipulation, what the most sophisticated advertising sells is not a tangible product, but an ideology. In Penn's case the most innocent expression of the particular ideology he represents is the most forthright one; thus in many respects his lip gloss and pudding ads are the closest he comes to artistic purity. The MoMA retrospective was, of course, designed to demonstrate the opposite.

Penn's work, whatever the subject matter, purveys the ideology of authoritarian beauty. Anchored in the reductive mental universe of the fashion magazine, this ideology is one of expropriated types, of "captured essences." It serves the delusions of a leisure class by presenting the world as a plenum of heterogeneous consumer goods and Dickensian characters. The diversity of Penn's subject matter is important in this connection. A class can only settle into its prejudices comfortably if it thinks it has seen the world; Penn's travels to faraway Peru, his descents to the lower depths of manual labor and petty trade, have yielded abundant proof that the world is full of colorful characters, and Beauty too—even crushed take-out containers, plucked in quantity from the nearest dumpster, will yield at least one attractively squished, Archetypal Take Out Container.

The idea of delectation as a modus vivendi is not unrelated to art, as Oscar Wilde and Ronald Firbank amply demonstrated. That it appeals more frequently to vulgarians is one of life's little ironies. In general contour, Penn's career reflects his public's fear of appearing vulgar. Penn has provided this public with dreamy images of distant lands from time to time (*Cretan Landscape*, 1964), in soft focus, keeping the particulars of daily life at a discreet distance from the viewer. The people, considerably dolled up and arranged in compositionally pleasing clumps, produce an effect of psychological miniaturization.

Penn's ethnic typecasting is closely related to the negation of personality effected in his fashion pictures, where the model's face is usually larded with makeup and garishly lit, heavily shadowed, or stylized into a hard mask. Most of Penn's fashion plates would have been just as effective if he'd used display mannequins. In fact, the ones that do use them are more expressive than the others. The only pictures indicating any involvement with the subject as a person are—predictably—Penn's celebrity portraits; here, it's as if the mystery of character were expected to reveal itself in epidermic details, each acne scar the evidence of a preordained destiny, like a tea leaf. Here, as elsewhere, Penn seems to have had, at best, three distinct ideas. Stand the subject in a corner. Sit the subject on a chair. Tell the subject to put his hand to his face. Tell the subject to look directly into the camera. Excuse me, four ideas.

Of course, these celebrity snaps do stir more interest than the numbing perfection of technique that seems, in so much of Penn's other work, the sole reason for its existence. The subjects themselves bring more to the picture than a nameless native or fashion model is permitted to. Interestingly, the star treatment works not at all on non-celebrities: *Hippie Family* and *Hell's Angels* look like every other cleaned-up magazine rendition of same that appeared in 1967; *Saul Steinberg in Nose Mask* (1966) could be anybody in nose mask, and is just as leaden. One can further measure the extent to which the celebrity shots are revelatory as photography, rather than as self-icons "captured" by a deft technician, by judging how long a celebrity one isn't interested in holds one's attention. For example, if you never regarded Anaïs Nin as the creature of mystery she seemed to herself, Penn's portrait is unlikely to change your mind; if you consider Tom Wolfe somewhat ridiculous, a quick glimpse at his picture is sufficient reminder.

Perhaps some nascent, or perhaps repressed awareness of the limitations of Penn's work accounts for John Szarkowski's desperate-sounding fatuities on behalf of Penn's "artistic vision," and his overstrained discovery of "artistic" preoccupations in Penn's early work. One example of the former: describing Penn's early guru Alexey Brodovitch, a director of *Harper's Bazaar*, exemplifies a rather ill-advised strategy for establishing Penn's creative lineage:

"Brodovitch was the son of petty Russian gentry. . . . Those who have known privilege, once relieved by revolutions of the traditional obligations that accompany the ownership of land and its peasants, sometimes enjoy for a generation or two the best of two worlds: their sense of natural authority remains intact, while

tedious responsibilities have been lifted from their shoulders."
(*Irving Penn*, Intro., p. 17)

This incredible statement is typical of Szarkowski's essay, and it
can only be hoped that its chillingly autocratic sentiment issued
from haste rather than from long reflection. It segues into further
disagreeable pensees, half hagiography, half apologia. Rooting
about for some plausible evidence of Penn's interiority, Szarkowski
casts a knowing eye over the antiseptically "gritty" portraits of the
late '40s and detects:

"the omnipresence of decay, imperfection, corruption, of
dustballs under the beds even of princesses. The raveled carpet or
its equivalent is a recurring motif in Penn's work" (p. 36).

But that's not all. Eureka, in fact. It seems that everywhere in
Penn's inner universe, decrepitude nibbles away at the garishly
protruding edges of luxury:

"The elegant still life is compromised by the stain of spilled
coffee in the demitasse saucer, or by a rank ash tray. The fairy-tale
kitchen of 1950 with prosciutto and provolone hanging as
prescribed from the wall, has a mouse at the baseboard. The burlap
sack of grain has a beetle on it" (p.36).

In short, Penn is way too much the artist not to see that even a
world of petty Russian gentry, princesses and prescribed provolone
has its dark side. But no amount of curatorial lyricism can really
enlarge the puny impression these dabs of cosmeticized morbidity
leave on the viewer. The rank ash tray suggests, not decay, but a
concept of decay, arrived at after four days of screaming at the art
director. The mouse looks like he just waltzed over from makeup
at Disney Studios.

There is plenty to suggest that the "quiet dissent from . . . perfect
elegance" Szarkowski sees as Penn's guerrilla-style tactic, at *Vogue*,
for infiltrating the fashion world with his personal angst (pursued
more darkly on his own) is precisely what Penn himself has been
counting on posterity to recall. A good deal of his noncommercial
work looks like a hyperinflation of successful gimmicks from his
fashion shots. The "Cigarette Series" of 1972—massive close-ups
of scarred, crunched, cracked and stained butts—is plainly out to

shock viewers with its surreal suggestions of death, putrefaction, the ugly beauty of blown-up filth. Penn had previously exploited the cigarette motif to great effect in his portraits and fashion layouts (*Tennessee Williams*, 1952; *Carson McCullers*, 1950; *Woman in Dior Hat with Martini*, 1952; *Woman in Chicken Hat*, ca. 1949); it was hardly peculiar, though, to see fashion models holding cigarettes at the time, and portraits of writers without them are still a rarity. The fashion and portrait cigarette detail, then, does not indicate a full-blown fetish, sucking attention away from the human subject—which would indeed be unusual, suggesting a strong psychological link between the incidental Chesterfield of 1948 and the monumental lung cancer totem of 1972. The adventitious quality of imagination on display here leads one to envision, instead, the photographer methodically researching decades of his own slides and contact sheets in quest of a suitably characteristic prop to heroicize.

The eminence assumed by detritus in Penn's late work has an almost welcome quality of innocence: *Edifice*, 1979, for instance, with its two vertical stacks of bone slices, or *Still Life with Shoe*, 1980, a veritable deathorama of shriveled fruit, skull, unsavory-looking bottles, rotten shoe, a pewter mug straight out of Washington Irving and what appears to be a pretty ripe ham bone. What could be *more* evocative of death, short of stamping the word in black ink across the print?

The idea of Penn as an artist perking with inner ferment who happened to do fashion photography—fashion photography that reveals a veiled consistency with Penn's esthetic itinerary—is quite inimical to Penn's actual work. Penn's photographs of street debris, aborigines, flowers, celebrities, and assembled still lifes are indeed consistent—with the superficial glamour of Penn's commercial work. There is an obvious reason why Penn seems driven to include marginal hints of desuetude in his pictures, and that is that any icon of luxury looks positively radiant when something odd or ugly is placed in its vicinity. Enlarged pores on a famous face make its more attractive features even more redolent of fame, charisma, and difference from the norm. The thing that really unifies this work is not a preoccupation with decay, but an unwavering assumption that anything, anything at all, can be appropriated and given the beauty treatment. The darker zones of reality that exist just beyond the threshold of consumer consciousness can be transformed into "memorable," "moving," "powerful ," "challenging" pictures for leisure delectation.

This brings us back to Penn's forays into the disturbing realm of the less-than-affluent. Penn has ratified the presumption of noblesse oblige and moral immunity that art and fashion photographers (and journalists) blandly acquire as their expected privilege. While many photographers have perpetrated inanities while attempting to ennoble the downtrodden or create sympathetic images of aboriginal tribes, few have approached humanity's underclass with anything approaching the glacial insensitivity of Penn's "beautiful" trophies from New Guinea, Morocco, and Peru. These ethnographic studies, so called, are among the most flagrantly exploitative photographs ever to grace the walls of MoMA: vanishing cultures ransacked for fashion ideas after a slow season on Seventh Avenue, their inhabitants posed against the inevitable seamless backdrop and coaxed into various Condé Nast fantasies of native behavior. Szarkowski wriggles free of the obvious issues raised by these photos rather unconvincingly, with a bit of formalist artchat wrapped in yet another, but in this instance misplaced, allusion to royalty:

"The fundamentally aesthetic issue Penn confronts with seriousness, skill, precise attention, and admiration, but it would be ingenuous to suggest that his art will be of greater use to them (New Guinea tribesmen) than Fragonard's was to Marie Antoinette."

Or David's was to Marat. Or something like that.

Penn's "Workers" series (1950–51) rivals his "natives" in obtuseness: here we find a chimney sweep, a tree pruner, a sewer cleaner and other laborers transformed into generic human beings, their faces obscured by dark lighting suggestive of soot or frozen in cliché expressions—temporary fashion models, again. Penn makes no attempt to plumb the reality of his "exotic" subjects; he reduces them, instead, to the status of objects. Human cigarette butts, so to speak. It's no surprise to leaf through this show's spectacularly well produced catalogue and find *Two Men in White Masks* (Cuzco, 1948) and *Couple with Dog* (Cuzco, 1948), followed immediately, and hilariously, by *Still Life with Watermelon* (New York, 1947). Certainly nobody intended the racist's symbol of ethnic food preferences to look like a gloss on an "ethnography" series. A more generous view of the sequence seems truer: everything pictured is offered indiscriminately for consumption, and everything equals everything else. The show itself makes the point unambiguously.

This is the message of Penn's retrospective. Only beauty pertains, only beauty endures as Art. Since perfecting his exclusive platinum-palladium technique (which gives a burnished, hand-rubbed appearance to the balder gray tones and harder blacks and whites) Penn has been recycling his earlier images of more pedestrian beauty—producing new, older-looking, larger versions that say "high art" in no uncertain terms. *Duchamp* and *Cigarette No. 17*, *Vionnet Back Tie* and *The Spilled Cream*, *Harlequin Dress* and *Coal Man*: it's all material, it's all beautiful, and it's all the same to Irving Penn.

1985

9.

The P and I

The Haldeman Diaries:
Inside the Nixon White House
by H. R. Haldeman

The publication of *The Haldeman Diaries* immediately after
Nixon's funeral is the kind of prosaic justice our cooling 37th
president most enjoyed: a coincidence that looks like a vendetta.
Unrecognizable in the somber eulogies to the architect of detente,
the canny elder statesman, and the man of peace, our Nixon—the
mad Christmas bomber, scourge of Alger Hiss and Helen Gahagan
Douglas, a loser in victory as well as defeat—has been restored to
us in all his daft and whimsical glory: unlovable, paranoid,
congenitally dishonest, and, like Richard III, entirely aware of his
own wretched nature. "P was fascinated this morning to get a
report on the Kennedy Center opening of the [Bernstein] Mass last
night . . . he paused a minute, this was over the phone, and then
said, 'I just want to ask you one favor. If I'm assassinated, I want
you to have them play "Dante's Inferno" and have Lawrence Welk
produce it,' which was really pretty funny."

And so it is. H. R. Haldeman's genius at playing straight man to Nixon's japes has been underappreciated in early reviews. Haldeman owes a little to James Boswell, a bit to Cosima Wagner, and quite a lot to Joseph Goebbels. Swirling in decaying orbit around a black hole, he too mixes the sublime with the tawdry, the monumental with the petty, the public gesture with the private tic. As diarist, however, Haldeman's perfected absence from his own narrative most resembles Andy Warhol's. Warhol said that he stopped having emotions when he bought his first television; for Haldeman this apparently happened when he became Nixon's chief of staff, if not earlier. There is hardly a trace of personality in Haldeman's day-by-day account—except, at the very end, a touch of asperity and disappointment. There is only the P, the P's lofty musings and valiant deeds, and the P's wacky collection of allies and adversaries.

This slightly posthumous work (Haldeman cooled shortly before P) is a comic masterpiece to place alongside Keynes's *The Economic Consequences of the Peace*. Yet the media, unable to wrench itself out of the somber/elegiac thing, has so far treated it with a leaden austerity. The *Wall Street Journal* notes "shocking anti-Semitic and anti-black bigotry" along with "fascinating glimpses of Mr. Nixon as a leader," as if they were different, reserving most of its contempt for Henry Kissinger—a/k/a K—"an incredibly petty and insecure man." Jonathan Schell, in *Newsday*, sees Nixon's career, per Haldeman, as "a titanic struggle between concealment and revelation," though Haldeman renders it as an effortless manic-depressive segue. In the *Daily News*, William F. Buckley, Jr. sniffs that the "supposed" "racial and ethnic prejudices" of Nixon were not "lethal," and were therefore not "the kind of racism we properly worry about." Ted Koppel, in a two-part *Nightline* program, plucked some of the juicier bits, e.g., "[Billy] Graham has the strong feeling that the Bible says that there are satanic Jews, and that—that's where our problem arises," but trod very lightly upon K, the book's second largest character and Koppel's favorite talking head. Michiko Kakutani, in the daily *Times*, does note "moments of out-and-out farce," but concludes that the diaries "can only depress and perturb the reader." Oh, please.

Such tidings reflect a nervous discomfort with the obvious fidelity of Haldeman's portrait. Kakutani, for one, seems to believe that most Americans actually swallowed the funereal makeover of Nixon as "a visionary foreign-policy maker," etc. and recites his major crimes as if disclosing them for the first time. It is rather jejune to find anything shocking, or for that matter arguable, about Nixon's ethnic phobias, his inexhaustible resentment, his compulsive lying, or the fact that he was, in the only sense of the word, a crook. Haldeman's ideal reader takes all that for granted and basks in the author's hilarious, total identification with P.

Nixon's zesty drollery and hijinks are there from the beginning. Within a month of inauguration, he and K are cooking up the secret bombing of Cambodia, giving it the festive code name "Operation Menu." The sudden intoxications of power put P into scary overdrive. "Fascinated by Tkach report of people who need no sleep at all. Hates to waste the time. . . . Thinks you have to be 'up,' not relaxed, to function best." Even the White House staff's gift Irish setter, King Timahoe, feels edgy around P. "Had Tim in the office, both of them pretty nervous." K, like P, "swings from very tense to very funny."

Haldeman strikes the note of farce with recurring comic minor characters. "Poor Agnew slipped on the icy runway during troop review and smashed his nose. Then went on TV to introduce P with huge cut on nose bleeding profusely." "Almost unbelievable conversation at dinner as J. Edgar went on and on about his friends . . . and his enemies. . . . A real character out of days of yore. . . . P seems fascinated by him and ordered me to have lunch with him twice a month to keep up a close contact." A theme of omnipresent enemies is also sounded with Warholian deadpan. "Interesting to watch Eunice Shriver last night and tonight, she obviously hates seeing Nixon as President. She talked to herself and winced all through the toasts, both nights, and must have been thinking back to JFK." "Big flap about proposed Ambassador to Canada. Turned out to be a guy P had met in '67 in Argentina. He was Ambassador there, and Nixon stayed at the residence, he left anti-Nixon literature and Herblock cartoons on bedstand. So now P has blocked this appointment, or any, for this guy."

The gang around P—an ever-shifting cavalcade of poltroons, buffoons, and sleazy opportunists, with a boorish core of constant retainers like Ehrlichman, Mitchell, Buchanan, Moynihan, Haig and Connally, along with the largely irrelevant cabinet, the almost invisible Pat Nixon, and the spectral Bebe Rebozo—is soon swept up in the charade of rulership. Like the court of the Medici everyone harbors little secrets, everyone "leaks" this and that to the press, and all important decisions take place in an atmosphere of psychotic secrecy. "P issued strict orders that Ziegler and White House staff are to say nothing about Vietnam until further orders. Has to keep complete control and not let an inadvertent comment play into their hands." "Later called over, all upset because K making an issue out of State reluctance to bomb Laos. Rogers wanted a meeting, to argue P's decision. P told me to tell K to go ahead and bomb, don't make announcement or notify State just do it and skip the argument."

Even in an actual crisis, Haldeman's tongue-in-cheek rescues his pen from excessive melodrama. As South Vietnamese troops entered Cambodia, P "reviewed DDE's Lebanon decision and JFK's Cuban missile crisis. Decided this was tougher than either of those . . ." Minutes later, "Called again to discuss problem of locating his new pool table. Decided it won't fit in solarium, so wants a room in EOB."

After a few unsatisfying meetings with civil rights leaders and antiwar groups, P and his team decide to ignore the demonstrations and other unpleasantness occurring outside the White House. "Need to reexamine our appointments and start to play to our group, without shame or concern or apology. Should feel our way, appear to be listening to critics, but we have now learned we have gained nothing by turning to the other side." From Haldeman's marginalia, however, the reader gradually surmises that just below the immediate circle of P subluminous worker ants with names like Liddy, Hunt, Krogh, and Ulasciewicz are scurrying around the troubled countryside, planting spooks at leftist get-togethers, burglarizing offices, forging letters on other people's stationery, and delivering large amounts of cash in brown paper bags.

Meanwhile, the inner circle serenely goes about its imperial business. "The Apollo shot was this morning; the P slept through it, but we put out an announcement that he had watched it with great interest." The P is preoccupied with keeping the kooks, hippies, niggers, and yids at bay, holding the line on school desegregation, nominating ghastly judges for the Supreme Court, and planning nasty shocks for an ever-growing list of enemies. Despite his ingenuity in these domestic areas, the P feels unappreciated. "K, at Congress, didn't make the point regarding the character of the man, how he toughed it through. . . . Why not say that without the P's courage we couldn't have had this? The basic line here is the character, the lonely man in the White House, with little support from government, . . . overwhelming opposition from media and opinion leaders, including religious, education, and business, but strong support from labor. P alone held on and pulled it out."

We will never know exactly how long the Vietnam War was protracted by K's on-again, off-again Paris Peace Talks, which in Haldeman's account seem mainly hobbled by K and P's capricious habit of following up each session with massive bombing raids. "The mad bomber" was Nixon's own term; he thought if the Communists believed he was really insane, they would be desperate to negotiate. K apparently agreed when it suited his mood, squabbled when it didn't. Haldeman's K is a Molièrean figure of fun, an incessantly grumbling, pompous, infantile worrywart who demands constant stroking from the P, threatens to resign every other day, and spends much of his time upstaging Secretary of State William Rogers, who he's convinced is "out to get him." What K and P share, aside from a child's love of secrecy, is the delusion that they function best in crises, which they frequently manufacture to rouse themselves from the torpor of omnipotence. They detect Soviet influence in various affairs the Soviets have little interest in—the India-Pakistan conflict, for example—issue blustery ultimatums, and work themselves into a prenuclear lather; when the bewildered Soviets acquiesce, K and P congratulate themselves on having forced the enemy to "back down."

They're equally gifted at spawning tensions within their own circle. "So I asked Henry to come in and join us. E then jumped on him pretty hard, on not only that, but also the intelligence thing, and the international drug problem. . . . At this point Henry blew and said as long as he's here, nobody's going to go around him . . . E got a little more rough on him, and that resulted in Henry saying E couldn't talk to him that way, and getting up and stalking out of the meeting." Squalid internecine rivalries and craven favor mongering permeate every small and large issue, conference, meeting, state visit, and memorandum. From Haldeman's micromanaging perspective, the epochal Nixon visit to China and the Moscow signing of SALT I are slapstick, almost accidental triumphs of business over venality and pettiness. And after Moscow it's all downhill.

Haldeman first notes the Watergate break-in on Sunday, June 18, 1972. "It turns out there was a direct connection (with CRP), and Ehrlichman was very concerned about the whole thing. I talked to Magruder this morning, at Ehrlichman's suggestion, because he was afraid the statement that Mitchell was about to release was not a good one from our viewpoint." At first the little tapping of Plumbers is muted by the roar of P's landslide election victory. For a time, the gang is confident that the problem can be "contained," even turned to advantage. "He wants to get our people to put out that foreign or Communist money came in in support of the demonstrations in the campaign, tie all the '72 demonstrations to McGovern and thus the Democrats. . . . Broaden the investigation to include the peace movement and its leaders, McGovern and Teddy Kennedy." In fact, freshly mandated P feels nearly invincible. "He wants Ziegler to put a total embargo on *Times* and *Newsweek*, there's to be no background to Sidey regarding election night or anything else at any time. He wants total discipline on the press, they're to be used as enemies, not played for help."

As late as February 1973, the P still had other things on his mind. "He said, 'Don't discuss this with anyone else, but we've got to cover the question of how to handle the Nobel Peace Prize. It's a bad situation to be nominated and not get it.' Maybe there should be a letter to Miller, who is nominating him, saying the P feels he should not be honored for doing his duty . . . He wants a report on the Nobel Prize—who's on the committee, what's the process, can the P withdraw his name, and so on." By April, however, even the P's unflagging prankishness has waned. "The P had me in at 8:00 this morning. Said that if this thing goes the way it might, and I have to leave, he wants me to take all the office material from his—ah—machinery there and hold it for the library."

With impeccable comic timing, Watergate begins to unravel the P at the very moment that K secures a negotiated settlement in Vietnam, snatching defeat from the jaws of defeat. Just when K and P should be preening in the funhouse mirror of world history, unsavory drones surface from the netherworld for urgent nocturnal covens, scrambling to get their stories straight. Each story is quickly shredded by someone else's story. No one can recall exactly when and where who told who to do what to whom. "Talked to Dean on the phone this morning. . . . He's back to his cancer theory, that we've got to cut the thing out. Cut out the cancer now and deal with it." ". . . Jeb said that he and Mitchell were afraid Colson was going to take over the intelligence apparatus, so they went ahead, and Dean feels it was probably with Mitchell's OK." "Caulfield gave this letter to Dean, Dean told Mitchell about it, Mitchell told Dean to have Caulfield see McCord and take his pulse." ". . . some evidence that Colson had put Hunt into the Plumbers operation to spy on Krogh, and so on."

As all the P's men are hauled before the grand jury, P recalls—too late!—the trap he set for Alger Hiss, involving the question of perjury. P realizes with horror that he's walked into the same trap! Here, Haldeman's narrative brilliantly captures the lunar panic of the final days, when one by one, sometimes two by two, the White House gang is thrown to the wolves by P. Frankly unable to recall his own lies, prevarications, secret meetings and the like, Haldeman starts to report other people's accounts of "Haldeman," as if he and the author were two different people.

Happily for us, Haldeman, along with Ehrlichman, is pretty much the last to go, unless you count the interim staff, special prosecutors, defense attorneys, and of course K, who surrounded the P when he was, at long last, forced to climb aboard his final presidential helicopter. Only a day before Haldeman's departure, P "shook hands with me, which is the first time he's ever done that." After announcing H's and E's resignations on TV, the P "asked me if I thought I could do some checking around on reaction to the speech as I had done in the past, and I said no, I didn't think I could. He realized that was the case." But the P just wouldn't be Nixon if he didn't ask.

And there Haldeman's delightful account closes, with the Vampire of Yorba Linda still clutching the frayed reins of power as he gallops toward . . . a full presidential pardon, his pension, and the mulch of historical relativism, shameless and saucy as the lounge comedian and used car dealer we, the people, always knew him to be.

1994

10. Writing Dangerously

Mary McCarthy and Her World
by Carol Brightman

A writer, Joan Didion observed somewhere, is always selling someone out. No other profession demands of its practitioners a flair for betrayal, an insatiable appetite for other people's weaknesses, flaws, inanities, crimes, and misdemeanors, all in the service of prattling a higher truth. Unavoidably, the rigors of the job require the writer to be as merciless to himself as he is to others. We mistrust a narrator who smells like a rose, especially when he's draining a cesspool. It's not enough to spill the beans about your alluring, enviable vices, à la Henry Miller; copping to the seven deadly sins can be a sly method of showering yourself in glory, cf. Benvenuto Cellini. What the really good writer brings to confession is a deep sense of embarrassment, shame, and contrition.

Despite having lost her faith at age 12, at the Forest Ridge Convent in Seattle, Mary McCarthy remained, throughout her life, a compulsive penitent, like most ex-Catholics. In Carol Brightman's biography, *Writing Dangerously*, McCarthy appears to have done exactly as she pleased much of the time, guilt and expiation emerging when the backward glance suggested a need for absolution. At times, though, a convoluted strategy for deflecting guilt may have dictated her behavior, against her rational judgment; decades after the fact, she could still not account for marrying Edmund Wilson, except by speculating that not to do so after he'd seduced her would have meant that she was promiscuous. That this odd scruple surfaced as the trigger of a major life decision at a time when McCarthy was sleeping with anyone she felt an attraction to makes perfect sense to an ex-Catholic, though it's probably opaque to anyone else. Those of us born or shanghaied into the Church at a delicate age are forever starving for grace, which usually requires some ghastly sacrifice. The worst thing about a Catholic childhood is that its mechanisms continue ticking inside, like the dynamic between one's parents, after they've been consciously repudiated. I wasn't surprised by McCarthy's final word on her liaison with Wilson, but rather, familiarly depressed: "If he had not shut the door firmly of the little room [at Trees] . . . I would not be the 'Mary McCarthy' you are now reading. Yet, awful to say, I am not particularly grateful." Brightman's book is almost everything a biography should be: sharply written, comprehensive, unpedantic, sensibly analytical, novelistic. Her account of McCarthy's childhood, Vassar years, and early days in New York is, somewhat unexpectedly (since these are twice-and-thrice-told tales), as compelling as her intricate retracings of literary-politics among the *Partisan Review* crowd before, during, and after the war. Brightman illuminates McCarthy's ambivalence about believing, for example, that her father continued to have an alcohol problem after "getting cured." She recreates the oddly stratified Seattle of McCarthy's girlhood, a port city where certain Irish and Jewish families were part of the gentry rather than slum dwellers; the fatal family move to Minneapolis during the flu epidemic of 1918 is painted in richly garish hues, as are the dreadful strap-wielding poor relations Mary and her brothers were parked with, after their parents' deaths, until their providential Grandfather Preston whisked them back to Seattle.

McCarthy's memoirs of Seattle and Minneapolis reflect the workings—some would say overworkings—of a skeptical and judicious mind. The judicious part is McCarthy's glory as well as her frequent downfall. The appeal of her sensibility resides as much in her willingness to doubt her perceptions as in the devastating conclusions she often draws from them. Yet the decline of McCarthy's literary fortunes in the 1970s and '80s can easily be attributed to a late failure to cast a cold eye—a drying-up of vitriol. She gives the characters in *Birds of America* and *Cannibals and Missionaries* far too much philosophical baggage, far too many brains; the latter book, especially, shows an incomprehension of the contemporary world's irrational passions and inarticulable impulses, an unwillingness to admit how truly awful people are. McCarthy may well have understood what mass media has done to people's minds and personalities, but she disliked it too personally, and gave her characters the faux-Socratic consciousness of an earlier period—specifically, the consciousness of the 1930s and '40s.

Residue of Catholicism aside, McCarthy's sensibility began to jell at Vassar, where Latinist and Elizabethan studies revealed the virtues of a classical prose style. With Elizabeth Bishop, Muriel Rukeyser, Margaret Miller, and others, McCarthy founded *Con Spirito*, a maverick alternative to the *Vassar Review*. Later, after her marriage to the actor Harold Johnsrud, her *Con Spirito* writings helped persuade Malcolm Cowley to let her review for *The New Republic*.

In the fullness of time, the marriage to Johnsrud seemed to her as much a mistake as the later one to Wilson did. A private preoccupation with finding error in her choices eventually registers, in Brightman's book, as an almost boorish tic—McCarthy's way of proving that she's larger and smarter than her own life, that things which didn't work out all issued from temporary lapses in taste. McCarthy was, among other things, an incorrigible snob whose populist politics invariably smacked of noblesse oblige. No one she discarded turned out to have been good enough for her, yet they were, for a writer, almost always beneficial. The connection to Johnsrud, for instance, proved useful: through him, she met the key personnel in the New York theater world, and was therefore able to write from inside when she began her "Theater Chronicles" in *Partisan Review*. She also got scads of material for her novels; Johnsrud is a major character in *The Group*.

Perhaps the cycle of error and regret Brightman reports as a chronic theme in McCarthy's conversations amounts to displaced guilt over the sour use she made of friends, lovers, Vassar classmates, and family throughout her fiction. The author of *The Company She Keeps* was hardly unique in the practice of serving an intimate up for dinner after giving him or her a slight change in hair color, or making "composites" out of two or three readily identifiable friends. But McCarthy, quite unfortunately, equated imagination with not telling the truth, and stayed closer to her models, and actual events, than was prudent or kind. According to Brightman, McCarthy had great difficulty, in *Cannibals and Missionaries*, rendering a character who was three-quarters Jewish, simply because she herself was only one-quarter Jewish and couldn't imagine what being three-quarters was like.

The most interesting sections of this book elucidate politics and literature in New York from shortly before the Moscow Trials to the end of the '60s. The prodigious cast includes Dwight Macdonald, Philip Rahv, Wilson, Hannah Arendt, Alfred Kazin, Sidney Hook, Clement Greenberg, Arthur Schlesinger, Delmore Schwartz, Nicola Chiaromonte, Simone de Beauvoir, and, ominously, Lillian Hellman. Somewhere during her affair with Rahv, which segued into her marriage to Wilson, McCarthy became, on the strength of her critical writing, a significant person in the mostly male world of *Partisan Review*, *The Nation*, *The New Masses,* and *The New Republic.* A signer of petitions, a presence on the picket line, an organizer of those noble open letters that still appear, with increasing pathos, in the rearmost pages of *The New York Review of Books.*

By her own lights, McCarthy never did anything especially brave, except to defend Trotsky's right to a fair trial. She was a sort of fellow traveler, but too much the patrician to commit herself to the CP. Her troubles with Hellman began at a dinner party in 1948, where Hellman made disparaging remarks about John Dos Passos. McCarthy and Dos Passos were no longer friends, but she felt honor bound to defend him. The following year brought the Cultural and Scientific Conference for World Peace at the Waldorf-Astoria, which Hellman helped organize, and at which McCarthy and Dwight Macdonald used their two minutes of speaking time to denounce Stalinism.

Brightman has a firm grasp on the ideological conundrums of the (Joseph) McCarthy period: intellectuals like McCarthy, Macdonald, and Rahv were anti-communists, but also anti-anticommunists, and attempted, not always successfully, to frame their opposition to Stalin in a way that gave no succor to the forces of domestic repression. There were Stalinists like Hellman who had, in fact, belonged to the Party, pleaded the Fifth Amendment when called before the McCarthy Committee, refused to name names, yet also stipulated that they had not belonged to the Party. There were the ex-Communists who had seen the light, eager to identify the enemies of the Republic. There were the ex-Communists willing to name themselves but nobody else. As Brightman points out, no one who came before the McCarthy Committee ever defended the constitutional right to be a Communist, and the scramble to take positions everywhere outside such a defense fueled the collective hysteria.

What's most revealing in Brightman's retelling is the feebleness of the nominally leftist response to McCarthyism, the expedient and self-protective mechanisms that determined the behavior of Mary McCarthy and her circle. They risked little, bending to circumstance like reeds in the wind. This was not so much a matter of hypocrisy as an expression of bedrock American values that had, a decade or so earlier, been occluded by the romance of becoming a Trotskyite or a Stalinist—romance in the true sense of falling in love with something one didn't understand much about, something that could produce feelings and convictions and reams of material too.

The book-burning honeymoon undertaken by Roy Cohn and David Schine through USIA offices in Europe in 1953 was an anomaly; the Inquisition was, rather presciently, more concerned about Hollywood than the printed word. "Freedom of expression" was good advertising abroad, and toward the end of the '50s most of the old *Partisan Review* crowd were junketing around the world to USIA-sponsored writers' conferences and striking brave leftist poses in magazines secretly funded by the CIA. It seems doubtful that these writers, adroit wrestlers in the ring of conscience, would not have found a noble reason for being government puppets had they known their publisher's identity. Though Brightman doesn't say so, the easy complicity of the Old Left with the "progressive" branch of The Company was one of many sclerotic symptoms that caused the '60s New Left to repudiate just about everybody from the Rahv-Macdonald-and-et al. set.

There are odd lacunae and ellipses in Brightman's book. McCarthy's third husband, Bowden Broadwater, apparently manifested homosexual tendencies after their separation, when McCarthy was living with her soon-to-be-fourth husband, the diplomat James West. Brightman lays no groundwork for this revelation, and after it's sprung, wraps it in ambiguity, reporting only Bowden's subsequent affairs with women. While almost all McCarthy's occasional prose is accounted for, along with her major essays, the decline in her perspicacity, evidenced throughout the '80s, goes mainly unmentioned. (I'm thinking specifically of McCarthy's woefully lame writings on Henry James, and a review of Joan Didion's *Democracy* in which McCarthy claimed to have ransacked Joseph Conrad in search of a reference to the Tropical Belt Coal Company; said company appears on the first page of *Victory*.) For that matter, Brightman's discussion of McCarthy's best novels, *A Charmed Life* and *The Groves of Academe*, is strangely perfunctory. The biographer seems, often, too ready to accept the negative appraisals of McCarthy's reviewers as gospel; she quotes Norman Mailer's self-serving hatchet job on *The Group* at undeserved length.

Brightman has mercifully spared us yet another précis of

Norman Podhoretz's venal autobiography, *Making It*. However, Podhoretz's claim that Susan Sontag's ascension to the role of Dark Lady of American Letters prompted McCarthy's graduation to Grande Dame, fatuous as it may be, carries a valid, unconscious indictment of a literary world that for decades made room for only two women as intellectual eminences. It's hardly accidental that both of them exhibited an extreme hostility to feminism—explicitly, in one case, implicitly in the other—and embraced the condition of being "the only woman on the panel," basking in the effusions of male colleagues pretending to be pussywhipped at symposia and colloquia.

The life Brightman records became rather uneventful after *The Group* and marriage to James West. McCarthy left America for Paris, where she entertained friends like Nathalie Sarraute. After some years, she felt marginalized, and saw her crowd as inferior. She had written things against Sartre and de Beauvoir. The beau monde disliked her. Her reports from Saigon and Hanoi, her coverage of the Medina trial and the Watergate hearings, were the best writing she ever did, but the resulting books were ignored. The Wests bought a house in Castine, Maine, where they spent several months every year. McCarthy's routine became rigid: breakfast at eight, lunch at one, etc. Her health was failing. With the debacle of *Cannibals and Missionaries*, she slid into obscurity.

McCarthy had become an anachronism. Her tastes were adventurous enough, as her championing of William Burroughs at the Edinburgh Festival of 1962 demonstrated, but her notions about writing fiction belonged to the 19th century, the novel of manners. Her attitudes about women, homosexuals, race relations, the way to seat people at dinner, were weirdly frozen in some '40s Smart Set configuration that never yielded to subsequent shifts in mores and cultural tropes. The evident nostalgia in her last books for the wholesome vanished America of her childhood—an America free of television, frozen foods, and labor-saving appliances (in other words, frontier America)—was much too corny, too class-conscious, too condescending to be taken seriously. Mary McCarthy seemed to have regressed to her convent years.

Then, fortuitously and disastrously, she was rescued from oblivion, with a single sentence uttered on *The Dick Cavett Show*, about Lillian Hellman: "... every word she writes is a lie, including 'and' and 'the.' " Hellman's subsequent $2.5 million libel suit, designed to ruin McCarthy, backfired; magazine writers began cannibalizing McCarthy's legal papers for articles like Samuel McCracken's *Commentary* piece, "'Julia' and Other Fictions by Lillian Hellman." Brightman's account of the lawsuit and surrounding controversy is as gleeful as a biographer can allow herself to be. The downside of the Hellman-McCarthy war, of course, is that the written word no longer has sufficient authority to set off such a conflagration. Only TV can do it. Indeed, it is hard for a "young writer" (in America, as McCarthy observed, a young writer is any writer under 50) to read Brightman's book without a mournful feeling, since so much of it covers an era when books, and writing, made a difference. If few people under 40 know who Mary McCarthy was, this is no fault of an exceptionally rangy, rich body of work, but a pathetic comment on the culture we live in.

1993

11. Paul Schrader's *Mishima*

Paul Schrader's *Mishima* is about Yukio Mishima in somewhat the same way that Fassbinder's final film is about Jean Genet's novel *Querelle*—a meditation on a piece of fiction. In Schrader's case, fictions: not only the excerpts from the three Mishima novels dramatized in the film, but Mishima's life story as well. What we see of Mishima's progress from childhood to hara-kiri is drawn almost entirely from the mythology Mishima spun around himself; he was a tireless self-promoter. After years of flogging the bizarre idea that Japan's lost glory would revive with a return to emperor-worship and the samurai code, Mishima formed his own army. Powerful connections in the military gave Mishima's Tatenokai, or Shield Society, access to training facilities at Eastern Army Headquarters, where in November 1970 Mishima and several comrades paid a call on General Mashita, tied him to a chair, and demanded that the garrison's troops assemble in front of the building and listen to a speech. Mishima's harangue, intended to spark a coup d'état, instead provoked catcalls. Mishima withdrew from Mashita's balcony. Back in the office, he disemboweled himself in the classical seppuku manner, but his second, a young man named Morita (who was Mishima's lover), flubbed the decapitation on first try, and failed to completely sever Mishima's head on the second. Finally, Furu-Koga, a fellow cadet with better kendo training, took the sword and did the honors. Morita then made a fainthearted attempt at hara-kiri himself, but couldn't quite cut it; Furu-Koga was obliged to lop his head off as well.

In the time of the samurai, Mishima's death might have been a supreme assertion of honor; in 1970 it was correctly perceived as a grotesque publicity stunt. In light of Schrader's film, it might almost qualify, like the death of Elvis Presley, as a good career move. The moment Mishima plunges the dagger into his abdomen, three other moments of death (hanging threads from the three fictional set pieces viewed earlier) flash on screen, woven—or, rather, hammered—together by Philip Glass's generically "Oriental" score. Then we see a blistering orange sun on the rise (or the wane) bubbling away on a near horizon. End of movie. The fact that we don't see the desperate, bumbling mayhem that followed Mishima's hara-kiri is consistent with Schrader's hagiographic intentions. The film has no time for the lesser foibles and banalities that comprise most of any lifetime, and no taste for the messy particulars a life like Mishima's leaves in its wake.

Schrader demolishes anything resembling real time, creating a continuum of past, present, and fictional present-perfect, each mode delineated by a distinct, elegant cinematographic style. *Mishima* flashes forward and back between color docudrama, black-and-white "past," color fiction. The "past," usually framed at low angle (the "pillow shot" favored by Ozu), is oneiric, its scenes full of visceral subtleties (Mishima's grandmother's legs under blankets; the slicing of fingertips in a blood-oath sequence), the camera generally static. The "present," alternately crisp and grainy, is characterized by a peripatetic camera that emphasizes the conceit of "action" as Mishima's ultimate art form: he puts on his uniform, leaves his farewell manuscript out for the publisher, gets in the car with his accomplices; from then on, this thread of the narrative is all motion and propulsive military music on the order of a drum roll before an execution.

The fictive dimension was shot on a sound stage, on wonderfully artificial sets designed by Eiko Ishioka—on whom the legacy of Leni Riefenstahl has not been wasted. The camera dips down into these sets from a towering vantage point, recalling courtesan prints and Mizoguchi movies. Eiko's sets are operatic masterpieces, monumental and more than slightly vulgar, but appropriate to the material. They frequently split apart or collapse with terrific drama; movement inside them is orchestrated in splashy patterns. The lurid colors of the "Kyoko's House" sequence are particularly effective in conveying the look of '60s Cinemascope gangster films like Nicholas Ray's *Party Girl*. Despite its hallucinatory vividness and extreme spatial closure, the theatrical excerpts from Mishima's novels achieve the peculiar effect of "opening out" the adjacent passages; while the present-perfect is saturated with the stuff of Mishima's obsessions, it's also the tense least obliged to sound true.

These studio sections are, on the whole, more dramatically energized than the black and white "reality" that brackets them, in which Mishima evolves from a sheltered, sickly child into a withdrawn, bookish adolescent, and finally into a protean lout who churns out prizewinning books, hangs around gymnasiums, patronizes student leftists, and issues fatuities to an ever-avid press corps. *Mishima*'s bio-pic aspects are quite punchy, but coercive in the manner of heavily stylized propaganda. No one has ever been so purely a product of personal obsessions as the Mishima of *Mishima*; reducing the man to the creature of his own publicity leaves Schrader with a pretty unsavory hero, a boorish right-wing crackpot whose unquenchable narcissism demands progressively grander manifestations (posing for photos as St. Sebastian, directing himself in films about ritual suicide, etc.)—pathological symptoms which Schrader accepts as talismans of spiritual truth.

One is more convinced by Mishima's art than by Mishima's life, however, and Schrader uses the novels as psychological stuffing for this publicity ectoplasm. The protagonist in each fictional episode is a troubled young man. In "Temple of the Golden Pavilion," it's a temple acolyte who stutters; oppressed by the perfect beauty of the Golden Pavilion, he finds salvation by destroying it when, at war's end, American bombers have failed to do so. In "Kyoko's House," it's an actor who takes up body-building, then meets an older woman who turns him on to heavy s&m, whereupon he realizes that art is a pale substitute for bondage, discipline, and death. "Runaway Horses" features a young kendo master, dissatisfied with the spiritual joys of martial arts training; driven by a need for purgative action, he assassinates a politician, then disembowels himself.

From these attractively fleshed, slightly nauseating passages, it's all too easy to extract the same messages: hatred of one's own physicality, desire for nobility through "action," inability of art to provide a sufficiently heroic raison d'être. The inductive leap to the psyche of Yukio Mishima presents no big difficulty, either. As if to prove that Mishima's life was really all about the stuff we see in the fictions, Mishima's own reflections on himself accompany the "past" in voice-over. But for many viewers, the smooth transitions from art to life will register as far too facile.

Mishima's concentration on the public Mishima leaves the viewer in considerable confusion (especially since even well-publicized aspects of his life have been suppressed, allegedly to placate his widow; still, the film was banned in Japan). In the opening scene, for example, we learn that Mishima is married, has children; we never hear another thing about them. A flashback in which Mishima dances with another man in a gay bar is the only explicit reference to Mishima's homosexuality. Mishima writes, gives press conferences, trains with his army; we never see him at ease, in what press photographers like to call an "unguarded moment." His biographers describe an often congenial, pleasure-loving man, but Schrader's Mishima is a stodgy, uncomfortable person who lacks any sort of spontaneity, a compulsive striker of attitudes who seems, at all times, to have frozen into the demeanor of one of his publicity photographs. He is so much his own cliché that one finally wishes Schrader had gone all the way and cast Jerry Lewis.

Avoiding any critical probing into the private Mishima, *Mishima* wraps a consistent, unsatisfying myth in flattering visual tissue. Schrader accepts the sword-and-sun hyperbole of Mishima's writing at face value, substituting its grandiose contradictions for the more prosaic ones that influenced Mishima's behavior. The film relentlessly searches for a metaphysical essence of Mishima; what it invariably finds is a perfect vehicle for Schrader's own obsession with rituals of male violence. Mishima's life, in this heavily colored version, confirms a hard, knotty "truth" that Schrader has already tried to pin on blue collar workers, fancy call boys, porn stars and taxi drivers: Purity is won only in murderous catharsis. Since masculinity is defined by the ritual of bloodletting, art can serve only as meager simulation, a shadow of the real thing. Mishima's suicide was supposed to fuse art and action in a moment of terrible beauty; in actual fact, the event was an absurd mess. Mishima set himself up to die of embarrassment, his insatiable lust for fame having finally consumed every other possibility. *Mishima* enshrines this tacky passion without a whisper of irony.

It can be argued, however, that while Schrader's hermetic sobriety in representing Mishima fails to debunk or aerate any myths, it does offer those myths without amelioration or special pleading, and lets us see them with optimum clarity, in the full sensual glory that is, unfortunately, truly theirs. Mishima was hardly alone in his necrophilic absolutism and his conflation of manhood with an attraction to weapons, injury and self-destruction. For the like-minded, *Mishima* is loaded with genuine Ur-substance, but opposing sensibilities are free to view this film as a richly articulated fabric of appalling ideas.

1986

12. The Sex Factory

Mulholland Drive, 8:30 a.m.

On a switchback lane off the west side of Mulholland, several ranch houses perch at the edge of a curving cliff, their barbecue pits and swimming pools facing the toxic morning glare of Beverly Hills. Wild mustard furs the hills. Funereal cypresses rise to mossy points above the rooftops. A home on this street ran as high as a million-five two years ago, but the current migration of the well-off from Los Angeles has dropped property values in all the fabled neighborhoods around here. The place I'm meeting Sam looks to me like $700,000, tops. Plain white ranch, electric gate, jade plants and assorted succulents in the courtyard.

A red subcompact swerves up to the curb in front of my rented Pontiac. A ropily muscled black man in jeans and a maroon T-shirt steps out, eyes me neutrally, says hi. His head's shaved up the neck and sides, leaving a blunt disk of hair on top. It's a dead California Sunday: no joggers, no dune buggies in the hills, no helicopters. Just the faint stirring of medflies in the lemon trees.

Inside the house, a kind of controlled chaos is kicking into motion. The black man and a tall brown-haired man mill around in the entrance hall with a boyish guy with heavy beard stubble and a cropped ponytail, who sorts through the contents of a nylon duffel bag. The owner of the house, a sixtyish party named H. Randall, sips coffee and chain-smokes at the kitchen table with a much younger man whose large, soft body and blandly handsome face suggest a certain louche variety of Californian male hausfrau.

The scene has the flavor of another time, though I couldn't say when. The house is full of things, things everywhere. Vases, carpets, paintings, sculptures, reconditioned antiques, shelves of hand-painted porcelain, commemorative dishes, Native Americana, dolls in cases, hideosities jumbled together with rare-looking objects. Later in the day, when all the chaises are occupied by naked bodybuilders waiting to do scenes, the poolside patio has a look of inevitability, of cliché, of something dreamed after a night of hard drugs and bleary sex.

A procession of young men invades the place, carrying grocery bags and equipment. The man with the ponytail introduces himself as Ed—"Mr. Ed"—the makeup artist, and starts laying out tubes and pots of goo, spray bottles, an enema bag, and a blowdrier in the bathroom. Then Sam arrives. Sam is a short, solidly built man with a Northern Italian face and short dark hair.

We chat. The last time I saw him, Sam had a mop of blond ringlets and was playing a prison doctor on a set in Queens ("Open wide . . ."). He hands me the day's shooting script: *Temptation*, a Gino Colbert film. Sam is also Gino Colbert. The day's stars are Mitch Rabida, the black man; Bill Marlowe, the brown-haired fellow; Ryan Block, a Hispanic actor who's just come in, and, replacing an actor who's canceled, a lean Argentinian boy who's been doing some still modeling for H. Randall and wants to break into the business.

The business, X, adult video, is something I have been mildly curious about for years, partly because it brazens what's usually concealed, and partly because of its mimicry of the legitimate film industry. Like Hollywood, the adult-entertainment business has producers, directors, agents, technicians, and stars; it has professional organizations, critics, galas, award ceremonies, and trade magazines.

Sam has been in the business since childhood. From ages four to 14, he ran errands every weekend at his aunt's burlesque house. A few years later, he answered a casting call for a Samantha Fox vehicle, *Tramp*, landing a bit part as a bellhop. Since then, Sam has done it all, straight and gay, as actor, stunt dick, producer, director. At the moment, he directs gay and straight product for Video Exclusives, a major porn company with offices in the Valley. Everyone likes working with Sam: he's rather amazingly good-natured, patient, polite to the talent. Today's shoot, he says, is a "one-day miracle": except for an already-shot, four-way scene with Joey Stefano, Rod Garetto, Nick Manetti, and Ryan Block (all familiar faces, etc., in current porn), he'll shoot the whole film today, in this house.

Poolside, 9 a.m.

While one of the bedrooms is prepped for a sex scene between Ryan Block and Mitch Rabida, Bill Marlowe stretches his legs in a poolside chair and says, "It's a lot more Hollywood than people think. You see these things onscreen and think, wow, it must be so great to be there and film that."

Irony is perhaps the least developed trait among porn stars, though they're consciously defensive, and funny, about how their profession is regarded by much of the general population. Jim Steel, who directs and produces gay product for Vivid Video, works it out like this: "Some people think you're scum, and those are the ones that are always renting the videos when they're drunk and alone."

Like everyone in this movie, Bill Marlowe has the physique you get from religious daily workouts: rippling muscles and defined, squarish breasts. He's also the butch type most heavily featured in California porn. The California aesthetic, which dominates the industry, tends not to discriminate between the reasonably streamlined body like Bill's, and the massively pumped one, like Mitch's. Later in the day, Bill will be inserting a gargantuan dildo into a blond actor who himself resembles a weird rubber inflatable.

"It's definitely work," he says. "I did a film for Matt Sterling about five years ago. I was working with an actor I didn't like very much. He just wasn't my type. We shot over at Springboard Studios in the Valley, in May, it must've been 110 degrees.

"Every time they turned on the air-conditioning it would stay on a 45-minute cycle—this is freezing air blowing on you, and they're spraying us down with water and glycerine all day. We were doing this scene with an ice cube running up my stomach to my mouth, with the other actor following it with his tongue. I could tell it was coming out gorgeous. We get that done, and the makeup man behind the deck says, 'What's that flashing light?' They had the cameras on pause.

"I had a tirade. I went in the dressing room, came back five minutes later and said, 'Okay, let's make some magic.' It took two days. I've never done a scene that took two days. I've never done a scene that took more than an hour and a half. The ironic part is, I won the 1989 Best Sex Scene Award for that scene. So it just goes to show, this is like the legitimate business in many respects."

Bedroom, 9:30 a.m.

Sam and a photographer named Lee Jennings are pondering a scene where Mitch, fully dressed, awaits Ryan, who enters in a bath towel. The room contains a four-poster bed, dressers, and an assortment of novelty lamps, statuettes, and things hanging on the walls. A curtained glass wall with sliding doors looks out on the pool.

Ryan Block, Sam tells me, is "straight," though he's a familiar top in gay porn.

"Straight in what sense?"

"He's straight," Sam repeats emphatically, ignoring my question. "The novelty here is, it's the first time he's playing a bottom. A lot of people are gonna want to see that."

The bedspread is black, with a splashy pattern of jungle orchids. Everything in the room is a study in bad taste.

"He's never been fucked in a movie before?"

"It's a delicate thing," Sam muses. "I've got to let him take his time. He'll be fucked by Mitch. In all my movies, I always have one black actor and one Latin actor, even if it's a white movie. I think I'm the only person who does that."

"Have him enter," Sam tells Mohammed, the video cameraman, "and Ryan comes out of the shower—"

"You're not using the pool?"

"I'm not one to shoot outdoors. It's more uncomfortable to shoot on pavement, or on a kitchen table, or a carpeted floor, than in a bed. A bed guarantees they're not gonna get a carpet burn."

Sam shows me a laundry hamper behind the monitors and recording deck where I can sit during shooting. It's wedged in the bathroom doorway. In the bathroom, Ryan Block stands in his underpants looking nervous.

"Have you shot in this place before?" I ask Sam. I'm imagining dozens of porn videos featuring the same grotesque bedspread.

"I've been here four other times. I've seen this house in a lot of other movies, but that doesn't bother me. We change things around to make it look different. If the viewers noticing the surroundings, there's something wrong with the scene. I'm using guys who've never worked together, and that guarantees me some form of chemistry.

"A lot of directors criticize me for always shooting in beds. But I look at their stuff, which is creative, like fucking in a helicopter or an air shaft, and the heat isn't there. If the actors are doing a specific position, one guy's on his back in the missionary and the other's on top of him, I'm not gonna tell him to flip over and do doggie, and then go into spoon on his side and lift up his legs—I'm not out to get creative sexually. I'm out to capture heat. I want to get that facial reaction where you can see the orgasm traveling up through his body right up to his neck, to his face. I want to get the real thing. Not the prettiness. I don't care if you see lube all over somebody's ass, or sweat, or spit. My stuff is more real."

"We're douching at the moment," Lee Jennings tells Sam.

"We're ready," the sound tech says.

"The guys know their lines," Sam says.

Ryan Block hovers naked in the doorway.

"How you doing?" Sam asks him. "You might want to run your body through the shower."

"My dick, definitely."

"That, and wash the other end. . . . "

Stars

You couldn't be cuter or blonder or more evenly tanned than Danny Sommers in a green bikini bottom, stretched on a chaise beside his apartment house swimming pool, teeny Walkman earphones blasting out the world. Danny Sommers is short and perfectly proportioned, a golden youth from the cornfields of Middle America, if Pittsburgh had cornfields. Sometimes described as a "greedy bottom" for his receptive roles in such Vivid Video offerings as *True* or *Blue Collar, White Heat*, Danny Sommers radiates an aura of uncomplicated sensuality and accessibility that becomes almost unnerving in person.

We go up to his minimally decorated apartment, which contains a Matisse print carpet and a Picasso poster and simple good furniture. His balcony offers a direct view of the driveway where Sal Mineo was stabbed to death. We settle on what feels like a miniature couch. As we talk, Danny smiles relentlessly. He projects both innocence and a seen-it-all, done-it-all weariness that brings out my protective side.

I ask the obvious question: How did a sweet boy like you, etc., etc.

"I'm 27. I got started in the business two and a half years ago. Certainly by surprise. Somebody came up to me in Pennsylvania and told me I could make a lot of money in California. It was January, the weather here was beautiful. I expected this to be a very short thing until I could get a job. I didn't even know they had awards or anything like that. My first year I won Best Newcomer. My second year I won Best Actor. All the money started coming in, and all the opportunities.

"But," he adds, conspiratorially, "I'm quitting. You're the first person to know."

Somehow I doubt this, but no matter. Is it true that he's in medical school?

"Pre-med. My problem has never been with grades, my grades have always been top-notch. The problem is that after doing what I've been doing for the past two and a half years, do I want to be stuck inside, in an office, a building, a surgery, or do I want to try self-employment, where I can open my own business and set my own hours. That's the type of freedom I like."

I suggest that being a doctor might have more long-range advantages than whatever self-employment he has in mind, and Danny agrees: "If I do finish med school, I'll never kick myself in the ass for it. 'You dumbass, you should have been a porno star!' "

A favorite of Vivid director Jim Steel, Sommers spent two years in the army as a model soldier. Two months before his stint was up, he took a joyride with a jeep and was put in detention for a year. He describes himself as "spontaneous."

"Most people don't treat this as a profession," he says. "No one expects it to last long. So they take the money, they blow it. When I came in, I had no idea how much money I could make, either. But if you're smart you invest it and do something for yourself. At first I just . . . well, I refurnished my living room, then I refurnished my kitchen, then the bedroom, and then I started taking trips.

"Then I entered Phase Two of pornography, which is dance tours. I've done all that. San Francisco, Florida, Texas, New York. You build up money from that. The life in touring stinks because you're up late, you usually end up staying in the club until the bar closes. You don't get to the gym, you don't eat right. You get to the point where you're fed up with it, which is where I am now."

I ask him to give me an idea how much money is actually involved.

"People exaggerate. When I started I made $500 for a movie. Now I make anywhere from $500 to $2000 for a scene. It depends on the movie and the budget. To be honest, it depends how desperate I am for money."

Many porn stars make their real money from the dance circuit, and from what is euphemistically known as out-call:

"We're all the same. 'Never will I do anything like that.' And then never becomes, 'I've gotta buy groceries.' Once you get into out-call, it's, 'Wow, I'm going to Paris, Europe, all these places.' At times I'm upset with myself that I've been foolish with my money. Luckily, I have a lot of things to show for it. Two cars that are paid off, beautiful furniture."

A question about craft: does he have an unusual ability to sustain an erection for hours at a time?

"It's not what it appears to be in the final product, obviously. But I'm very lucky in that, whether it's a woman or a man standing next to me, kissing me, I'm going to get erect. Whether I care for them or not. It was a lot easier when I first started, though. The more I know about the business, the more I want to get away from it."

Bedroom, 10:30 a.m.

"Scene two and three we're doing right now. You have one line, and Three is sex. So you've got on your towel, strip down. Put on your towel. This is a good towel."

"Sound test."

"Are you ready, sir? Let's rehearse this. You got a good shower? We'll rehearse it and then we'll spray you."

"'You sure took your time getting here.'"

"Okay. They're in frame?"

"Ed? Spray him down."

"Nonchalantly he's checking you out while you're drying under your arms, and then he can't wait any longer, he starts playing with the tits. And as he's doing it, you start stroking your dick. And, you know what I didn't do? I didn't slate. I haven't done a feature since January, just that catalogue stuff where you don't slate."

"Rolling."

"Action."

"'You sure took your time getting here.'"

"Shirt."

"Oooh, yes, baby, yeah . . ."

"Can you freeze there? Actually, you can lose your pants now."

Stars

Busty Belle, who sometimes appears in Sam's movies, was a stripper for eight years before doing videos. Before that she was a dental assistant. Her first video featured just herself and a vibrator ("a piece of cake") and then came some softcore work. When she got into hardcore, she insisted that her costars wear condoms.

"I found that it was very hard to make a straight movie and have that happen. Now I do gay and bi porn. Girl-girl, and also boy-boy-girl, where they're together and then have a threesome. I don't even do straight movies anymore. Why? Because the bi and gay movies have protection. I'm bisexual in my personal life. In my professional life, I would do either, but I'll only do what's healthy. It's important to know the straight movies don't use protection. It's very, very dangerous."

"What are the bisexual movies like?"

"Most are boy-boy scenes, and they'll throw in a boy-boy-girl scene to make it bi. I go on the set, and everybody there's a man except me. Lots of times, they just put me in the background as scenery. There's two guys doing each other, and I'm using a vibrator, getting off looking at them. Which I do, actually."

"Is having large breasts important for women performers?"

"For some parts of the business. Obviously, you can do big-busted videos that girls without big busts can't. For dancing and doing naked scenes, those assets help out a lot. You get paid more dancing if you have a large chest, usually. I'm naturally big, though."

"How big is the fetish video market?"

"I know that Bizarre Video does a lot of the s&m and leather videos. Sam does a few of the fetish things, I don't know exactly who they go out to. I've done a foot fetish one, where men are sucking on the heels of my shoes, coming on my feet which is, you know, extremely safe sex. And, I'm in a lot of tit fetish videos, where I'm being tit-fucked. Then they have a few really weird videos, like, black women who have shaved pussies and no tits, things like that. They're all fun."

"What are your long-range plans?"

"Oh, as long as I'm looking good and have the public wanting to see me, I'll keep doing this. I'm only 27, so I have a couple of good years ahead. Then I'll probably go back to school and get into something."

Politics

Ron Sullivan's apartment is in a large stucco building in the Valley. It's full of generic furniture, lots of glazed dark wood, furry carpeting, and mess—clothes and papers everywhere. He has, he explains, just moved in, his girlfriend got in at six in the morning, and he completely forgot our appointment. I notice, in the bookcase, copies of Tony Robbins's *Powertalk* seminar tapes and a biography of Jean Renoir.

Ron Sullivan (a/k/a Henri Pachard) is 54. He founded the Adult Video Association, which merged with the Free Speech Legal Defense Fund to form the Free Speech Coalition. He has the frazzled appearance of someone who's not doing badly but who's had to hustle every penny. His ample hair has a lot of silver in it and his body, in a purple bathrobe, has a mild middle-aged sag.

"I guess I've been 25 years in the industry," he says. "I certainly wasn't a pioneer of the business. They're all dead now. This industry really was an offspring of people who were into carnivals and circuses, always promising the world but not giving it to you. Like in the '50s, with burlesque. I grew up in Kansas City. I remember seeing Blaze Starr and Candy Barr, and many of the highly talented strippers of the time.

"There were these silly black-and-white movies of nudist colonies, and things like that. Someone finally came along and said, Why don't we give them their money's worth? Let's show people having sex.

"The Free Speech Coalition is a trade association. I always thought we should be the ones to finance a national organization involving the public. There are 7 million supporters of the Second Amendment who pay $15 or $25 a year to the National Rifle Association, which is really motivated by gun manufacturers.

"Now, we promote pornography, we manufacture pornography, dirty movies. So we need to raise about 7 million people to create a First Amendment organization. We're losing the battle. We haven't gained crap in 25 years. What we release today is so watered down, it's vanilla porn compared to what we used to do in the '70s.

"There are legal opinions that say we can't use certain language like, 'Suck my dick, bitch.' Unless you say, 'Would you please suck my penis, Miss Such-and-Such.' What we're getting in these movies are a half dozen scenes of happy couples that will bore the shit out of you.

"All of us pornographers are not necessarily trained political-action freedom fighters, though we have the greatest motivation. I sort of equate it to our Founding Fathers, who created the Revolution 200 years ago. These people were slave dealers, rum sellers, tobacco merchants, and they were making a lot of money. So they said, 'Let's create our own country, because we'll make even more money.' And these guys who created this great country were a bunch of smugglers and sellers of flesh.

"Yes, we exploit the First Amendment. We make money off of it. Therefore, we're the ones who should be financing everyone else's First Amendment freedom. There are groups in California like NCAP—the National Coalition Against Pornography—which have lots of splinter organizations, to make it look like a massive force. It's really a handful of people in Lancaster, Santa Clarita, and Palmdale. For instance, there's the California Care Coalition, which is also the Concerned Citizens of Antelope Valley, which is all part of NCAP."

Sex Factory

Video Exclusives is a $20 million-a-year business. At company headquarters in Van Nuys, which from the outside looks like an electronics plant, Sam and I pass through a foyer that belongs on a space station, into a warren of offices that would not look out of place in a Madison Avenue high rise. There are tasteful executive suites with tasteful executives gabbing into telephones. Conference rooms in soothing colors. Secretaries with framed baby pictures and Smurf dolls on their desks. A cubicled accounting department with 10 full-time accountants. An ad department that could service a large-circulation magazine, drafting boards and light tables covered with glossy color photos, sheets of transparencies, strips of press type.

Chromes, still photographs, and detailed distribution and financial histories on each film are filed in a bank of metal cabinets. You need a full-boner color transparency of Matt Windsor in *Lords of Leather*? It's all cross-indexed and there at your fingertips. Forthcoming product is digitally spliced and sound-mixed in a suite of editing rooms where shapeless men puff Marlboros in the darkness, synching grunts and splotches of mood music into close-ups of people jamming parts of themselves into holes in other people.

Everyone knows Sam. He moves through the building dispensing sardonic charm and bawdy jokes, a showman displaying a well-oiled machine. An editor runs a few dozen feet of current video for Sam's approval: it's a four-way romp in a standard porn bedroom, and Sam notes that he had a bitch of a time with one of the actors who couldn't stay hard. While we're here, he picks up several CDs of merengue and salsa music to which Video Exclusives has bought the rights. None of it sounds all that wonderful, Sam says, but it's wholly owned, they can put it on any movie they want.

We go through a warehouse of bins full of flattened box covers. When the product hits the video store, the box cover sells it, a lot of thinking goes into box covers. (Best Box Cover is an awards category.) Then we head down a corridor where several hundred Panasonic duping machines flip videos in and out of attached VCRs and into a shipping dock where dozens of Hispanic workers pack and crate thousands of videos. Sam inspects shipping forms, invoices, checks out the size of orders to New York, Chicago, Kansas City. He shows me an order for $26,000, from one video store: "That's a good order. That's very good."

Video Exclusives makes something for everyone. Fetish video.

Bondage. All black. Trisexual. One series specializes in "giant dick," i.e., actors with abnormally large prosthetic penises attached to their bodies.

Sam used to produce straight porn as well as gay, but the two branches of the industry are now pretty much segregated except at the financial end. Capital-intensive companies like Video Exclusives and nearby Vivid Video cover the waterfront sexually, but there is less and less crossover among actors and directors. I ask Jim Steel of Vivid how the straight side of the business views the gay side.

"The girls certainly don't want to work with the guys who do the gay stuff," he says. "Even though they'll sit there and get fucked repeatedly by eight guys not wearing condoms, they're quite sure if they do gay movies they'll get AIDS and die."

Straight pornographers consider gay porn a marginal product, though I've heard gay directors say their own market is larger. The annual industry galas have, Steel says, snubbed gay videos, giving out a handful of awards every year as a sort of afterthought. The gay industry now has its own awards. Safe sex practices are only haphazardly used in straight films, except at certain companies like Vivid that acknowledge the health risk of unprotected vaginal intercourse. In the straight industry, AIDS is often viewed resentfully, as a problem brought into the business by homosexuals.

"I think the hetero society thinks they're free from getting AIDS," Busty Belle says. "I don't know what other reason there could be, because it's sheer stupidity. And everyone else I talk to, unless they're doing that for a living, agrees with me."

"When I started at Vivid," Steel tells me, "I explained to them there would never be any unsafe sex in my movies. My reason being that, being gay, I'm not going to ask someone to do something for money that I wouldn't do myself. Some people complain that they like the older films, because the minute they see a condom it turns them off. Well, it's a fact of life, if you're gonna fuck these days you're gonna use a condom. I think it would be more abnormal now to see a video where they don't use condoms."

This is true for nearly all current gay videos. Typically, the penis is lit so that it looks unsheathed except for the telltale ring of rubber near the base, just enough to let you know it's there. In straight porn, however, the condom issue remains, as Ron Sullivan puts it, "pro-choice."

"In straight videos," Sam says, "they're still doing anal sex with no rubbers. They don't care."

Makeup

"My life in porn? What would you like to know?

"I've been doing it for 10 years," Mr. Ed says. "I started in straight porno, then progressed into bisexual, gay, transvestite, transsexual. I enjoy what I do. I started by doing special-effects makeup, but this is less stressful, and in the long run more fun. I make more friends doing this than when I was doing legit makeup.

"A lot of dates? God, no. Friends, but not dates.

"Usually, I make up the guy's faces, cover any imperfections. Circles or bags under the eyes. As gay men, they're very finicky about fixing their own hair. I cover scars and pimples. There's always a pimple on somebody's butt to cover up.

"Very little body makeup. Once in a while I'll have to do a full body makeup for a guy who needs a tan line and doesn't have one. That takes time. I make sure they're all shaved in the proper body areas, and douched for the scene.

"How much is shaved varies from director and company, but almost everybody wants the butthole shaved. Aesthetically, it's just more pleasing to see a smooth butt, especially when you get in there for rimming or fucking, and there's all that lube and everything. It starts building up in the hairs and looks really gross and ugly.

"Almost all models have their balls shaved. Usually, they do it themselves.

"Faking come shots, that's few and far between. You use Jergen's hand lotion and whipped cream. In some of the VE stuff they have a guy who makes prosthetic dicks and stuff that shoots through the prosthesis. He uses creme rinse.

"The fake dicks have gotten to be quite huge: 12, 15 inches. The same guy makes prosthetic tits and pussies. I don't do that. I have made fangs for vampire videos."

Bedroom 11 a.m.

"Turn your face towards me a little bit. Worship his cock. Turn down off the bed a little bit, and turn over. . . . "

"That's fine for the moment. Thank you guys. Are we ready for the oral?"

"You were down more. Come out just a hair, Mohammed. Medium. Right there. Put your head down like it was, and we are gonna roll. Action. And roll."

"Oooh, yeah. Oooh. Oh baby."

"More cheek to the camera. Let me see nuts."

"Go for a close-up of sucking."

"Good."

"Ryan, stay right there, I want to milk the cocksucking and keep jerking your dick, because we're going to—"

"I can get more wild."

"You bet you can."

"Get back as you were, men, ready to suck. Let's see that foreskin over his dick as well. And keep your head right there, Ryan, not much more out of frame."

"Freeze. We're gonna do it wide and then you'll be able to put them on the bed. Excellent so far. Keep sucking, when I say move, just move in. You can't force him. We have to obey our guidelines. There you go. Come down on it. Put your thumb on the foreskin. Pull the foreskin up. Lower it down for the camera. React. Now let's see the tip of his cock. Work on the nuts. Closeup of Mitch's face. Go in a bit tighter sir . . . come out just a hair. Lock it there."

Guidelines

Ever since the Meese Commission failed to deliver a plausible, national definition of obscenity or pornography, the Justice Department has refused to issue a standard set of guidelines for the adult-entertainment industry, leaving most of the pertinent legal questions up to individual states, which means that exactly what you can and can't do in porn, and where you can and can't sell it, is extremely fuzzy. As a result, every company has generated its own set of Byzantine rules, based on its legal counsel's reading of local prosecutions.

"Our lawyers are very strict about certain things that are considered obscene in various states," says a Vivid executive. "You can't have bondage and hardcore sex in the same movie. Bondage movies have to be softcore. No visible penetration. That's obscene. No insertion of inanimate objects—technically, you're not allowed to insert any inanimate objects, but they're not as strict when it comes to sex toys. Probably because they can be considered educational, or therapeutic."

"You'll notice, when they prosecute these cases they don't pick L.A. or New York or San Francisco," says Jim Steel. "They'll pick Memphis.

"The guidelines vary, but I assure you, if I have to defend what I'm doing to 12 people in Memphis, it will certainly stop me from shooting certain things.

"Interracial porn will be prosecuted in the Southern states. I know one company that made the mistake of sending a tape where this white boy was getting absolutely pounded by this black guy, who then pulled out, called him a whore, and shot in his face. And they shipped it to a city that's regarded as the birthplace of the Ku Klux Klan. To me, this is sheer stupidity."

The old-style loop, which simply shows sexual acts without a dramatic context, is currently considered equivalent to prostitution. Most companies agree that porn videos must have "stories," with dialogue, to be defensible as having "redeeming social value." On the other hand, fictional scenarios permitted in legitimate and softcore films (e.g., kidnapping, rape, assault, murder) can't be simulated in hardcore: because the sexual acts are "real," states may consider the fictions built around them as "real," or as incitements to criminal behavior, and therefore legally obscene. Several companies have their material vetted by psychiatrists at UCLA, who decide whether the videos could cause psychological damage to the consumer.

Among the many narrative genres that saturate popular entertainment, advertising, and journalism, porn is uniquely restricted to a set of established narrative conventions. Its legal status places it between fiction and nonfiction, potentially illegal if it's strictly documentary, and also if it's too imaginative.

Stars

Randy White is tall and solid-looking and has a long, introspective face and quick eyes and a frisky dog named Shoko who often pulls him along on his Rollerblades through West Hollywood. Randy White lives in a modest house he's remodeling in his spare time. We talk in a white living room that gets good light, interrupted several times by calls from strangers answering ads. One wants Randy to describe the kind of massage he gives. Another gives him a hard time about his out-call rates, which are decidedly upmarket. Randy White seems slightly oppressed by these strangers.

"Sometimes you meet obnoxious people," he says. "People who want something from you but don't see why they should pay for it, or don't understand how it can be a job. People think, 'That's not a job, sex is something everybody does.' It can be fun or it can be work. It depends on a lot of different things."

"You're a porn star, that's what you mainly do?"

"Yeah, I guess. We can use the term loosely. I started doing videos a couple years ago. First, I was stripping in Waikiki. I was a pretty good stripper, on the circuit, but it's getting harder for nightclubs to bring performers in. Everybody's starting to get more and more in shape, so when you go to a club in Wisconsin or Iowa, on a given night there will be some hot local boys who want to dance semi-naked anyway, so why should they pay a lot of money to bring in a porno model?"

"Is it hard to maintain the kind of attractiveness you have to project?"

"I'm getting into the production part now. I'm really over that whole thing. I used to teach English in Tokyo. When I lived there I was really skinny. I was not in great shape, and that's when I set out to build myself up. I always had this fantasy about stripping. I've always had a bit of exhibitionism in me. So I started lifting weights. When I got up to 185, I was still a little thin, but tight and defined. That's when I started to get the attention.

"I was never the most beautiful guy or had the total body, but I was a pretty good stripper. I put a lot into my act. You can't keep it forever. Now that I'm pushing 30—at some point in your life, you've peaked out, you have to start going downhill. You can spend a lot of money on cosmetic surgery or hair, all those things, but . . ."

"What are the nice things about being a porn star?"

"Let's see. It's really great fun for me if somebody recognizes me. The good thing about this business is, it helps a person get over his hang-ups. You get really liberated—it's easy to say hello to people. It's made me really easy going."

"Did you learn a lot about the production side of the business from being in front of the camera?"

"When you're in front of the camera, you're just thinking about, Am I getting this right? Do I look stupid? I used to worry about being six three. Shorter guys who are really buffed up, on film they look really great, and nobody knows they're five six. Being six three, on video, you don't look tall, you just look skinny." The phone rings again. Randy patiently explains to the caller which hours he will be available.

"I guess most porn stars also do out-call?"

"That's no big secret. When I get an appointment to see somebody who's seen my videos and wants to see me, that's pretty cool. They're usually nice, and kind of glad to meet Randy White. People in the business can't help getting a bit of an ego. They're getting the attention, they're getting some money. But it doesn't affect me all that much. You have to remember there's always somebody better looking than you, there's always somebody who will do a video or see a private client for a little less money. There's no reason to get a big ego about it."

The Boy Next Door

"Minority people? Some people say we don't use as many as

they'd like," Jim Steel says. "I have no problem with anything. A lot of people who come in just aren't attractive. I'm certainly not going to use someone just to satisfy somebody's scream that they want to see more Latins. A large majority of the buying market is apparently interested in the 'blond boy next door' ideal.

"I subscribe to probably 15 magazines, and I look at the ads, the new kinds of looks and everything, and try to introduce them in the films. When the goatee thing started, Falcon was doing it, and Vivid was doing it, and everyone else was making the guys shave. I figure, shoot it so if you were to go to a bar, and see something current or trendy, that's reflected in the film. It's very subjective. There are people I hire just because they have a sparkle in their eyes and I know it'll show up on film.

"I don't shoot what I want to see, but what I know sells," says Sam. "You want the guy with the nicely chiseled body, or the young chicken type. Those are the two sellers."

H. Randall

"You get some companies that don't really respect the homeowners or the neighbors. I keep a list of the ones that are good to work with. They have to have permits. IDs and AIDS tests on the talent. You have to be kind of low-key, make sure there's no kids around, keep the sex scenes quiet.

"The straight companies are a little harder to deal with because it takes them longer. They usually want 15 to 20 hours. I try to cut them off after 12. Especially with the girl-girl scenes, they get a little too loud. You've got directors who will sit in the dining room with a monitor and scream back and forth across the house. After an hour of that, everybody's got a headache.

"It's a four-bedroom house, it's a view home. It's got a Victorian living room with fireplace, a country French kitchen, a southwestern living room, formal dining room with fireplace, three bathrooms, one we use for makeup. It's got a swimming pool, and we're putting in a jacuzzi, outside waterfalls and showers, so it looks like different locations on the outside.

"I treat it as a business, to pick up a lot of the bills and stuff. I know quite a few people aren't renting anymore. You have to figure, if they pay $500 for 12 hours, is it really worth it, by the time you figure your utility bills and everything else?

"Some of the companies furnish their own towels; a lot of them don't, so you're washing towels, you're changing sheets.

"I rent to one guy who does fetish videos. They're hysterical to watch, because they have these fake enemas. When they told me they were gonna do these, I said, 'Oh, well, do them in the bathroom,' and they said, 'No, we're doing them in your living room.' And I had white carpet then. I said, 'No, I don't think so.' And they said it was all done in the camera. They show the enema bottle full, they show the water going down to the rectum, then they cut, pull the tube out, and drain it. They show it going down the tube, but it's going into a bucket on the floor. The girls love doing it, because they get good money, they don't have any sex at all, and then they freak out when they have to sign the release and it turns out they're going to be on the box cover. They don't want to be on a box cover with a tube in their butt."

The Incident, H. Randall

"One of the big talent agents sends his people every three months to their doctor to get AIDS tests. A new girl went in and tested with three other girls. The doctor later called the office and said one of the girls was HIV-positive, but he wouldn't give the name. So this agent called everyone in, all the guys and girls and told them. The girl broke down and said it was her.

"So they narrowed down how many people she'd worked with, because she'd just started. And they isolated those people. Nobody would work with them until they went through, I don't know what the test was, but the blood was sent to New York.

"I had the house booked solid for eight days when that happened, and everybody canceled, because half the talent wouldn't work. Now the girls and guys are being tested every month and a half. The talent pays for their own AIDS tests, which I don't think is right.

"I know for a fact there are guys in the business with HIV. I do a lot of copying of the IDs and the AIDS tests, and I've noticed how many different labs are used. Some of these labs I've never heard of. It doesn't mean they're not out there, but . . ."

The Incident, Sam

"What happened in April is, this girl walked into a producer's office, and she was so attractive he sent her right out on a call. I don't know how it was discovered that she was HIV-positive, she must've told someone. Everyone she worked with, no one's using. She had four scenes that day; maybe they made an exception, letting her work, but told her she still needed to bring in her test results. Maybe she did, not realizing, or maybe she sent someone to the doctor's office to get them. Anyway, there was a little panic going on."

The Incident, Ron Sullivan

"Late in April, a woman who was living with a musician was sent in to take her HIV test, which every performer has to have every three months. She worked her first job the day her results came back. By the time she was contacted, she'd worked with one guy who, later that day, worked with another girl, who the next morning worked with another guy, who worked with another girl . . . Within 24 hours, 16 people were, I don't want to say infected, but conceivably exposed.

"Well, the shit hit the fan. We ended up quarantining 20 people. They could not work X number of weeks until they'd been tested again, twice. We're all terrified of HIV. Then the actors and actresses created their own factions and got organized, ad hoc, brilliantly. People who couldn't remember directions to get to a set all had skills to mobilize; it was something they believed in.

"Some of the groups are prochoice. We'd been using condoms in our industry more than any other group, but we didn't use them exclusively. We used them for anal sex. The gay product, they've been using them since 1984. We've used them since 1985, but not for oral or vaginal penetration. In the hetero product, there are three orifices to contend with. . . . Some movies are now made all-condom with any kind of penetration, and others . . . it's all divided up. We've increased the rate of testing from three months to six weeks.

"None of which guarantees us anything."

Busty Belle

"I don't care if you had an AIDS test two weeks ago, who were you with last night? I can say—and this is very, very true—I've been doing movies since 1988, and nobody has ever asked me to take an AIDS test. Ever. Okay? Therefore, if they haven't asked me, I don't think they've asked a lot of other people. I just had someone call me today to do a straight movie. They didn't ask me a word about it. They just said, 'When can you work?' "

Bedroom, Noon

"I want to see your balls. Go ahead and do that transition, where you raise his legs . . ."

"Do we have any more reflectors?"

"Slowly, slowly."

"No, but I'll go in an area where the sun's just right. I'm easy, nothing's storyboarded. I can play it by ear. Like the real filmmakers."

"Back up a hair with your dick."

"Come down a bit lower with your pelvis so I can see your dick going in his butt."

"Right there is good framing. I need it faster. Keep those eyes open, Ryan. I want to see you looking right at him, saying how it feels so good. I want you to say, 'I want you to stick it in me.' "

"Stick it in me. Oh, yeah."

"Great."

What's My Motivation?

"We have to accept the fact that we wouldn't be in this business if we weren't somehow socially dysfunctional, codependent, fucked up," says Ron Sullivan, echoing the prevalent psychiatric opinion of industry participants.

"Some research says that over 90 per cent of the women performers in the business were sexually abused as children. Can this behavior be turned into a constructive behavior that's positive, or at least nondamaging? Are you going to keep validating whoever abused you? Validate that person to be sure your self-esteem remains at a very low level?"

Jim Steel disagrees: "Incest survivors, that sort of thing, I think it's another version of the Mafia. In eight years, I have not encountered anything that really links this business to organized crime. It's ridiculous to make any generalizations about these people when you look at how much product is out there. Certainly, a lot of people I meet are fucked up. People have dependency problems with drugs and alcohol—for gay people, that's part of a process where we live in ghettos and mainly meet in bars."

"A lot of people think because you're having sex for money there's some sort of major dysfunction going on with you," says Bill Marlowe. "I don't think that's the case for a lot of people anymore. It used to be, but there's more respect now between actors and producers and directors. It's all business now; it's not playtime the way it was in the early '80s and the '70s. Then it was 'anything goes.' The AIDS situation has sobered things up. One day, when this is all over, hopefully, this kind of responsibility will carry on. I think it's taught us a lot about family and friends and the respect we should give to life and love and sex. That it shouldn't be taken for granted. You can turn it into a good thing, and make money out of it, and . . . that's great."

Bedroom, 1 p.m.

"How are we doing the shot? Am I just putting it in?"

"I'd go in right now, and then pull out, and then keep going."

"Mohammed, you're gonna have to move more to the left."

"Deep strokes. No, not yet. We're gonna wait till you get a couple strokes."

"It doesn't look good. We've got to give it more light."

"We need to see when you're going in. Can you keep your chest back? Not uncomfortable but just as far back as you can."

"Like that?"

"You're fine. Keep those legs pinned back, buddy. Watch your left arm."

"Aaah, oh, oh . . ."

"Left arm up, Mitch . . . that, or hold his legs. We're gonna roll on some of that. Perfect: Keep going."

(Airplane noise.)

"Eeegh . . ."

"We'll get it. We'll get it."

"This goddamn dialogue. And it was perfect, too . . ."

"I'd rather have you in missionary. I want to make it easy on you. One hot position is all I need. I can see your face, I can see the sex."

"Mohammed? I want to see penetration now. You're on the wrong side."

"Just tell Still Boy to get the fuck out of the way."

"This is all good stuff."

1993

13. Otto Hypnosis

Thirty-one films directed by Otto Preminger are running at Film Forum over the next seven weeks, a prodigious chunk of American cultural history. Preminger's best movies are unforgettable, and so are his worst ones. It is often difficult to tell which are which. He made appealing garbage as well as prescient, thoughtful drama, and a number of hybrid things like *Bunny Lake Is Missing*, which has some ineluctable family resemblances to *Dementia 13*, *Night Must Fall*, and Visconti's Claudia Cardinale incest pic, *Sandra*: Carol Lynley and Keir Dullea are siblings who may or may not have an imaginary daughter; Noel Coward plays a vulpine landlord; there's a creepy primary school with a nutty old bag in an attic flat and lots of footage of the Zombies, in Liverpool haircuts, crooning on the TV.

Bunny Lake is from 1965, and it feels like it. Many of Preminger's pictures shrewdly exploited the cultural moments they appeared in. In some cases, Preminger broke whatever Hays Office or Legion of Decency rules prevailed at the time to deal with material the audience was primed for: drug addiction in *The Man With the Golden Arm* (which shows Frank Sinatra, as someone once quipped, as a man with an insatiable craving for candy bars), rape in *Anatomy of a Murder* (the long courtroom disquisition on the word "panties" and the casting of Joseph Welch as the judge were like red flags waved at the right wing), and homosexuality in *Advise and Consent*.

Advise and Consent provided this author with an especially plangent childhood moment. I saw it with my father. There was a scene lasting all of a minute and a half, maybe less, in a gay bar. A Sinatra tune was playing on the jukebox. Otto, God bless him, had managed to contrive the most sinister imaginable tableau of butches and femmes at play, without really showing anything. Yet I, a mere infant, knew immediately what was going on. And my father knew that I knew what was going on. After the film we had a sincere chat. We agreed that Communism was a terrible thing.

Preminger is not a director one thinks of as having an intense personal vision, obsessive themes, or a signature style. He favored a cool, distancing eye, scenes rendered in wide shot. This is, of course, a style, but an empirical one that resists complete identification with the characters. Preminger is an intellectual artist rather than an emotional one. Even in Cinemascope, Preminger's p.o.v. is complex and ambiguous instead of sweeping and didactic. The effect of an epic like *Exodus* is to leave the audience with fewer certainties than it came in with, whereas Stanley Kramer's *Judgement at Nuremberg* makes an airtight case through grueling emotional manipulation.

Looking at *Advise and Consent* again after 30 years, I notice how truly ambiguous it is: the ambitious demagogue who should be a Joseph McCarthy prototype is blackmailing the once queer senator to get a peacemonger confirmed as secretary of state; the otiose curmudgeon played by Charles Laughton turns out to be a man of principle and compassion; the ineffectual vice-president readily and willfully assumes the throne after the much-beloved president, who turns out to be a nasty old prick, dies. Nothing is what it seems; Preminger gives the contradiction of an institution a complete airing, without stacking the deck in favor of his own political beliefs. There is perhaps some nod given to the notion that people should behave "decently", but *Advise and Consent* defines decent behavior in a very elastic fashion. Preminger was, after all, a man of the world, and even in his sentimental moments bore no resemblance to Frank Capra. The gay bar scene, today, looks entirely benign, unless you imagine yourself as an over-wrought closet case walking into it.

Anatomy of a Murder maintains the same sort of distance from its subject: Lee Remick may be a slut or just a nice woman who likes to dress sexy and hit the local juke joint; she may have been raped or she may have had consensual relations with her supposed rapist; Ben Gazzara might well have beaten her up and then killed the guy in a jealous rage instead of acting from an "uncontrollable impulse"; Jimmy Stewart's court-room antics could easily be read as narcissistic dementia rather than impassioned lawyering on behalf of an innocent client, etc., etc. In the end we know all the contradictory facets of the characters but we really don't know the truth of what happened. Maybe the panties were planted in the laundry chute by Eve Arden. We just don't know.

The exemplary Preminger films noirs like *Laura*, *Angel Face*, and *Where the Sidewalk Ends* are, of their genre, perfectly carved scarabs of postwar neuroticism and structured, like much noir, according to the bulletproof "Yes, but" school of script writing. Yes, we love each other more than anything, but I have just killed your husband and dumped his body in the East River. Yes, I could get away with it, but I have to confess because your father has been accused of the murder. Though Preminger never favored the close-up, these films are about faces – Gene Tierney on the cusp of nervous-lipped apotheosis, less porcelain and rangier in the eyes than in *Shanghai Gesture,* Jean Simmons as an ectoplasmic slate of sulky shadows. Dana Andrews with weltschmerz and peasant cunning engraved on a mug you could add 10 pounds to to make Eddie Constantine. Preminger knew about faces: decades later, in *Tell Me That You Love Me, Junie Moon*, he had Liza Minnelli made up to look like she had been doused with battery acid. It's the only movie where you literally can't take your eyes off her.

We usually search the work of an obsessive artist for

consistencies that fill out a picture of the artist's mind. In the work of someone like Preminger or Sirk, we're more likely to glean a sense of the world the artist was passing through, however ample the artist's idiosyncracies. *The Man With the Golden Arm* will always be remembered as the first Hollywood movie about heroin addiction, but it's not always remembered as an Otto Preminger film.

Sirk, of course, had a more slyly subversive method than Preminger. Sirk took potboiler scripts and made intelligently downbeat films from them. Preminger frequently took first-rate scripts of whatever genre and delivered something a bit overblown or slightly miscast or downright mediocre. The event quality of a Preminger movie often had little do with the actual film. He made not one but two all-black musicals, *Carmen Jones* and *Porgy and Bess*, and they're both horrible. *Forever Amber* was Kathleen Winsor's three-boner bestseller of the '30s, transformed by Preminger into a no-boner Linda Darnell flop in the '40s. *Saint Joan*, for which a worldwide star search turned up a then awkward ingenue named Jean Seberg, is notable mainly for an embarrassingly elfin performance by Richard Widmark as the dauphin of France. *River of No Return*, Preminger's sole Western, is a dreary blizzard of process shots with a drenched Marilyn Monroe and scowling Robert Mitchum bobbing around haplessly in the foreground.

While Preminger enjoyed the reputation of being an extremely brutal and unpleasant director, one had to allow that his trashiest pictures are fun to watch and oddly good-natured, too. He played the autocratic buffoon in public and suffered, I suppose, from having to be more eccentric and disagreeable than Stroheim in order for people to tell them apart. If he was no day at the beach in person, he did prove himself a loyal friend to Gene Tierney, hiring her on *Advise and Consent* after her long bout of madness, when no one in Hollywood would give her the time of day, and a principled maverick when he broke the blacklist and gave Dalton Trumbo his rightful script credit on *Exodus*. After staging the disaster of Seberg's debut in *Saint Joan*, Preminger hired her again for *Bonjour Tristesse*, proving to the world that she really was the remarkable actress he'd taken her for in the first place. Preminger's flaunting of the Legion of Decency and the MPAA Production Code expanded creative freedom for everybody in Hollywood. Whether he was being brave or just obdurate or egomaniacal, or all three, really doesn't signify. After all, he's dead. And even if very few Hollywood movies today actually deal with abortion, homosexuality, addiction, the structures of our institutions, or social issues of any sort, even Steven Spielberg fearlessly uses the word "panties" whenever he pleases.

1993

14. Jonathan Ned Katz's Gay Science

The Invention of Heterosexuality
by Jonathan Ned Katz

This handy little book turns the tables on a century of theorizing about "the nature of homosexuality." It complements the (to some) late-breaking news that the homosexual is not an authentic category of persons but an ideological artifact, invented to define "deviance" at the moment when sexuality became an object of scientific scrutiny in the late 19th century. As it happens, heterosexuality was invented at the same time—Webster's gives both the same year of origin, 1892—to identify "the normal."

Like other social constructs of the normal, heterosexuality serves the needs of the dominant group. It's an ideology masquerading as a sexual practice, occupying a position thought to be above inquiry; all other sexualities must define themselves in relation to it, but it never has to define itself. The same can be said about whiteness, or maleness: those who dominate in power relations place themselves beyond the narrow, largely punitive definitions assigned to statistical minorities.

As Katz demonstrates, a great deal of tinkering occurred before different-sex-desiring people and "heterosexuals" became the same thing. Once they did, though, a massive campaign was launched to make "heterosexuality" appear an immutable fact in human history. Like the Scottish tartan, it was rapidly detached from the concrete historical circumstances of its invention, its origins pushed back to the prehistoric mists. But heterosexuality was unknown among the ancient Greeks, who knew about procreation, sex between men and women, sex between men and men, and sex between women and women, without perceiving any two of these things as "opposites." Same-sex and different-sex desires were recognized as existing in the same person, and none was thought to be, eo ipso, inferior to the others.

While procreative sex became privileged in later Western societies, usually to ensure a steady birthrate, and to install the family as an instrument of social control, nonprocreative desires and sexual acts, whether between different-sex or same-sex people, were seldom regarded as "unnatural." Quite the contrary. They were seen as urges just about everybody had, which needed to be proscribed because they wasted precious seeds and eggs. Katz quotes an early American cleric: "Every natural man and woman is born full of sin ... atheism, sodomy, blasphemy, murder, whoredom, adultery, witchcraft, [and] buggery"; Katz notes that, "As a universal temptation, not a minority impulse, a man's erotic desire for another man did not constitute him as a particular kind of person, a buggerer or sodomite."

Katz's examples include the New England colonies between 1607 and 1740, where the need to stabilize the agricultural base and multiply the labor force produced extremely harsh laws limiting erotic activity to reproductive sex within marriage. The death penalty for sodomy was established in all the colonies, even though their rulers acknowledged that "it might not involve the same 'degree of sinning against the family and posterity' as some other 'capital sins of uncleanness.' "

"The operative contrast in this society was between fruitfulness and barrenness," Katz observes, "not between different-sex and same-sex eroticism." In this system of maximized growth, even masturbation was a criminal waste of capital-intensive energy. The churches, of course, played their customary grotesque role, disseminating an economic policy as the word of God. Katz's point, however, is that early New England was not a society dominated by homo/hetero binarism, any more than early Greece was.

What seems to have propelled the essentialist division of individuals into normal and deviant, hetero and homo, was the rise of the middle class and the slackening of the reproductive imperative—in other words, the late Industrial Revolution. With the rise of the middle class, marriages based strictly on the transfer of property and the need to reproduce gave way among many Victorians to an ideal of "true love." According to Katz, "true love" enabled erotic relations to flourish among unmarried different-sex couples between, roughly, 1820 and 1850; only the fusion of penis and vagina was prohibited before wedlock. "True love" was not simply eros, but a higher and nobler type of sensuality; men and women could and did express it toward members of their own sex, arguably oblivious to its sexual implications. As for sexual acts, Katz notes that "sodomite" and "sapphist" are thinly scattered terms in documents of the period, and that "sodomy laws defined a particular, obscure act, referred to in a limited legalese, not a common criminal, medical, or psychological type of person, not a personal, self-defined 'identity' and, until the nineteenth century's end, not a particular sexual group." Soon, however, this idyll of invisibility came to an end, proof if it be needed that the middle class is Satan's spawn.

In the late nineteenth century, as the white Protestant middle class pursued its early happiness, its attitude toward work shifted in favor of pleasurable consumption. By century's end the ideal of true love conflicted more and more with middle-class sexual activity. The invention of heterosexuality publicly named, scientifically normalized, and ethically justified the middle-class practice of different-sex pleasure.

Katz gleefully charts the daft, bumpy trail of witch-doctor

theory as well as the doomed efforts of early liberationists like Karl Heinrich Ulrichs, who coined the notion of Urnings (fags) and Dionings (dikes), according to which the desire for a particular gender, "natural" to the opposite gender, could as naturally inhabit someone of the same gender. In other words, a man who loved other men was thought by Ulrichs to have a female libido, and so forth.

It seems that in the earliest formulations of the hetero/homo split, heterosexuality was not a synonym for successful erotic adjustment, but a term indicating an excess of libido, or an "unfettered capacity for degeneracy." This usage, coined by Karl Maria Kerbeny, was copied by Krafft-Ebing in the fourth edition of *Psychopathia Sexualis* in 1889, by which time the medicalization of sexuality was under way. Kerbeny's heterosexuals were unnaturally endowed with libido, so much so that in the absence of licit sexual opportunities they were "likely to assault male but especially female minors . . . ; to indulge in incest; to engage in bestiality; and even to behave depravedly with corpses if their moral self-control does not control their lust."

Heterosexuality only gradually became identified with "normal sexuality," homosexuality with "contrary sexual feeling" and "inversion." With Freud the pathologizing of same-sex desire becomes institutionalized, with penis-and-vagina intercourse, procreative or otherwise, elevated to the status of a religion. Katz is especially good when interpreting the famous case of Dora, and in demolishing the Oedipus complex. He applies simple logic and common sense to lay bare the considerable twaddle larded into Freudian theory, though he also finds in Freud's writings the seeds of a critique: "Freud's repeated reminders are necessary to call our attention to a phenomenon repeatedly repressed. That is, that exclusive homosexuals are not the only ones whose erotic objects are restricted to one sex. Heterosexuals are just as limited."

Katz doesn't limit his inquiry to the higher theoretical plane. *The Invention of Heterosexuality* traces the development of the heterosexual idea in popular culture, particularly in literature and theater, often using *The New York Times* as a barometer of prevailing attitudes. This is absolutely on target, since the media reception of watershed events like the Kinsey report tells us as much about social norms as the events themselves. Katz takes us from *Tea and Sympathy* to Kate Millett in a breezy style that misses few significant twists in sexual politics. His account of feminisms, and of hetero backlash against women's and gay liberation, is a valuable primer for anyone who imagines him or herself "post" anything.

The AIDS epidemic—along with the quantum increase of women in the work force, with their demands for equal pay and promotion—has been a pretext for heterosexualist retrenchment under the banner of family values, and although history can never really run backward, the progress gays and women have made needs to be defended on a daily basis. The right-wing anathematizing of political correctness and multiculturalism expresses the resentment of a heterosexual establishment forced to question its legitimacy; works like Katz's expose that establishment as a transient historical phenomenon and obliterate its claims to eternal truth. *The Invention of Heterosexuality* is a wonderful weapon against self-contempt, among other things, and while it explicitly "does not doubt the value of anyone's heterosexuality," it does demolish a hierarchy of sexual desires that was never much use to begin with, and which, in a grossly overpopulated world, has long outlived even its original, malignant premises.

1995

15.

The Dark Side of Gilbert and George

An extensive view of Gilbert and George's 18-year collaboration is currently available in a traveling retrospective now at the Guggenheim Museum (1071 Fifth Avenue, through June 16) and at Sonnabend Gallery (420 West Broadway, through June 1) in a show of recent works. The artists commenced their mutual career in art school, first exhibiting themselves as "living sculptures"—identically dressed in worsted suits, their exposed flesh areas and hair painted to resemble bronze or colored polystyrene. Apparently, Gilbert and George have sustained this dandyish presentation of themselves, publicly and privately, right up to the present day. According to their retrospective's catalogue essay (by Brenda Richardson), Gilbert and George ". . . move through life in the same uniforms which have become so familiar from the self-portraits that recur in the photopieces, and they project into the world an impression of theatricality which can be frightening in its consistency."

Besides appearing in museums as objets d'art, Gilbert and George initially showed large display pieces fashioned from postcards. These often contain serially repeated images arranged in symmetrical cross patterns. Other early works feature individually framed photographs linked by an overall design scheme. Though Gilbert and George refer to these collages as "sculptures," there is actually nothing in their entire output that strictly qualifies as such. But the artists' insistence on this term to describe two-dimensional objects is significant, and I'll return to it.

Gilbert and George's present exhibitions offer dozens of large photo-pieces in their current manner, the lion's share of which are, or contain, self-portraits. George is a tall, bespectacled, balding man whose physiognomy might be that of an embittered bank clerk, while Gilbert is stubbier, mildly handsome, and slightly less portentous-looking. Their recent works consist of photographically derived, square images, assembled in imposing square and rectangular grids that form large, cohesive pictures. The formal complexity of the work is formidable, even in a relatively simple piece like *Coloured Black*, in which a crude stencil drawing of an African mask is translated into a four-panel (red, blue, greens and yellow) image. Larger works evidence a staggering sophistication of technique, a blaring audacity of visual language that mixes black and white with voluptuous color, tinted photographs with photographed drawings and designs, and the rigidity of the regular grid with expressionistic internal material.

This said, I should affirm that the content of Gilbert and George's work is no less striking than its spectacular formal quality. Their early efforts in black and white with the later addition of red, then yellow, playfully treat subjects such as intoxication, loneliness, fear, race relations, and urban desuetude. However, since 1980 the artists have narrowed their focus, in increasingly splashy colors, to a limited range of material: themselves, crosses as religious symbols, adolescent working-class men, flowers, monumental sculpture, and urban architecture. Or, more descriptively, adolescent working-class men depicted as sex objects, Gilbert and George leering at adolescent working-class men from various elevations, Gilbert and George mooning up at adolescent working-class men from supine positions, Gilbert and George bowered in flowers and gazing at flower-festooned adolescent working-class men, the compositions sometimes decorated with religiously symbolic crosses, sometimes not, Gilbert and George looking at each other, Gilbert and George praying, an occasional chunk of photographed sculpture or modern building thrown in for heightened suggestiveness, and so on.

Perhaps the smell of dank tenement hallways and boiled cabbage that pervades these works would be less acute if Gilbert and George were themselves comelier as objects. Perhaps not. Their gelidly pederastic interest in the extremely junior youths in their pictures might then appear less masochistic, and at the same time less exploitative, than it obviously is. Leaving aside the strong impression that the formal elaborateness of their art making must somehow mimic whatever intricate, predatory formalities are involved in luring these teenage Adonises with rotten teeth home to the studio, the lurid obeisance to formal religion displayed throughout G & G's recent work is consistent with a long tradition of dandyism, traceable to Oscar Wilde and the more turgid, cloying passages of *De Profundis*. This, in turn, echoes the normative hypocrisy of a conservative yet sexually liberated age, in which any desire is permissible if the desired performs as an economic object rather than a human being, and the desire is gratified by exploitation rather than parity—hence providing a source of sadomasochistic guilt, and therefore available as a religious experience.

While Gilbert and George have been widely praised for their boldness of subject matter, the sensibility infusing its treatment is the most self-abnegating and destructive mode of homosexual dandyism, infatuated with religious ceremony as the spiritual equivalent of furtive seduction. Beautification is the necessary first step toward guilty orgasm. One can't simply be a person, one has to be a "living sculpture." All those icky urges must be filtered through the damp handkerchief of Art, ritualized into a pattern of deadly sameness. Image must be conflated with substance—ergo, the labeling of postcard collages as "sculptures."

The diminishing lack of vitality in Gilbert and George's work is partially concealed by a desperate burgeoning of technical novelty.

As the iconographic routine becomes deadlier, the colors become abrasively active, vivid, autonomous, like an accelerated putrescence. Quantity overwhelms fastidious articulation. Where formerly a single boy, or two, lent mystery and magic to the shorted narcissism of yet another regressive self-portrait, now 10 or even 20 bare-assed or besneakered youths fail to convey anything besides anonymous victimization. *Life Without End*, the central work at the Guggenheim, represents the giantism typical of contemporary artists whose content has become repetitive. If you can't make it different, blow it up. Here we get a stiffening dose of everything: droopy flowers; a lineup of pedo-objects in windbreakers; spooky Gilbert and porcine George glowering amid the overhanging vegetation, elsewhere praying and posing; a Nude Youth, hands clasped across his kissy-smooth fanny, agape at the portal of what is surely the Chapel of Love; an impassive, standing youth in T-shirt and jeans projecting the vague belligerence of rough trade; another one squatting on his haunches; yet another who looks like Roger Daltry as a child; a few other faces, some sparse streaming tendrils of plant life, scattered branches of winter trees, budding phallic vegetables strewn about like tumescent garni.

This theatricality is indeed frightening in its consistency, of a piece with reactionary modernism in its late, post-Warhol phase. It appeals to the period's unhealthiest obsessions, i.e., moronic religious piety and lust without content. Its frank avowal of dandyism—the stylization of the self and others into aesthetically consistent objects—has always been read, and exonerated, as ironic, just like Andy Warhol's obsequious portraits of fascist politicians and the superrich. These seemed ironic in a critical sense when they first appeared, because of the kind of artist Warhol was widely taken to be, and perhaps at one time was: a sexual and economic outsider equipped with class-instilled liberal sympathies, suddenly operative, via art stardom, as a subversive parvenu in the world of power. Warhol's was the mingy irony of mere reflectiveness, eager to become whatever it beheld, whether it was Candy Darling or the Shah of Iran.

In a rather more committed way than Warhol's, Gilbert and George's early work deploys the outsider's ironic relation to official art culture, investing obscene graffiti, urban detritus, and proletarian boys with beauty and dignity. This work was rapidly embraced as high art. The artists became rich, a circumstance that has clearly altered their relationship to their own working-class backgrounds. They retain an ironic tone, which now conveys the sarcasm of the vampire towards his victim. Irony without criticality is a sacred tusk of reactionary modernism, the ne plus ultra of the modern dandy. It's the nature of dandyism to shrink into fetishistic preciosity or to swell into authoritarian loutishness, if it goes anywhere at all. Gilbert and George, and Warhol, have done both without ever budging very far.

I didn't go to the Gilbert and George shows expecting to find any of this in their work. I'd always thought I "liked" Gilbert and George, and in a radically qualified sense I still do. The power of their art seems indisputable: it has the kind of overpowering beauty that coats its liminal messages with anesthetic as they travel into your brain. But beauty isn't enough, and it certainly isn't everything.

At a different time these works might meet us in a different way. Today, when the male body has replaced the female as the primary fetish object of the culture industry, Gilbert and George's work resonates with the empty sensualism of mass advertising, emitting "desire" in the form of sexy asses, firm pectorals, and big dicks. It reflects a century-old canon of "the beautiful" that needs to be overthrown, to be defeated by a more knowing, more subtle appreciation of what human beings are. What this art celebrates is a class system in which the victims are redeemed by artistic ministration, rescued from the obscure squalor of their lives for a few glamorous moments, their bodies pictorially captured and consumed by the class that keeps them down. One can admire Gilbert and George for the artlessness of their art. Technically superb, it shows what artists can do without any urgent insights and how much they can tell us without intending to.

1985

16. Hervé Guibert's *To the Friend Who Did Not Save My Life*

To the Friend Who Did Not Save My Life by Hervé Guibert

To the Friend Who Did Not Save My Life is a species of intellectual thriller, its premise not far removed from movies like *D.O.A.* or *The Incredible Shrinking Man*, in which the protagonist's actions are circumscribed and dictated by his own imminent death. In this case, the possibility of reprieve is bruited on the first page, with the bald manipulation characteristic of both very bad and very good writers who are sure they've got a live wire on their hands:

I had AIDS for three months. More precisely, for three months I believed I was condemned to die of that mortal illness called AIDS. . . . But after three months, something completely unexpected happened that convinced me I could and almost certainly would escape this disease, which everyone still claimed was always fatal.

Hervé Guibert sucks us into the theater of his distress, mapping his perceptions of the illness from the time of its appearance in his friend Muzil, who eventually dies through numerous glitches in his own early warning system (an attack of shingles, etc.), the megatrauma of diagnosis and its aftermath, the later stages clocked by his dropping T4 cell count. Afflicted and unafflicted friends make up a rarefied, rapidly decimated Parisian milieu where the worlds of writing, filmmaking, and medicine overlap. (This book features lots of doctors: quacks, homeopaths, GPs, AIDS specialists.)

The novel ranges polyphonically back and forth in time. Guibert incessantly compares "the time before" this and that complication with the nuance of, say, an attack of mouth fungus or a drastic dip in his blood count. He is determined to claim his experiences and view them clearly, without flinching. A fastidious, archival sense of his own life, and those of Muzil and others who've died, immunizes this novel against sentimentality, as do Guibert's splendid gifts as a writer: fluidity, unflagging intellect, and eclectic sensuality.

Read through the pseudonyms, *To the Friend* . . . chronicles the last days of Michel Foucault and satirizes a difficult friendship with Isabelle Adjani. (For French readers, perhaps, the other lightly veiled figures are equally obvious.) Guibert's lover is married, with children, and the instabilities set off in this ménage by both men's seropositivity provide a smartly underpainted domestic background, a floating familial anchor in a narrative of incessant motion. Some of Guibert's best effects occur out on the street—crossing Paris to get to a hospital, standing on line at a testing center, roaring through town in a friend's Jaguar—and on trips (Portugal, Rome, Sardinia, Japan). Rather than a sedentary meditation on death, *To the Friend* . . . conveys the sense of a mentally and physically peripatetic life, a young writer's life, in process of rapid erosion.

One of the glories of Guibert's book is its intense specificity: the narrator's plight isn't generic, its extremity doesn't lead him to abandon the habit of precise observation (if he shows us a bottle of yellow goo used to treat candida, we get the exact flavor and smell, as well as the label), he spares us none of the casual, monstrous betrayals and selfish failures of compassion that human beings perpetrate.

The incubus of the book, Guibert's friend Bill, is a pharmaceutical manufacturer working with a Salk-like researcher on a promising vaccine. Bill says he'll get Guibert into clinical trials, then traduces him at every turn, disappears for months at a time, secures the vaccine for his comparatively healthy new boyfriend, while Guibert's T4 cells drop below the level of the vaccine's efficacy. Bill even hints, albeit in a joking way, that Guibert would be better off dead, anyway.

At the same time that he records a fecklessness worthy of Caligula, Guibert recognizes Bill as exactly the sort of appalling, bigger-than-life character he needs for his writing. For this book, in fact. In a keenly evident sense, Guibert's writing is his life, and what Bill withholds on one plane of existence he lavishly provides on another: material to keep going. The fact that people are terrible, frail, solipsistic, fickle, and even capable of playing God with their best friends' lives is not exactly news to a writer; if things were otherwise, literature would be largely restricted to the pastoral lay. Guibert's schizoid willingness to locate his salvation in literature, in writing up the last bits of his own annihilation, informs this book with startling nobility, as well as startling absurdity.

Much of To the Friend . . . describes Guibert's scramble to balance the demands of his work with the escalating needs of his deteriorating body, and to get some pleasure out of life even as its end becomes ever more immediate. (Guibert is a sensualist; his pleasures are ambitious and fullbodied. He lets us know that he practices safe sex in one phrase, instead of stopping the book dead for a school lesson.) Although Guibert inspires questions on every page about what is autobiographical and what's invented, the refreshingly adult quality of mind at work also renders these questions moot. (Guibert did, in fact, succumb to AIDS-related illness earlier this year.)

Guibert's voice has an outrageously seductive assurance. He

makes us complicit with his anxious haste to finish this book, complicit with his inexorable awareness of life slipping beyond rescue. In his bleakest hour, hilariously, he persuades us to take his side in a verbal skirmish with Thomas Bernhard, no less, "this lousy Viennese traitor to everything who endlessly proclaimed his genius all through his books, which were just little tiny things, little bitty ideas, itsy bitsy gripes, eeny weeny images, eentsy weentsy inabilities over which this amateur diddled and dawdled for two hundred pages, without budging an inch from the fragment he'd decided to polish, in his incomparable way; until it gleamed like the sun or was totally eclipsed by the static on his lines . . ."—all the while maintaining the suspense of a *roman policier* over the McGuffin of his own survival.

Like David Wojnarowicz's memoir *Close to the Knives*, Guibert's *To the Friend Who Did Not Save My Life* refrains from pushing all the easy buttons, abjures kitsch emotions, and slices through to something truly hard to take. Both books demonstrate that a high level of artistry is the only lastingly effective form of propaganda. In very different ways, both authors uncover the sublime as well as the irremediable in the burgeoning certainty of death.

1992

17. Death Notices

1981

Not very tall, less thin than he looked, with the kind of stage face that's all geometry, wild surrogate hair sometimes twisted into implausible cones resembling the spires of that Gaudi cathedral in Barcelona, flashy outfits knocked together from shards of purple Mylar, sequins, torn-up opera costumes: he'd appear in Mickey's or the Mudd Club with an entourage of demented-looking freaks, install himself as a visual challenge exactly where the light was strongest. Hours later, the black lipstick and scab-colored eyeshadow creamed away, the wigs and costumes tucked in a closet, he entered the bar like a wisp, in ordinary denims and a plain khaki T-shirt, settling in the corner of one of those benches running under the windows, as if trying to merge with the burlap curtains.

His voice was a curiosity of nature, like Siamese twins. Years after he died, someone asked if I'd ever heard of him.

It began, someone said, with a hissing sound, like Enzensberger's iceberg-thumbnail scraping across the Titanic's hull: garish rumors, talk of impossibly grotesque pathology, and, as always in the face of the unknown, jokes, recounted with a modicum of nervousness, as if the efficacy of jokes in keeping things at tong's length could not be assumed in this case, but only wished for, with fervor.

1982

Supposedly, she had access to realms he couldn't reach with his own imagination. We knew her only vaguely. Delicate bones, high hair, a definite way with a cigarette, muted presence that could amplify without warning. Fey. Not shy, exactly. At times, cooler-than-thou. Her friends were in the music business.

The only thing he could do with her was make a movie about the pose. The look. The easiest available obsessions, transposed from a suburban Catholic girlhood. It turned out something like the George Romero vampire film set in Pittsburgh. You felt that everyone involved with it was choking underwater, even the musicians on the soundtrack.

The film was prophetic of the later idea that having Catholic saints rattling around in your brain could figure interestingly in your biography. Much of it revolved around fantasies of her martyrdom.

Then she died, spectacularly and by accident, the same day the film opened. He showed up at the premiere, in a hazy conflation of art and life. The event had an ugly, opportunistic taint that clung to him afterwards. Even people who understood that this was, in fact, his life, did not entirely appreciate the lack of conventional sentiment.

It was said to be some phenomenon of the nether fringe, a molecular revolt bubbling up from damp "Third World" environments, an exhaustion of the flesh by postmodern forms of mortification. The first descriptions of wounds, lesions refusing to heal, pedestrian ailments mushrooming into lethal afflictions, resembled the shocking litany of saints' impalements, dismember-ments, self-infection with leprosy.

1983

He maintained a novelty jewelry company out of a Tribeca loft while raising money for another movie, to be based on sadomasochist comic books published in Paris in the '30s. I, who disliked him, was rehearsing *Salome* with an actress he wanted to play "Claudine" in his movie. For reasons that remain mysterious, he contacted me and asked me to write the script.

We met twice. Once in the loft full of tacky punk mail-order paraphernalia, the second time in an apartment where she had lived, a block from my house. At the second meeting I realized that he was . . . haunted, what other word is there? Her dresses lined the open closets, her makeup was spread out before a giant round mirror on the vanity, compacts open awaiting her fingertips. The place was heavy with her scent, her aura; her presence was so emphatic that he seemed powerless and confused in the midst of it, as if he were clumsily obeying her residual wishes.

He had an affair, around that time, with a man in a theater group we were friendly with. It's only worth mentioning because he and they were emphatically "sensitive macho" types. Anyway, then came the bowling craze.

Everyone went every night to a bowling alley on University Place to throw bowling balls while wrecked on coke. About him, there was . . . a lot of talk. Then no talk. In the spring, a lot of talk again. Finally he just came out and told everybody, "I've got it." It was still far from clear what "it" was. Four weeks later he died of pneumonia.

1984

I did him in the toilet of an afterhours, then took him home. I'd desired him for months but this happened unexpectedly, in a blurry fever I knew practically nothing about him. He'd been the lover of a friend of mine. He had drifted onto the scene. You'd sometimes find him sitting at your table with six other people, if you went for breakfast after the bar closed. He left town, much later he came back. I wanted him again "like anything," as I told him in my irritating faux naive manner of the period, but he asked me to write him a poem instead. He dropped from sight, sparking the usual true rumors. If you had heard that someone had been carried away by a spaceship, it would not have been different. I tried writing a poem for him, but nothing I came up with was any good.

Money fever. Jokes about Haitians. Cold city. A paradise for empty people, slickness without end, and here and there, suddenly, an unexpected person disappears following a brief, wasting illness.

1985

His former lover had the looks of a WASP in the marines, teeth so perfect they seemed false. A gossip of genius, he knew stories about all the old queens of New York literature, and had had his prong spit-shined by most of them at one time or another, too. We often nagged him to write his memoirs: what a pity if all that precious dish got lost! He had money troubles right up until the end, the end being accompanied by dementia, drastic weight loss, etc., etc.

1986

She bounds home from the hospital after days of hovering at his bedside. She calls: Oh, come over, I've got to read you something, it just started writing itself in my head! She reads what sounds like a verbatim transcript of what she's overheard, her soon-to-be-prizewinning story. "Well," I tell her, "I wonder how he'll feel about it." "Oh, he won't mind," she says, "he's a big user of people himself." After eons of writer's block, she's frighteningly avid these days. It's becoming obvious that she thinks the epidemic could put her back on the map.

He'd been a sailor in the Australian Merchant Marine for 10 years, in places like Rangoon and Singapore. Then he hooked up with a film company in Africa, met a man he adored, moved to Munich with him. He became the assistant to a famous director, who occasionally tried stealing him from the lover. They both had affairs, but nothing too serious.

He later moved back to Sydney to start a distribution company. He and the lover now commuted between continents. He turned sick in a matter of months. They brought him back to Germany. A certain friend met a doctor who operated a private clinic. The doctor had a plausible sounding, quack theory, that the disease was really something else, and offered treatment on an "experimental" basis.

The experiment was torture. He was not allowed painkillers and the virus had gone into his nerves. He became incontinent and bloody from bedsores. When they visited, they could hear his screams from the clinic parking lot. Next the friend suggested to an actress we knew that the doctor, overworked to the point of collapse, needed sex to revive his diagnostic genius. The insanity of the situation eclipsed everyone's judgment. The actress found herself banging the doctor every day while listening to her friend's shrieks in the adjoining room.

1987

The lover blamed himself for everything. "All the time he was dying," he told me, "I was sexually obsessed with someone else, and fucking that person whenever I could, and now he has died too."

He said there was nothing left to do but kill himself. And we both laughed. I said: Oh, there are treatments now, things are much better than before, they can do a lot. Soon they'll be able to do more. Do you really think so? he said, and I said, Absolutely, yes. I want you to promise, if anything . . . develops, you'll come here and let us take care of you. All right, he said, fine. Then he killed himself.

1988

Waiting for miserable acts of faith to fail, we take some sort of proprietary comfort from the fact that he is still alive. There is always something further to do, and because he's suddenly well-off, always money to investigate new medicines, underground treatments, expert mental programs.

Memorials. A new way to be unhappy in a group. I visit a friend who can no longer speak. A few days later he's dead.

If you ask after people you haven't seen for a while, be prepared. Sometimes, horribly, it was like this: someone you wanted to sleep with but didn't got sick, and along with the horror came this ugly relief that you never scored. Or: relief that someone who died was only a distant acquaintance instead of a close friend. Later, none of that made any difference.

1989

After he died I started to see people in the street who looked like him. Not just from behind, but sometimes the face, the hair, the style of the jacket even, and one night on 23rd Street so close to where he lived the association was automatic, I followed the person for three blocks thinking I'd catch up or get close enough to call his name and when I did snap out of it I realized it didn't matter if someone was alive or dead because every street in the city was now full of ghosts that I couldn't distinguish from living people.

She told me over the phone that she didn't think she would die.

"As far as I can figure out," she said, "there's only one or two things—one thing, really, that could get me, and unless it does—"

I remembered sitting behind her on a motorbike on the Amalfi Drive, both of us so drunk we could've driven straight off the cliffs with the tiniest flick of inattention. And we hadn't, so why should this other thing be so impossibly final? Especially since we had pulled ourselves together, grown up, and had started living such responsible lives.

What I mean is, it would not surprise me if I saw her through a crowd on a busy street, with a dozen bracelets flashing on her arms, eyes shadowed in green, pink lipstick, her first words a brilliant exegesis on the nature of cabdrivers—why shouldn't that happen in the city of the dead? If I tell it now this story begins and ends in a glass of wine, in a sense, with every detail present in a single moment. It's the fate of all of us to persist in the mortal dreams of those whom we haunt.

1990

18. Emma Tennant's Higher Powers

When she was 26, Emma Tennant published a novel called *The Colour of Rain* under the pseudonym Catherine Aydy. The name and title were both arrived at by manipulations of a Ouija board. The book was well received. Her publishers submitted it for the Prix Formentor, a literary prize given every year in Majorca. "There," Tennant later wrote, "the novel was held aloft by the Chairman of the Judges, the distinguished author Alberto Moravia, who denounced it as an example of the decadence of the contemporary British novel. Some reports have it that the book was then hurled into a wastepaper basket . . . ."

This daunting reception by a world literary figure caused Tennant to flounder for 10 years, making numerous attempts at the kind of naturalistic fiction then favored in Britain. What eventually issued from her typewriter, though, was a startling procession of novels unlike anything else being written in England: wildly imaginative, risk-taking books inspired by dreams, fairy tales, fables, science fiction, and detective stories, informed by a wicked Swiftian vision of the U.K. in decline.

Tennant found the way back to novel-writing through contact

with J. G. Ballard, Michael Moorcock, and John Sladek, three writers who used the conventions of science fiction to chart the psychological landscape of a technological society. (Booker Prize British fiction was still marveling over the invention of the telephone.) Tennant says Moorcock taught her to plan her books precisely, "to see the writing of a novel as a fast, essential, bill-paying activity." An antidote to literary precocity, this new approach suggested that "like Silenus's box, as described by Rabelais, a real work of art should—or could—be gaudy and vulgar on the outside (a box with a painted harlot on the lid, for example), but inside, once opened, would reveal the gem of truth, the philosopher's stone."

Tennant's fiction belongs to what Calvino, writing of Gore Vidal's *Duluth*, termed "the hyper-novel or the novel elevated to the square or to the cube." This kind of book ranges across several species of literature, lays waste to seamless narrative, and piles on improbabilities with surreal abandon. In *The Crack* (1973), for example, a gigantic fissure rips the city of London in half, draining the Thames, inundating entire districts in mud, creating a cosmic disaster area. In *Two Women of London* (1989), a mentally disturbed crone leads a second life as a glamorous career woman by taking large doses of an antidepressant drug. As in Ballard's apocalyptic scenarios, Tennant's characters inhabit the space between verisimilitude and farce vehicles for ideas colliding on a narrative expressway loop. In *Hotel De Dream* (1976), characters from a novelist's manuscript materialize in real space from time to time, intent on murdering their creator to avoid the dreary denouement she's planning for them.

The realist novel, anchored in the 19th century, proclaims its seriousness by depicting heavy emotions, credible situations, characters that invite empathy and identification. Practitioners of the realist novel tend to view it as the only permissible kind, its hegemony threatened by experimental fiction. One thinks of Katherine Mansfield's reaction to *Ulysses* ("This is obviously the wave of the future. Thank God I'm dying of tuberculosis"), Mary McCarthy's preachy essay "The Fact in Fiction," and Tom Wolfe's recent advocacy of a return to the literary practices of 1820. Broadly speaking, the realist novel is a novel of rules, proscriptions, morality with a big M.

The hypernovel, which includes books like *Naked Lunch*, *Myra Breckinridge*, *Crash*, and *Vineland*, has its true roots in the picaresque literature of the 18th century, which chronicles ghastly events with sardonic detachment and tends to dispense with "sincerity." Its material is often the flotsam and jetsam of popular culture, aporias of mass media, the junk of disposable civilization. Pastiche and parody are at home in the hypernovel. Tennant's *The Adventures of Robina* (1986) recounts the life of a hapless debutante "at the court of Queen Elizabeth II," pursued for a fortune she doesn't have, in the style of Defoe's *Roxana* and Smollett's *Peregrine Pickle*:

> *In the Dark, and with his Flies now undone and a small Prck sticking out, the Prince now came at Full Speed (fearing perhaps that his Staff would Outstrip him) and then Fell, Cursing and Groaning, and then I'm sorry to say Screaming in Fear which wasn't Manly (for a male Member of the Royal Household must set an example to his Subjects and in the Case of War must be ready to lead them into Battle without Timorousness), none of which the Prince showed on his Coming Across the* Glass Jellies *I had placed in his Path, all unseen by the* Contessa *and glistening there with the Moon Coming in through the Roof of the Conservatory.*

Conflating hypernovels and "postmodernism" probably ought to be resisted, if only because the latter term presumes an *a priori* concern with theory. Willfully postmodern fiction of a certain type seems locked in an eternal argument, simultaneously abject and condescending, with other literature, and with language—and somewhat etiolated in its deconstructive epiphanies. The hypernovel is above all *written*, taking obvious pleasure in language, form, the dance of events, and is usually as much concerned with the world as with literature.

The Bad Sister (1978) and *Two Women of London* reinvent existing books, Hogg's *Confessions of a Justified Sinner* and Stevenson's *The Strange Case of Dr. Jekyll and Mr. Hyde*. *The Bad Sister's* main narrative is bracketed at either end, like Hogg's, by an editor's commentary; *Two Women of London* parallels Stevenson's overlapping narrators with a succession of clinical notes, descriptions of videotapes, answering machine messages, and an audio cassette. Women characters have been substituted for men, the stories updated.

Despite the elaborate play of resemblances, Tennant's books avoid becoming glosses or deconstructions of their Scottish sources; she isn't interested in co-opting the "patriarchal voices" of Hogg and Stevenson, but instead does something wittier, wheeling familiar literary structures into a feminist context. Gender-switching the (veiled) male homosexual cast of *Dr. Jekyll and Mr. Hyde*, she produces a sly melodrama of women's lives under Thatcherism, showing how class and advantage color political convictions and personal behavior. *The Bad Sister* replaces the Calvinism satirized by Hogg with a fanatical brand of '70s feminism that endorses the killing of men. This account of a lost soul armed with a bad idea is brilliantly compassionate, nasty, and hilarious by turns, its ambiguities precisely echoing the occult strains of Hogg's diabolically funny novel.

These two books explore the theme of the Double, and are themselves doubled or mirrored. Several of Tennant's novels spin off from one or more Ur-texts: *Queen of Stones* (1982) from William Golding's *Lord of the Flies*, *Woman Beware Woman* (1983) from Merimée's *Colomba*, *Wild Nights* (1979) from Bruno Schulz's *The Street of Crocodiles*. The distance from text to source varies—*Wild Nights* has the mood of Schulz, the child's magical perception of the everyday world, and little other direct relationship—but in each a form of mythmaking has been redreamt, as in J. M. Coetzee's *Foe*.

Another hypernovel strategy is the use of genre as a container for serious writing—"a box with a painted harlot on the lid." (If the kind of novel John Updike writes were recognized as merely a genre, American fiction would be in much better health.) Burroughs uses detective novels and Westerns as the mulch for those wild carnivorous flowers, *Cities of the Red Night* and *The Western Lands*; Vidal's *Duluth* is a satire of the TV series "Dallas," among other things, and includes a running pastiche of a Harlequin Romance novel set in "Hyatt Regency England."

Tennant has written straight social satire—*The House of Hospitalities* (1987), *A Wedding of Cousins* (1988)—but much of her best work streaks across various genres like a chameleon bolting through a densely variegated jungle. *The Last of the Country House Murders* (1974) is part SF, part detective mystery, set in a British dystopia where massive overpopulation has eliminated the privacy and isolation that typify the "country house murder" genre. The cozy Agatha Christie sort of mystery, saturated in homely stereotypes of class and an England that has long disappeared, is torn apart into free-floating elements the narrative dangles in front of us, ridiculous anachronisms waiting to be pasted down to effect some sort of narrative closure, which the whole thing finally achieves in the most grotesque fashion possible.

The useless ex-rich, shut up in state-run retirement mansions, relive their florid memories of more gracious times, while a new class of postrevolutionary bureaucrats plan diverting spectacles for a restive (and physically stunted) proletariat. Jules Tanner, the last remaining private owner of a manor house, will be murdered by an assassin of his choice, as part of the conversion of Woodiscombe Manor into a tourist attraction. A government detective is dispatched to the scene to plant clues, screen assassins, and orchestrate the murder for optimum aesthetic effect.

Any reader of Hobsbawm will recognize the gem in this particular box as the invention of tradition, a fact of life in the rudderless and joyless democracies of the West. Writing at a time when an especially corrupt Socialist government was devastating one sort of England, Tennant was canny enough to show that actual power remained in the same old hands. The ritual murder of the rich, witnessed by throngs of high-paying foreign tourists and assorted peasants, becomes a sleight-of-hand trick in which the actual corpse is provided by the intelligentsia.

Bits of fractured history are recited to the omnipresent tourists—Woodiscombe is claimed to have hosted the Bloomsbury Group, Sir Francis Drake, and Spenser, among others, its chapel said to be the very spot where "the Archbishop of Canterbury was assassinated by Samuel Beckett—" Half the characters are Jules Tanner's opium hallucinations, weirdly palpable to other people. As in a Grandville engraving, "differences in rank are made visible by differences in size." However often the narrative shifts on its axis, the prevailing dream logic carries the reader along. Tennant has a serene genius for making the reader want to believe anything, a deft hand at emptying the text and immediately refilling it with fresh absurdities—one trusts the voice, steadily pitched, while the story bounces all over the place.

Emma Tennant spent her childhood in Lowland Scotland, specifically in a fake manor house called Glen built by Sir Charles Tennant, "with pepperpot roofs, gargoyles, and unnecessary Victorian battlements"; her father came into the old monstrosity after passing his childhood in Wilsford on the river Avon, site of her uncle Stephen's decades-long retirement from the world. These gigantic houses haunt Tennant's fiction, in which the figure of the Double resonates with the duality of being foreign in your own country, Scottish and English; and with Scottish devilry, the legends of the Fethan Woods, where "it was only too probable that the idle walker would be transformed into a three-legged stool, or a jay, or maybe even a hare."

Tennant's fiction is a meditation on the strange destiny of the disinherited and the ill-disposed-of, in a country where manor houses and vast fortunes defined for centuries the manner of life, declined, but kept a firm ghostly hand clasped over people's dreams. Issues of class and gender attach to the bones of Tennant's plots like metal filings to a magnet; her characters double themselves in dreams of lives they should have had, miniature Englands dreaming of former glories, restaging the triumphs of Empire in their heads in the midst of disintegration.

The great house swims into view as a simulacrum with glass shrubbery and mechanical birds in *The Last of the Country House Murders*, a tropical folly in *Black Marina*, and a magical theater of decay in *Wild Nights*. This locus of wealth is forever embattled—by a coven of female guerrillas in *The Bad Sister*, by the hostile Irish townsfolk in *Woman Beware Woman*, by revolutionaries as well as the U.S. Marines in *Black Marina*. Often the melodrama of the Big House, the landed family, is a diverting puppet theater in the midst of chaos, since other forces have moved in and conquered the territory. In Tennant's fiction, the horrible status quo is always poised on the verge of fracture into something even worse. The apocalyptic upheaval of *The Crack* concludes with a balloonist's vision of the new country just beyond the disaster area:

> *What lay beneath him was—a termitary! Workers swarmed endlessly, tirelessly over the network of towers and passageways and cells-within-cells of the monstrous immobile organism.*
>
> *Soldiers with tiny red guns guarded the inner and outer ramparts of the structure.*
>
> *The digestive organs of the community lay directly under him now. Canteens five miles long and ten miles wide gave off a shrill clatter of spoons on plates. Cities of latrines spread out beyond, the walls gaily painted to resemble English summer gardens.*

One of Tennant's best effects is an overview of England as a flimsy, crumbling accumulation of Masterpiece Theater clichés piled over the squalid contradictions of capitalism. *The Adventures of Robina* is stuffed full of grasping, inane, impotent aristocrats desperate to replenish empty family coffers by marrying into new industrial money. In *Two Women of London*, the city's poor have become so reduced that they no longer resemble anything human. Sometimes the wealthy require so much room that a separate narrative space has to be invented for them:

Mr Rathbone was a person very visible indeed. A great swell of money ran beneath his feet, the wind running high sometimes and Mr Rathbone rocking slightly, then recovering balance, in periods of calm, when the deep waters only hinted at the turmoil under him, the snakes and flecks of currencies adrift and him upright, he was more evidently than ever in command and could be seen for miles around. If he was larger than life, then so were the objects he came in contact with, the pink horse chestnuts on the branches above him in the avenue made fat spears over his head, outsize dogs seemed always to be attracted to him when he went walking. Large women, richly dressed, strolled about on the horizons of his gaze.

Tennant's fiction spends a lot of time at the other end of the socioeconomic spectrum, especially in the world of single women. A Tennant novel is a locus for several concerns running together— feminism, innovative notions of literary composition, an analysis of society. The question of who profits and who loses is always central. What gives books like *The Bad Sister* and *Two Women of London* real bite is the perception that losing out is not an ennobling experience. Disadvantage makes people crazy, mean-spirited, depressed, and violent.

The central text of *The Bad Sister* is the notebook of Jane Wild, unacknowledged daughter of a rich man. Her sense of grievance is projected as a Double who persuades her to kill her father. Hallucinatory, replete with episodes of vampirism and out-of-body experiences, Jane's dry, precise sentences carry a freight of schizophrenic visions. ("Who knows but one day, unwrapping the bright tartan package, mile on mile of paper, some crinkled as corrugated iron, some transparent and horribly soft, membrane, caul, out will fan the doll with the pin in its heart, the scapegoat for all this.") Jane's experience is submerged in a gray zone below the level of volition; vengeance, coupled with idealism, drives her into madness and suicide.

Woman Beware Woman employs a different version of the revenge theme, this time extrapolated from Merimée's novella

Colomba, in which a deracinated Sardinian nobleman returns from the Napoleonic Wars; against his own wishes, he's driven to avenge his father's death by relentless pressure from his sister. In Tennant's version too, the modern and rational collide with the primitive, on the western coast of Ireland, when an Anglo-Irish novelist is murdered by an IRA man. The central figure is the dead patriarch, a parlor Communist whose family embodies the hypocrisy of the rich and radical; the voice of the excluded is represented by the narrator, a woman whose marriage into the family has been blocked by the mother because of class differences. The theme of exclusion is worked out like a geometric formula. Bitterness is seen gestating over decades into an implacable anger that demands a sacrifice.

Like *Two Women of London*, this is a book of women and their conflicting loyalties to families, careers, and their images of themselves. Tennant's characters are often people who wake up at a certain age to discover they haven't become what they thought they would; *Woman Beware Woman* flickers between then and now, showing fate as a steady accretion of details rather than a thunderbolt, the outcome of myriad small betrayals. The past breathes through people. Ruined dreams become idées fixes. The Gothic tendency of such ideas is mitigated in Tennant's fiction by a strain of farce, and here there is a particularly obnoxious daughter-in-law, a "post-feminist" documentary filmmaker named Fran, chewing up the scenery.

The embittered marginal who becomes central through an act of betrayal recurs in *Black Marina*, probably the only novel ever inspired by the Grenada invasion. The narrator is again a woman whose dreams have come to nothing, a late '60s expatriate who's settled on a holiday island and then watched months and years go by while others "scoop all the prizes." As in *Woman Beware Woman*, the depth of the narrator's rage against the past, at losing out to circumstance, is shrewdly underplayed until the violent finale.

One obvious and liberating aspect of these books is that they place women at the center of narratives in which we're used to seeing men as the prime movers; women as nurturers and vessels of sexuality. In Tennant's novels, men are obdurate, symbolically powerful totems of the status quo, but more or less irrelevant to the actual drama of living. *Two Women of London* nicely pares down the male world into two figures, a rapist and an industrialist.

Tennant's technical effects are as rangy as her choice of stories. *Hotel De Dream* and *Woman Beware Woman* are put together like jigsaw puzzles, following different characters or different chronological strata in alternating chapters, fusing the separate threads at the climax. Prologues, introductions, a cast list at the outset of *Two Women of London*, a page of tourist brochure come-on in *Black Marina*, psychiatric reports and newspaper clippings in *Queen of Stones*: Tennant likes distancing devices, interjections that cast doubts about the evidence presented. As a great refashioner of myths, Tennant lets us know whose filter is on the lens.

The effect is often one of observing a second reality behind the carnivalesque surface—the lowering drabness of upper-class adolescence through the archaic prose style and galloping farce of *The Adventures of Robina*, for example. Tennant doesn't want to be understood didactically, or simply, since her prodigious talents include a bemused knack for spotting the complexities in simple things, contradictions between the real and the apparent. The reality she conjures up is subject to gross intrusions of the unconscious, mystical happenings, miraculous transformations of matter. But perhaps her most salient talent, like Gombrowicz's, lies in showing the falsity of people's ideas of themselves, the bogus quality of public feelings, public forms, the unknowable perversity of our actual inner selves. The scandal of *The Bad Sister* is precisely its exposure of the dank, miserable emotions, instilled by a rotten society, that often masquerade as radical convictions and utopian ideals.

Shaking loose from an overliterary notion of writing in the '70s, Tennant's work began folding in ideas and techniques from science fiction, Marxism, and feminism. The English literary world had little use for the imaginative fiction being produced at the time. In

1975, as a way of bringing her diverse concerns together, Tennant founded *Bananas*, a literary quarterly in the form of a newspaper. She later wrote, "You could read stories as if they were the latest reports from the writer's brain rather than 'timeless' literature, and have the space for big, arresting illustrations and original drawings as well. We decided to have the occasional piece of criticism . . . but to eschew reviews."

Bananas mirrored Tennant's preoccupations, contextualizing them in a spectrum of other fiction and poetry. The magazine was completely irreverent towards the British establishment, from a leftist perspective. By sticking almost entirely to fiction, poetry, and graphics, *Bananas* avoided the hortatory and mediocre tendencies of Movement publications, opting instead for wit and imagination. It encouraged heterodox and heretical voices, the free expression of fantasy (without regard to political rectitude), humor. Tennant piloted *Bananas* through 11 issues; its popularity refuted the myth of a brainwashed and indifferent public. Tennant recalls:

> *Once* Bananas *was made available in newsagents and bookshops all over the country, people started to buy it. Subscriptions went up, from people and libraries. Manuscripts came in in large numbers. The magazine began to be attacked in critical quarterlies, always a good sign, and Auberon Waugh called it pretentious rubbish. Meanwhile people went on writing stories and more people went on reading them.*

Some of the best of *Bananas* was collected in a 1977 anthology, Angela Carter's "The Company of Wolves," Hilary Bailey's "Middle Class Marriage Saved," Peter Wollen's "Friendship's Death," J. G. Ballard's "The Dead Time," and Tim Owens's "The Night It Rained"; poems by Libby Houston, Ted Hughes, Marilyn Hacker, Daniel Brand, and Frances Horovitz; a memoir of Ezra Pound by Claude Cockburn. A brilliant essay by Martin Seymour-Smith, "A Climate of Warm Indifference," surveying the wool-gray literary scene, discussed the reception of Ballard's *Crash*:

Its critical fate was to be judged from the standpoint of SF; and many people felt that it was a fantasy and that, while "gripping," the author should "see a psychiatrist." SF is now sometimes called "speculative fiction." But all fiction must now be "speculative," in one way or another. This is no longer a special and inferior category. Who—if indeed there were more than a few dozen competent psychiatrists about—does not need to see a psychiatrist? Ballard's book is not a "fantasy." It is (broadly speaking) an expressionist novel describing the real, *the inner,* state of a certain important aspect of modern life.*

Things have changed in the last decade, primarily through the celebration of South American writers like Márquez and Rulfo, earlier Central European ones like Schulz and Witkiewicz, and of course Calvino. The appetite for novels of fantasy, myth, and imagination has burgeoned, though the latest Booker Prize winner has been duly gurgled over in *The New York Review of Books* for its "Victorian" qualities. American and British critics continue to rank their domestic fiction according to its faithful mirroring of bourgeois values; generosity towards foreign "exotica" doesn't cost them anything with the mediocre novelists they went to school with. Literary culture in both countries is dead, but people go on reading (Vidal's *Kalki* with considerably more pleasure than Vidal's *Lincoln*, I suspect) whatever disobedient books they can get hold of—Emma Tennant's, too. After all, most people now remember Alberto Moravia as Elsa Morante's husband.

1991

19.

Debby with Monument: a Dissenting Opinion

A package has arrived from the law offices of someone named Gustave Harrow. The enclosures relate to the proposed removal of a large piece of Cor-Ten steel from the plaza of a downtown office building. Testimony on behalf of this piece of steel has been extracted from nearly every bureaucratic luminary and bright star in the art cosmos.

These expert witnesses are unanimous on several points. The work was commissioned under contract by the General Services Administration's Art-in-Architecture Program. The artist states that removal of the work equals its destruction, as its aesthetic impact is site-specific. The public is slow to understand new art and therefore is unqualified to pass judgment on it. Removal of the work would set a dangerous precedent. The hue and cry against the work suggests "certain events, practiced in Germany's history between 1933 and 1945, which were addressed against modern art and literature." In case the public has any question about what exact dish it's been served by the GSA, European museum director Rudi Fuchs has this avuncular wisdom to offer: ". . . would the City of Rome ever consider to remove Bernini's fountain from

Piazza Navona because it takes away a bit of sunlight? Of course not. But Richard Serra might be your Bernini." And I, to paraphrase Dottie Parker, might be Marie of Romania.

The question that seems most directly relevant to these proceedings could not very well crop up in them, but it's more or less the same one that bubbled to mind when the DIA Art Foundation began closing up its "permanent" art installations and receiving lawsuits from its "permanent" artists. Who on earth did these people think they were dealing with in the first place? Granted, everyone in public life is somehow involved with power. But if you are so enamored of it that you regularly ornament its dinner tables, ride cackling through the night in its limousines, and sign worthless contracts with it, it is no problem of mine or anyone else's if power decides, one bored afternoon, to add you to the menu instead of inviting you to eat.

Artists lavishly favored by the status quo often acquire the mentality of naturalized debutantes, complete with the delusion that favor and *arriviste* Debbyhood will last forever. "Forever" is a word with all kinds of funny meanings on the Planet Debby, but none of them is remotely synonymous with "permanent." On the Planet Debby, "permanent" is strictly a noun meaning hairdo.

The excerpted testimony supporting *Tilted Arc* reads like Flaubert's *Dictionary of Received Ideas*. Every conceivable cliché about art's relation to society has been put to work for Richard Serra by a chorus of well-off, well-meaning art specialists, who naturally see the fate of the Republic riding on the GSA's decision. Some of the clichés are true, but in this matter they are largely irrelevant. The General Services Administration is not God. Neither is Richard Serra. Either entity is capable of making a mistake, and in this case they both have. It would indeed be a dangerous precedent for the GSA, which failed to consult the public in the first place, to blithely expunge the detested object without Richard Serra's agreement. Acting by fiat, the GSA neglected its duty—obvious in this case, since many of Serra's sculptures have encountered a hostile public—to protect its funding from the kind of right-wing attack that initiated this controversy.

But it is ridiculous to suppose that Richard Serra's pugnacious resistance to reasoned argument is a thing to be supported or blown into a political cause.

The only legible aesthetic argument favoring Serra's *Tilted Arc* as a site-specific work would logically demand its eventual removal, and that of everything around it: not a bad idea, depending on the methods used. The piece heightens the alienation effect of a hideous modern office building and further orchestrates the processional regimentation of the office worker en route to and from work. It is a physically abrasive, hateful piece of art. If its intention is to raise public consciousness of the surrounding architecture's inhumanity, a future public intent on overcoming its oppression would start by removing *Tilted Arc*. This enlightened public would then proceed to demolish the Jacob K. Javits Federal Building, the disgusting turquoise fountain in the plaza, and stop going to work.

This is not going to happen, and neither will *Tilted Arc* be removed, unless the powers that be perceive some unlikely, real threat to their own authoritarianism being generated by the sculpture. This public art piece does constitute an act of aggression by an individual in public space, similar to those permitted and encouraged in architectural construction by the government and various corporations. In this sense it could be interpreted as an individual's assertion of superior importance to the government and the corporations, and therefore admirable.

But this particular individual is not proposing anything terribly distinct from the aims of corporate and governmental hegemony in the public realm. He is, like them, assuming noblesse oblige over large numbers of citizens, who—hypothetically, anyway—own the space that this work occupies. Serra's unbudging insistence on the site-specific immobility of this work refuses all accommodation with the public he designed it for, and thus it becomes a fixed component in an ensemble of oppressive architecture. Moving the piece by even 20 degrees would afford better access to the plaza and the building, but Serra has obviously read *The Fountainhead* and thinks this would be deadly compromise with squat-minded office sheep. *Tilted Arc* is a prototype of what the government and the corporations would gladly do if they could get away with it in such a blatant manner, the dream-fulfillment of a macho universe of bigger and bigger ugly obstructions to freedom of movement.

Serra has nothing to fear: his dream will undoubtedly be realized throughout Manhattan, if not the world, even if the realization does not have his name stamped all over it. If he is a true idealist, as he seems to be, this absence shouldn't bother him. But since he is also an artist, it does. In his public utterances on this matter, Serra has come increasingly to sound like Albert Speer, though he probably imagines himself Thomas Mann, Bertolt Brecht, and Walter Benjamin all rolled into one. Perhaps the answer is to sell him the entire building complex for a dollar and let Serra pay the taxes on it.

Let me draw your attention for a moment to the notion of public sculpture. If public sculpture consists of aesthetic objects placed in public space by the state and by corporate boards, it is the duty of every citizen to pay attention to the myriad examples of public sculpture which the state and corporate boards have placed on the sidewalks of the Lower East Side and other New York neighborhoods, without fanfare, since the election of Ronald Reagan.

I am referring to that genre of public sculpture known popularly as "the Homeless." These lifelike sculptures are positioned on every street, and typically solicit money "to get something to eat," "to buy a drink," and for other less intelligible purposes. Anyone who has observed the proliferation of these objets d'art and listened carefully to the messages they emit will have noticed certain refinements in the genre over the last five years.

In the late 1970s, most of these sculptures were decrepit, caked with grime, and seemed to display the latter stages of terminal alcoholism. Since the election of our current leader, however, fewer and fewer of them have been hopelessly incoherent. This is because there are thousands more of them, recently dispossessed. But the people who occupy their former homes know enough to regard them as nonhuman entities, to confront them as aesthetic objects—

untouchable vehicles of "aura," worthy of investment on the basis of their degree of cleanliness and lucidity. A sculpture that pukes its guts out in a gutter cannot be compared in aesthetic value with one that dresses with a certain flair and has an engaging rap programmed into its circuitry.

These public works wear down, exposed as they are to the elements and to the indifference of the human swarm that passes by them: they die, in public hospitals or on the street—uncollected by avatars of aesthetic sensibility like the Thyssen-Bornemiszas who financed Hitler as well as Andrew Crispo; unremembered by the Gracie Mansions and Bianca Jaggers who have given so much, so unstintingly, to the society in which we are forced to live by the sheer accident of birth.

Yet they define the space of public sculpture in a sense that a hunk of steel emanating from a drawing board in Richard Serra's office never could. They occupy real space, as distinct from the space of idealistic projections, utopian fantasies, and masturbatory empires. They are the brothers and sisters of the people huddled in the halls of the Jacob K. Javits Federal Building waiting to be photographed for immigration documents. They couldn't care less if Richard Serra's contract with the GSA is abrogated. Their contract with anything has been severed at the nerve by the government Richard Serra expects to do the proper democratic thing. That government has demonstrated, for the past five years, that it is capable of any deception, any illegality, capable indeed of anything. Compared to what it does every day to those ordinary people who can't understand modern art, knocking over some egomaniac's prefab sculpture is a hilarious canard. In case Richard Serra never heard this from anybody else, I'd like him to hear it from me: lie down with dogs, get up with fleas.

1985

20. All I Need Is Love

All I Need is Love
by Klaus Kinski

Going out of print is only the last in a long series of humiliations inflicted on most writers by most publishing houses. Unless you are the most wildly popular public strumpet, or have written some vapid book about one, chances are your publisher—who, after all, is running a whorehouse, not a public charity—believes he is doing you a huge favor to begin with. Of the thousands of writers he could pluck from obscurity, it's you whom he's decided to favor.

Naturally, it would be base ingratitude for you to expect anything more than chump change in return for one, two, three, sometimes four or five years of work. You think your publisher doesn't have overhead? Who do you think you are, Belva Plain? Ads? Are you crazy, ads? Why should he do anything for you? It's no surprise that dozens of good books go out of print every year, when their publishers manifest no real support for them in the first place. I know one writer whose five novels are widely regarded as ground-breaking, fascinating works; they're all out of print. I know another whose two novels are universally considered plodding, mechanical, unreadable exercises in intellectual vanity; because of her enduring fame as a writer of jacket quotes and slender, precious meditations on contemporary aesthetics, her publisher has dutifully reissued the novels every few years for the past 20.

Arbitrary as it really is, authors naturally experience going out of print as a horrific form of judgment. Klaus Kinski, however, need feel no such qualm. *All I Need Is Love* would certainly have given Belva Plain a run for her money, but Random House stopped shipping after 10 thousand copies, reportedly out of fear of libel suits. Kinski collected a hefty advance and, if his book's self-portrait is anything to go by, couldn't care less whether anybody gets to read it. It is an astonishing document that makes Errol Flynn's *My Wicked, Wicked Ways* and Hedy Lamarr's *Ecstasy and Me* look exceedingly like *Rebecca of Sunnybrook Farm*.

Kinski grew up in hideous poverty. At age 16, at the desperate end of World War II, he was forced into army service and then became a prisoner of war. His account of childhood has a blunt descriptive brilliance. After a meal in a children's welfare home: "I barf right into my torturer's mug. I throw up everything in my stomach. Filthy shit comes shooting out of my wide-open throat in spurts like a sewage pump until I'm emptied to my very bowels and can't pump anything more. Doubled over by cramps, I rush from the table, as the jail-warden slut nearly chokes to death on my barf and bawls me out at the top of her lungs."

His adventures in the army are equally salient. Right after the war, Kinski starts his career as a stage actor. Everyone, including Bertolt Brecht, senses his genius. But that's not important to him. What he cares about, what consumes him, is getting laid. Starting at age 14, Kinski fucks virtually every female who crosses his path, in doorways, dressing rooms, public parks and toilets. His triumphs on the stages of Germany and Austria are mere background noise in the din of grunting, snuffling sex. "I haven't called Biggi even once from Prague. When she calls me, I lie and say that I'm shooting day and night. I am a pig. But I am rendered powerless by Dominique who has enslaved me with her cunt. Dominique is obsessed with me, too; she asks me to stay with her, live with her. I promise I will."

Like Henry Miller, Kinski is irresistibly attractive to everyone around him. Men and women both go crazy for his cock, though he has evidently avoided homosexual penetration. And while he's surrounded, like Miller, by a chorus of arty gargoyles proclaiming his genius, Kinski himself has nothing but loathing for his career. The money passage of this book describes the director whose films made Kinski an international star: "It's perfectly clear to me that never in my entire life have I ever encountered such a humorless, mendacious, stubborn, narrow-minded, pretentious, unscrupulous, bumptious, spiritless, depressing, boring, and sickening person— entirely unconcerned, he drives home the most uninteresting high points, finally falling to his knees like a sectarian, holding forth fanatically, waiting for someone to pull him up. Having unburdened himself of his garbage stinking all over the place and making me want to vomit, he pretends to be a naive child of innocence, talking about his dreamy poetic existence, as if he weren't living in reality at all and doesn't have the vaguest idea of the brutal material side of the world."

All Kinski needs is love, but the love he needs can only be had with a great deal of money. Offered a choice between "quality" films and high-paying trash, Kinski opts for the trash almost every time. This buys him villas and Rolls-Royces and epic weekend flights from cooze to cooze. His mania is aggravated by marriages, the birth of children, and ever-burgeoning fame.

It isn't so much the belated Beat Era anarchy, or Kinski's quirky compassion for animals and children, or the scads of amusing pornography that give this book its great charm. What distinguishes *All I Need Is Love* from other out-of-control, cunt-crazy, tell-all memoirs (cf. Miller, Bukowski, *I Jan Cremer*) is its operatic self-contempt, so blaringly sustained that it acquires a sacramental aura. Unlike the wild and crazy guys who pioneered this genre, Kinski knows that his "genius" doesn't redeem a single moment of his piggishness, and because he wallows in it on its own terms Kinski invests it with quixotic integrity.

1990

21. The Farewell Party

This month, in Sunday supplements and *Life* and wherever journalists tell people what the artifacts of American culture really mean, the retirement of Johnny Carson is featured as a national milestone, something akin to menopause, but affecting all Americans. Rich and poor, black and white, and all the other polarities of the Only Remaining Superpower have purportedly oozed together in anticipation of this seminal event. Perhaps Elizabeth Taylor, quoted on the cover of *TV Guide*, unwittingly said it best: "Even though we waited 29 years, it was worth the wait."

With tart nostalgia, the hacks of *Time* and *Newsweek* salute the departure of a titanic presence whose twinkling wit and winsome grace under pressure have given a whole nation the same thing every time for three decades, like Burger King and Florsheim Shoes. Encomiums from show-biz colleagues reflect that special zest for uninflected groveling exampled each year in the presentation of the Jean Hersholt Humanitarian Award. "I've been a little bit in love with Johnny all these years," confesses Angie Dickinson. "He speaks a language that all America understands," gurgles Milton

Berle. Watershed moments of *The Tonight Show* are lovingly charted. The marriage of Tiny Tim is fondly recalled as Johnny's biggest ratings share. The treachery of Joan Rivers is invoked as a caution to all who would be Johnny. Various bloopers and risqué episodes are resurrected to remind us just how much a part of our collective memory, our shared life, Johnny really is. The only thing missing from this Grub Street vomitorium is a flatulent salute from Jeff Greenfield on *Nightline*, and I'm sure one is in the works.

It's worth remembering that the editorial We who are everywhere in stories about Carson's retirement, enduring a uniform onrush of manufactured emotions about a figure very few of us have ever thought about for more than 10 seconds, are presumably the same We who were traumatized by the recent rebellion in Los Angeles. In that case, however, hardly any two of Us questioned by the media used the same language to characterize events. Instead of unanimity, the words people found revealed myriad shadings of class, education, personal character, ideology, and prejudice, the monadic movements inside each person that make reality less than consensual. You think canned entertainment is any different?

The sheer longevity of *The Tonight Show* has persuaded journalists that everyone, however unlikely, has a sentimental relationship to Johnny. He has always been there in his network time slot, embalmed in a dense magma of reassuring mediocrity, mugging behind his desk as if to guarantee the faceless millions that they, too, can repeat the same absurd gestures day after day, year after year, without an unbearable amount of suffering: entertainment is a factory like any other. Faces come and go on the assembly line but the power plant of fame and money and success will always occupy the same coordinates in space and time. *The Tonight Show* is a nightly reminder of who we aren't, which has its own negative fascination.

The multimedia festschrift, conducted with the affectionate yet trenchant humor of a Friars' Club Celebrity Roast, has brought the question of What Johnny Means To Us to the forepan of such soaring brains as Frank Rich, whose almost overgenerous Arts &

Leisure piece observes that "the actual content of a Carson show does not matter. At a time of anxiety who cares about the color and material of a security blanket?" Mr. Rich goes on to imagine himself, or "you" (whom he takes to be interchangeable with himself) "alone and exhausted in an antiseptic hotel room in a strange city," tuning into Johnny with the sound off, and becoming "tranquilized" by the predictable morphology of Johnny's face, the unchanging set, the soothing familiarity of Ed McMahon and the show's orchestra.

For Rich, whom anxiety promptly strikes at 11:30 every night for reasons unknown, the institutional obduracy of *The Tonight Show* serves as a safe and pleasant narcotic. The sense that nothing will ever change, that the magical taxidermy achieved by any guest's appearance on Carson will forever serve as a powerful index of celebrity, acts like a Quaalude on the distinguished theater critic's jangled nervous system. For others, understandably, *The Tonight Show* represents a kind of two-man time warp (let's not forget Ed), a charity ward for superannuated comics and occluded stars where regular visits from present-day celebrities sustain the illusion that they, rather than the inmates, gain from the encounter.

Like most institutions dominated by white men fond of big-tit jokes and locker-room camaraderie *The Tonight Show* has an atmosphere oppressive to anyone normally cast in the frying pan of "difference." The clubhouse ambiance was described in an excellent recent article by Diane Werts in *Newsday*, to which I can only add that if you collected all the limp-wristed, lisping pansy gags Carson has perpetrated over the years you would have several hours' worth of "Carson's Comedy Classics."

As Romy Schneider once said in a movie, it isn't the scandal, it's the banality—all those squalid farts with hair weaves on the cusp of 65 who've just opened for Steve and Eydie in Vegas, chawing their cigar ends and cackling about what bitches their wives are, drooling over starlets, forcing the supine, glazed audience Out There to imagine what gets such repulsive washed-up geezers hard. Through some strange process of osmosis, almost any guest who comes on the Carson show, however enlightened, is assimilated to the clichés of a bygone world where Frank and Dino and Sammy, to say nothing of David Brenner or Don Rickles, count as major personalities.

The heterosexual credentials of all guests are established as quickly as possible. If one is married, that's very good. If one's recently had a child, wild applause from the audience is called for. Single males must exhibit an interest in women, and, to settle any doubts in the pop mind, it's best to be cunt-crazy. (Harvey Fierstein has assumed the mantle of Truman Capote as the very occasional okay fag, a role Sandra Bernhard plays with more ambiguity and panache on Letterman.) Female guests, unless they are Julia Childs or nonagenerians with a gimmick, are an assortment of remarkable body parts with resumés. It makes no difference what they talk about. The whole framing of the show is angled for a viewer who wants to have sex with them.

A declared homosexual appearing on any late-night talk show becomes the immediate butt of fey jokes about not touching the host. In this era of heightened sensitivity, a guest's preference for his (rarely her) own sex can only be discussed in the solemnly dropped tones used at funerals. In that long-ago era when Capote, Gore Vidal, and Tennessee Williams were the only known homosexuals in the country, things were actually looser on the Carson show. Groucho: "I'd marry you, Truman, but I couldn't give you what you deserve." Capote: "What's that, the best years of your life?"

Talk shows began as improvisations and quickly jelled into formula. The old live Jack Paar show was almost aleatory, and its regulars—Dody Goodman, Oscar Levant, Genevieve—were true "characters" who probed the limits of acceptable expression on television. Paar's show was intellectually venturesome, even dangerously so; the personality types on display exhibited a neuroticism that was pure New York bohemia.

Carson's arrival shrank the space available for amusing marginals like Alexander King, mainstreaming down to a few intermittent weekly bursts of heterodoxy. For at least 20 years, the show has been targeted at middle-class white Midwesterners who believe in God and Bob Hope. Frank Rich credits Carson's monologues with turning the audience against Richard Nixon, pressuring LBJ out of a second term, and terrifying George Bush with a "steady barrage of ridicule." I, by the way, am Marie of Romania.

As far as mentality goes, from Carson to Letterman is a considerable dip down the evolutionary scale, from informed insipidity to sociopathic narcissism. What Letterman and Carson share is the viewer's suspicion that neither one exists off-camera— or, if there is someone there, he's the flip side of the video image, deeply antisocial and impossible to know.

Johnny's over-the-hill regulars like George Burns go over quite well on Letterman. On Arsenio Hall they look like not very funny geological relics, prone to embarrassing sex jokes and apt to betray unease at being seated next to a black man. Arsenio has his own problematic pathology, but his show speaks to vast numbers of people Carson never addressed when he was the only game in town. In a few years Arsenio should demonstrate the good sense Carson lacked, and quit while he's ahead.

1992

22. Hannah and Her Sister

Between Friends:
The Correspondence of Hannah Arendt and
Mary McCarthy, 1949-1975
edited by Carol Brightman

In her introduction to *Between Friends,* editor Carol Brightman tells us that Hannah Arendt and Mary McCarthy did not hit it off when they first met. At a party in 1945, McCarthy made a characteristic gaffe by saying she felt sorry for Hitler, who, in Brightman's paraphrase, "was so absurd as to want the love of his victims." Arendt replied, "How can you say such a thing in front of me—a victim of Hitler, a person who has been in a concentration camp!"

It goes without saying that McCarthy didn't feel any sort of pity for Hitler; she was just being Mary, provocateur of the then-Trotskyite martini set. And Arendt had never been in a concentration camp; she'd been briefly interned in France. What glitters in this anecdote, for a writer of my generation, is the fact that it happened "at a party": there were so very many well-chronicled parties during the seemingly endless tenure of the *Partisan Review-New Yorker-politics-Commentary-New York Review of Books* literary coven, so many confabs and cocktails shared by Cal and Lizzie and Philip and Dwight and the dreadful Trillings and Saul and Alfred and Harold. They lived in a time when literary people and their parties had some palpable connection to the great events of the day; they were taken seriously by presidential advisers, ambassadors, even heads of state. Thanks partly to their clannishness and partly to the invention of TV, the very idea of a literary party now has a ring of quaint anachronism: who, pray tell, would attend?

Theirs was, alas, the last, or perhaps next-to-last, generation of writers who could safely assume that their correspondence would be collected, or for that matter exist in sufficient quantity to be of interest. The telephone has made such communications rare and vaguely suspect: we live in an age that privileges the instantaneous outpouring of unmediated "feelings" over more delicate, dilatory sentiments. (The recent suggestion in *Newsweek* that faxes and e-mail might revive letter-writing is faintly absurd, since these pushy forms of human contact tend to demand immediate response, just like the telephone.) The McCarthy-Arendt correspondence has a solid, crafted thereness to it, the force of fluent prose applied to the business of daily life. The quick, sloppy missive is acknowledged as such: "Dearest Hannah: The next mail leaves in forty-five minutes, and I'm writing you this note for purely selfish reasons: because my heart is full of emotion and I want to talk." "My dearest Mary—I am writing not to write a letter but to do everything required to receive one."

But nothing here is truly sloppy—a certain lopsided urgency is the sole, rare infelicity—and most of the letters are fulsome, funny, keenly descriptive, written with one eye darting to, though happily not fixed on, posterity. There are so many things one can write about people, knowing that one will be safely dead by the time they read it, or that they will be dead by the time one publishes it. Arendt: "I was away from New York, an idiotic affair at Baltimore, honorary degree together with Margaret Mead, a monster, and

Marianne Moore, an angel . . . Mead (one better call her only by her second name, not because she is a man, but because she certainly is not a woman). . . . " And McCarthy:

> [Hans Magnus] Enzensberger's letter [the famous Wesleyan resignation in protest over Vietnam] is causing a great stir here . . . The fact is, far from being in Cuba, he is in California giving lectures. . . . From there he goes on to lecture in Australia, then to Tahiti and other pagan paradises, then back to West Berlin. His wife is staying with Nathalie Sarraute, which is how I know all this. Nathalie thinks it is a rather dishonest comedy. But don't repeat that. She gathers that what happened is that Masha, the young wife, got bored in Wesleyan; "Magnus" too.

Arendt was the ant, McCarthy the grasshopper: Arendt remained married to the same man, and pretty much rooted in New York City, throughout the span of the letters, while McCarthy had affairs, divorced Bowden Broadwater, and married James West, traveling incessantly for one reason or another. (This perfectly suits the separate natures of the philosophe and the novelist.) Comparing these letters with Arendt's to Karl Jaspers, one gets the impression that McCarthy brought out the bitchier side of Arendt, while Arendt had the opposite effect on McCarthy, who frequently sounds humble, awed by Arendt's intellect, and, like an assiduous graduate student, eager to win her approval.

As years go by and life delivers its usual insults to the heart and brain, both women's letters become increasingly tender, fretful, solicitous. McCarthy's dreadful remarks about "pansies" and "fruits," usually in relation to Auden or Spender, do little to allay the impression that her friendship with Arendt was the major love story of her life. A friend of mine who is an authority in these matters assures me that most of the raging neuroticism of the *Partisan Review* crowd sprang from repressed homosexuality— "Rahv, Macdonald, Lowell too for that matter," he says—and perhaps the same is true for the distinguished authors of, respectively, *The Life of the Mind* and *The Company She Keeps*. At any rate, McCarthy was vigilant about possible Sapphic rivals for Arendt's affections: "But I read that Susan Sontag was arrested [in an antiwar demonstration]. And what about her? When I last watched her with you at the Lowells', it was clear that she was going to seek to conquer you. Or that she had fallen in love with you—the same thing. Anyway, did she?"

Arendt was 43, McCarthy 37, when the letters began with a short note from Arendt praising McCarthy's recently published novella, *The Oasis*. There is a lapse of two years before the next— McCarthy's to Arendt, on *The Origins of Totalitariarism*. Letters have been lost, and there are sometimes months of epistolary silence between the two followed by blizzards of communication. Because they told each other "everything," *Between Friends* has the narrative pull of a novel. At times it reads like the kind of novel McCarthy wrote, though it has more in common with the works of two writers she admired, Ivy Compton-Burnett and Nathalie Sarraute: oblique, elliptical, proceeding as much by inference as by direct description. A rich cast of recurring characters, glimpsed first from one protagonist's view, then the other's, floats in a kind of annotated historical broth, while the actual meetings of the two heroines occur off-stage and swim into our peripheral vision as afterimages when the letters resume.

The vigilant politics of the principals gives this book one kind of momentum; we go from the McCarthy era to the Kennedy years to Vietnam and the civil rights movement, the student revolts in Paris, Watergate, up to the mid-'70s proliferation of terrorism that McCarthy treated in her last novel, *Cannibals and Missionaries*. Another current carries the personal dramas and daily trivia—the struggles with work, planning of travel itineraries, McCarthy's intricate negotiations for her divorce from Broadwater and James West's even more tangled dealings with his ex-wife, McCarthy's long spells in Venice and Florence, Arendt's conferences and classes, and, as time passes, the deaths of Arendt's husband and many mutual friends, illnesses, and other losses.

The personal intersects often with the public, most dramatically when *Eichmann in Jerusalem* and *The Group* appear a few months apart in 1963, bringing both writers wide fame and violent controversy. It would be too simple to say that McCarthy's response to events was to *do something,* sometimes recklessly, while the more sedentary and reflective Arendt tended to mull things over and often to let them go. But the Eichmann controversy does seem illustrative. Arendt, attacked by Jewish groups for describing the role of the Jewish councils in organizing deportations to the death camps, decided to wait until things had calmed down to respond to her critics. McCarthy found the hysteria of the attacks an intolerable provocation, especially Lionel Abel's *Partisan Review* piece ("The Aesthetics of Evil: Hannah Arendt on Eichmann and the Jews"), and worked herself up to a brilliant counterattack, "The Hue and Cry."

Arendt never publicly roused herself on McCarthy's behalf when the latter's books, after *The Group,* met with ever-frostier reviews, sometimes with critical silence (in the case of her Vietnam books, *Vietnam, Hanoi,* and *Medina,* and her book on Watergate, *The Mask of State*). I think Arendt's mentor status made it impossible for McCarthy to consciously expect that kind of reciprocity, but a shadow of resentment flashes out, a decade after the Eichmann furor, during their friendship's single (recorded) crisis of faith, which occurred over a trivial misunderstanding. After visiting the Wests in Maine, Arendt boarded her plane without "lingering over good-byes"—McCarthy believed Arendt had found her irritating, and in subsequent letters, plaintively, tried to coax Arendt into admitting it. She was less disturbed by Arendt's supposed irritation than by the possibility that her own perceptions were mistaken—and in a letter of September, 1974, insists on her version of events: "As for Aberdeen, I *know* you were cross with me some times (for instance when I brought you some fruit paste candies from Paris). . . . Then in Castine, feeling that I was on your nerves again, I wondered about that." This is followed by a rather devastating non-reproach:

> No, I am not suspicious of my friends. What an idea. It isn't a suspicion but a certainty, an objective fact, that when I got

*some very rough treatment in the press ... not a soul came
to my defense. ... It is not that I think A or B should have
come to my support; what astonishes me is that no one did.
And I can't help feeling, though I shouldn't, that if one of my
friends had been in my place, I would [have] raised my voice.
This leads me to the conclusion that I am peculiar, in some
way that I cannot make out; indefensible, at least for my
friends. They are fond of me but with reservations. In any
case, none of this involves you, because you were in the
hospital and then recovering when it happened, because you
weren't in the U.S. and didn't see those unpleasant pieces and
because, finally, even if you had been on Riverside Drive and
in the peak of condition, you* couldn't *have helped since
people would have said that you were repaying the Eichmann
debt, that we had dedicated books to each other, etc., etc.*

This explosion of petulance is uncharacteristic and therefore
notable; McCarthy detested self-pity in any form, though it must
be said that Arendt was generally much quieter about her own
complaints, or at least more stoic. (After a horrendous car crash in
1962—nine broken ribs, a concussion, hemorrhages in both eyes—
she writes, "[W]hen I awoke in the car and became conscious of
what had happened, I tried out my limbs, saw that I was not
paralyzed and could see with both eyes; then tried out my
memory—very carefully, decade by decade, poetry, Greek and
German and English, then telephone numbers. Everything all
right.") Arendt's side of the correspondence lapses for six months
after the Maine episode, perhaps because she didn't wish to thrash
out the misunderstanding on paper. It appears to have been
mediated by publisher William Jovanovich, who crops up from
time to time as a sympathetic, globe-trotting magus, gobbling up
subsidiaries to keep his literary division afloat.

Between Friends owes much of its charm to an assortment of
figures like Jovanovich, encountered on the trail, so to speak.
While Arendt was mainly busy with academic work and domestic
life, McCarthy, residing in Paris and much in transit, "the family"

(Norman Podhoretz's derisive term) established in the '40s is ever with them. However exasperated or betrayed they feel by the old perennials—Lizzie, Cal, Philip, et al.—it is clear that people in the family will never be permanently banished to outer darkness, and that certain enemies will ever remain in focus. The political is often the personal. Arendt, who had a stake in postwar German intellectual life, had a bug in her brain against Adorno, and denounced him for trying to make himself interesting, on one occasion, to the Nazis in 1933; he had apparently blocked Arendt's graduate thesis way back when, and after the war led the attacks on Heidegger, one of Arendt's mentors.

McCarthy's circle of enemies was, of course, wider than Arendt's: Diana Trilling, Simone de Beauvoir, and Lillian Hellman were but a few, and she seems to have loathed them mostly on principle—though the campaign against de Beauvoir, sustained over 30 years, had a quality of inexplicable excess. While it's always fun to read well-honed malice, both sides of this correspondence have their moments of cheap caricature and dishonesty, as well as egregious mutual flattery.

Like all good friends, they tactfully supported one another's prejudices, though not necessarily among other people. You will find, for instance, a much better opinion of Günter Grass's work from Arendt in her letters to Jaspers than in what she told McCarthy, and kinder words for Sartre from McCarthy, in a 1984 interview with Carol Brightman, than in what she told Arendt.

As this is an evolving record of two lives, inconsistencies, shifting attitudes and opinions, and sudden changes of heart are precisely what animate it. For two such eminent persons there are surprisingly few intractable hobbyhorses. The famous are often boringly fond of their own utterances, but in their letters, at least, Arendt and McCarthy were determined not to bore each other. Arendt was generous by nature, McCarthy by self-discipline (which finally mellowed into nature). They both had a moral commitment to truth-telling, which meant being (or trying to be) fair-minded, which meant, finally, that they were willing to be surprised by people they did not expect much of. If a genuine idea emitted from a horse's ass, they felt honor-bound to consider it seriously.

This gives even their idle gossip a certain respectable texture, as when, for example, the certifiably crazy Robert Lowell appears to get saner on lithium, but then has an unfortunate lapse. McCarthy: "He is still taking his pills. And he spoke with horror of his old mania. . . . If one has known him so long, one is alert to the signs. There was one ominous note, I must admit, during the evening we spent together: he mentioned *Hitler*. In a guarded but somewhat commendatory way. I said: 'Cal, if I hear the word "Hitler" again, that finishes it.' "

They want poor Cal to be sane, and feel it's a pity he just isn't. Of course, it is also true that McCarthy hits her best stride, prosewise, when encountering stark raving eccentricity, and Arendt, too, surpasses herself when the people around her are plainly out of their minds. Earthbound by the obligation to make sense of reality, both writers take hilarious flight when reality repudiates sense: the correspondence positively sizzles in the period around May '68.

Between Friends is an exemplary dialogue of two astonishing minds, set against a background of progressive loss—the decay of the body, the disappearance of friends, the coarsening of the public sphere, the ruin of nature—that serves as an effective primer in what Arendt saw as the three activities of human consciousness: thinking, willing, and judging. Anchored in the data of the everyday, these letters reflect a shared search for a modern, godless transcendence, an ethics, a tolerable way to live in the world we have now. To soldier on while knowing this quest is doomed to fail-ure is itself a quixotic triumph of mind over matter. "As a person and a writer, I seem to have had little effect on improving the world I came into," McCarthy told an audience at the MacDowell Colony in 1984. "Why should I care that I have lived my life as a person and as a writer in vain? Most of our lives are in vain. At best, we give pleasure to some."

1995

Index